Female Identity in Contemporary Fictional Purgatorial Worlds

Female Identity in Contemporary Fictional Purgatorial Worlds

Edited by Simon Bacon

BLOOMSBURY ACADEMIC
LONDON • NEW YORK • OXFORD • NEW DELHI • SYDNEY

BLOOMSBURY ACADEMIC
Bloomsbury Publishing Plc
50 Bedford Square, London, WC1B 3DP, UK
1385 Broadway, New York, NY 10018, USA
29 Earlsfort Terrace, Dublin 2, Ireland

BLOOMSBURY, BLOOMSBURY ACADEMIC and the Diana logo are trademarks of Bloomsbury Publishing Plc

First published in Great Britain 2023
This paperback edition published 2025

Copyright © Simon Bacon, 2023

Simon Bacon has asserted his right under the Copyright, Designs and Patents Act, 1988, to be identified as Author of this work.

For legal purposes the Acknowledgments on p. xii constitute an extension of this copyright page.

Cover design by Gita Govinda Kowlessur
Cover illustration © Wachirawit Thongrong/ iStock

All rights reserved. No part of this publication may be reproduced or transmitted in any form or by any means, electronic or mechanical, including photocopying, recording, or any information storage or retrieval system, without prior permission in writing from the publishers.

Bloomsbury Publishing Plc does not have any control over, or responsibility for, any third-party websites referred to or in this book. All internet addresses given in this book were correct at the time of going to press. The author and publisher regret any inconvenience caused if addresses have changed or sites have ceased to exist, but can accept no responsibility for any such changes.

A catalogue record for this book is available from the British Library.

A catalog record for this book is available from the Library of Congress.

ISBN: HB: 978-1-3502-2703-3
PB: 978-1-3502-2707-1
ePDF: 978-1-3502-2704-0
eBook: 978-1-3502-2705-7

Typeset by Integra Software Services Pvt. Ltd.

To find out more about our authors and books visit www.bloomsbury.com and sign up for our newsletters.

Contents

List of Illustrations	vii
Notes on Contributors	viii
Acknowledgments	xii
Prologue *Simon Bacon*	1
Introduction *Simon Bacon*	5

Part One   Purgatorial Space

1. Miasma Theory, Particulate Matter and Modern Horror
   Jeffrey Andrew Weinstock … 23
2. Between Hell and Hel: Gender, History, and Nature in Subterranean Spaces *Elana Gomel* … 41
3. La Llorona Hauntings: Storytelling Feminicide at the Purgatorial Mexico/US Border *Cristina Santos and Sarah Revilla-Sanchez* … 55

Part Two   Daughters, Mothers, Trauma

4. "I Lost All Hope of Going up the Hill": *Silent Hill* as a Female Specific *Inferno* *Dawn Stobbart* … 71
5. "Mother Is God in the Eyes of a Child": Doppelgängers, Punishment, and Maternal Otherworlds in *Silent Hill* and *Triangle* *Catherine Pugh* … 85
6. Pray and Obey: The Horror (and Purgatory) of Religious Fundamentalism *Nicola Young* … 101

Part Three   Female Development in Purgatorial Spaces

7. The New Eden? The Female-Centered Purgatorial Space of *Dollhouse* *Erin Giannini* … 117
8. The Vampire in the Attic: Constructing Monstrous Female Identities in Liminal, Purgatorial Spaces *Taryn Tavener-Smith* … 129

9 "Into the Further We Go": Exploring Gender, World-Building, and the Return of the Fantastic in the *Insidious* Franchise
Mark Richard Adams — 143

10 Coded Outcry: Margaret Atwood's *The Handmaid's Tale* (1985 and 2017–Present) and *The Testaments* (2019) *Gina Wisker* — 157

Part Four   Spaces of Female Resistance

11 Of Monstrous Spaces: Female Identity in *American Horror Story: Murder House* and *American Horror Story: Hotel*
Pembe Gözde Erdogan — 175

12 "This Time I'll Get It Right": Female Coming-of-Age within Purgatorial Time Loops *Shawn Edrei* — 191

13 The Trauma We Inherit: Sister Night, Black Female Identity, and the Parallel Racial Purgatory of *Watchmen* *Kevin J. Wetmore, Jr.* — 205

14 "We're Human Too, You Know": Tethered Journeys and Shadowed Struggles in Jordan Peele's *Us* (2019) *Nancy Johnson-Hunt* — 221

Index — 238

Illustrations

1.1 Pestilential air surrounds werewolf Ethan Chandler (Josh Hartnett) in *Penny Dreadful*, created by John Logan — 24
1.2 Children playing in the radioactive ash from Chernobyl in *Chernobyl*, created by Craig Mazin — 29
1.3 Rose considers the falling ash in *Silent Hill*, directed by Christophe Gans — 31
1.4 Rose entering the abandoned town of Silent Hill in *Silent Hill*, directed by Christophe Gans — 31
1.5 Eleven (Millie Bobby Brown) in *Stranger Things*, created by The Duffer Brothers — 32
1.6 Sheriff Hopper (David Harbour) and Joyce Byers (Winona Ryder) in the hazmat suits in *Stranger Things*, created by The Duffer Brothers — 33
1.7 The Big Bad, the Mind Flayer, creating its own weather in *Stranger Things*, created by The Duffer Brothers — 34
1.8 Chris (Daniel Kaluuya) in "the Sunken Place" in *Get Out*, directed by Jordan Peele — 35
1.9 Into the heart of the maelstrom in *Twin Peaks: The Return*, created by David Lynch — 37
3.1 Shot of desert dumping ground for victims of feminicide in *Narcos: Mexico*, season 3, episode 10, created by Carlo Bernard, Chris Brancato, and Doug Miro — 62
3.2 The search for the disappeared girls at the Juárez border in *Narcos: Mexico*, season 3, episode 10, created by Carlo Bernard, Chris Brancato, and Doug Miro — 64
4.1 Sharon stares into Hell in *Silent Hill*, directed by Christophe Gans — 72
4.2 Pyramid Head in *Silent Hill*, directed by Christophe Gans — 77
4.3 Colin the Janitor in *Silent Hill*, directed by Christophe Gans — 79

Contributors

Mark Richard Adams received his Doctorate from Brunel University for his study examining institutional contexts of *Doctor Who*'s Fan-Producers and historical research into the concept of authorship. He also has a Masters in Cult Film. Publications include chapters on masochism in *Screening Twilight: Critical Approaches to a Cinematic Phenomenon*, an analysis of Valentine's stylistic excess in Style and Form in the Hollywood Slasher Film, and "Clive Barker's Queer Monsters" in *Clive Barker: Dark Imaginer*.

Simon Bacon is an award-winning writer and film critic based in Poznań, Poland. He has edited books on various subjects including *Gothic: A Reader* (2018), *Horror: A Companion* (2019), *Monsters: A Companion* (2020), *Transmedia Vampires* (2021), *Nosferatu in the 21st Century* (2022), *Spoofing the Vampire* (2022), *The Palgrave Handbook of the Vampire* (forthcoming), and co-edited *Growing Up with Vampires* (2019 with Katarzyna Bronk). He has also published a series of books on vampires in popular culture: *Becoming Vampire* (2016), *Dracula as Absolute Other* (2019), *Eco-Vampires* (2020), *Vampires from Another World* (2021), and is working on the next *1000 Vampires on Screen* (forthcoming).

Shawn Edrei is a researcher of digital narratology, an avid gamer and observer of online fandom dynamics. He recently published *The New Fiction Technologies* with McFarland, exploring the latest developments in transmedia interactive fiction, storytelling and authorship. He currently teaches at Tel-Aviv University.

Pembe Gözde Erdogan received her BA, MA, and PhD from Hacettepe University's Department of American Culture and Literature in Ankara, Turkey. Her PhD was on Southern Gothic American Television series. Her research areas include Popular Culture, Cultural Studies, Film Studies, Television Studies, Horror and Gothic, and American Theatre. She has published and presented on race and gender in horror and postmodern horror. She currently resides in Cardiff, UK and is an independent scholar.

Erin Giannini, PhD, is an independent scholar. She has served as an editor and contributor at *PopMatters*, and her recent work has focused on portrayals of and industrial contexts around corporate culture on television, including a monograph on corporatism in the works of Joss Whedon (2017). She has also published and presented work on religion, socioeconomics, production culture, and technology in series such as *Supernatural, Dollhouse, iZombie,* and *Angel,* and is currently co-editing a collection on the novel (and series) *Good Omens*.

Elana Gomel is the author of six academic books and numerous articles on subjects such as narrative theory, posthumanism, science fiction, Dickens, and Victorian culture. She is currently working on a book about narrative representations of post-utopia and editing a *Palgrave Reader of International Fantasy*, along with several other projects. She is also a fiction writer who has published six novels and more than ninety science fiction and fantasy stories. Several of her stories won international awards and were featured in "Best of Year" anthologies.

Nancy Johnson-Hunt is a PhD candidate and popular culture scholar at the Auckland University of Technology. After a decade-long career within the advertising and marketing industry, both in Aotearoa, New Zealand and North America, she joins the Popular Culture Research Centre at AUT. She has been published in the *M/C Journal – Journal of Media and Culture* and the *Australasian Journal of Popular Culture*. She has also been featured in fashion and lifestyle media publications across Aotearoa, New Zealand. Her research interests include the construction of ethnic and racialized identities in popular culture, the diffusion of advertising culture, and as the influence of popular media in shaping everyday lives and stories.

Catherine Pugh completed her PhD at the University of Essex and is now a writer and independent scholar. Primarily writing about horror and science fiction across cinema, television, and theater, she is particularly fascinated by ideas of monstrosity and mental illness versus literary madness. Her research interests concern disability, mental illness/"madness," metamorphic monsters, and horror landscapes. She has contributed to various collections including: *At Home in the Whedonverse: Essays on Domestic Space, Place and Life*; *Politics of Race, Gender, and Sexuality in* The Walking Dead: *Essays on the Television Series and Comics*; *Vying for the Iron Throne: Essays on Power, Gender, Death and*

Performance in HBO'S Game of Thrones, as well as online journals including *Studies in Gothic Fiction*, and *Aeternum: The Journal of Contemporary Gothic Studies*.

Sarah Revilla-Sanchez is a PhD student in Hispanic Studies at the University of British Columbia. Her research lies at the intersection of gender and cultural studies, with a particular interest in gendered violence, contemporary Latin American fiction, and artivism (art+activism). She previously completed an MA degree in Sociology at the University of Victoria and an MA degree in Studies in Comparative Literatures and Arts at Brock University.

Cristina Santos is an Associate Professor at Brock University. Her work focuses on feminism and popular culture from an intersectional feminist perspective in the construct of "monstrous women" from an interdisciplinary and multicultural approach as seen in literature, film, television, popular culture, and mythology. She also researches the construction of the Other through testimony with a focus on the human experience of trauma, memory, and life that has been silenced and/or misrepresented. She is the author of *Unbecoming Female Monsters: Witches, Vampires, and Virgins* and the editor of books on testimony, monsters, and various topics in sexuality and gender studies.

Dawn Stobbart completed her doctorate at Lancaster University and is currently focusing on how videogames function in a trans and intermediary capacity for her second monograph. She has fingers in many pies, including queer studies, cultural studies, and media studies, as well as a focus on horror and the Gothic that bleeds into everything she does. She has an interest in contemporary media, and especially in looking at how narrative translates to videogames.

Taryn Tavener-Smith is a lecturer at Buckinghamshire New University. She holds a BA (Honors) in English Literature and Psychology as well as a Master's degree in English Literature. Her research interests extend to the Gothic genre with a particular focus on the monstrous-feminine, specters, madness, and vampires in contemporary British fiction. She also holds an affinity for the multidisciplinary application of Victor Turner's Theory of Liminality.

Jeffrey Andrew Weinstock is Professor of English at Central Michigan University, USA. He is the author or editor of twenty-seven books, the most recent of which are *The Monster Theory Reader* (2020), *The Mad Scientist's Guide* to Composition (2020), *Critical Approaches to Welcome to Night Vale: Podcasting between Weather and the Void* (2018), and *The Cambridge Companion to the American Gothic* (2018). Visit him at JeffreyAndrewWeinstock.com.

Kevin J. Wetmore, Jr. is the author of over a dozen books, including *Post-9/11 Horror in American Cinema, Eaters of the Dead: Myths and Realities of Cannibal Monsters,* and *The Theology of Battlestar Galactica,* as well as over a hundred book chapters, journal articles, and essays, on topics from ghosts on the Japanese stage to African Adaptation of Greek tragedy to Shakespeare in graphic novels. He is also the twice-Bram Stoker Award-nominated editor of books such as *Uncovering Stranger Things* and *The Streaming of Hill House.* He is an actor, director, and fight choreographer who lives and works in Los Angeles.

Gina Wisker is Professor Emeritus of Higher Education and contemporary literature, University of Brighton, Associate Professor supervising doctoral students in ICHEM, University of Bath, and Open University Associate Lecturer on A 233 "Storytelling: realism and fantasy." She has written or edited twenty-five books and published 140 articles. She specializes in twentieth-century women's writing, postcolonial, Gothic and popular fictions. Her published work includes *Margaret Atwood: An Introduction to Critical Views of Her Fiction* (2012), *Contemporary Women's Gothic Fiction* (2016), *Contemporary Women's Ghost Stories: Spectres, Revenants and Ghostly Returns* (2022).

Nicola Young is an independent scholar whose key research interests are the intersections between philosophy, religion, and film. Her published work includes contributions to *Breaking Down Joker: Violence, Loneliness, Tragedy* (2022) and *The Undead in the 21st Century: A Companion* (2022). She has also published in Transnational Cinemas, Fantasy/Animation and the Journal of Popular Television.

Acknowledgments

This book came about from a shared love of the film *Silent Hill* on Facebook and the discussions that came out of that, so I'd like to thank all those that shared that love and helped inspire this book that eventually evolved from it. I would like to thank all who have taken part in this collection at its various stages. It's been quite a journey with one thing and another, not least the pandemic, and unfortunately not everyone was able to stay involved to the end, yet this end would not have happened without them. To those who did reach this point, a huge well done for doing so under such difficult circumstances, it is no mean achievement, and you deserve a huge pat on the back for doing so. Also, many thanks to the always helpful team at Bloomsbury, and Laura in particular who has helped get us over the line, even with last-minute setbacks and delays. Most importantly I want to thank my forever wife Kasia without whom none of this would get done or be worth doing, and our two little monsters Seba and Maja that always manage to remind us of what's important in life. And of course, Mam i Tata Bronk for their continual support and endless supply of sernik Magdi.

It is only fitting that the main thanks for this book should go out to those women, like my own mother, who have endlessly and tirelessly railed against the limits arbitrarily set upon them by a patriarchal world and who have worked twice as hard, twice as long and for substantially less money, rights and recognition in almost every sphere of life, and often more so if they're not white, wealthy, or of the dominant social group. Purgatory in this sense is often not the lack of hope, but of hopes constantly and consistently deferred, denied, and destroyed. The hopes aroused by #MeToo seem to have suffered a similar fate as a system under threat reinforces its own version of the "natural" order and obfuscates the need for change behind "more important" things. And yet, it is the silencing of a woman (Mahsa Amini) and the subsequent backlash that has destabilized one of the strictest patriarchal, religious regimes in the Middle East. Even the silenced will be heard, and change will inevitably come. It is to them and the women who remain undeniably themselves that this book is dedicated.

Prologue

Simon Bacon

Since first writing the original Introduction to this book at the start of 2020 it feels as though the world has significantly shifted and that the feeling of the inevitable and significant change—in spite of the start of the Covid-19 pandemic—that still filled the air following Black Lives Matter (BLM) and #MeToo had not only stalled but been and so a Prologue seemed necessary. The pandemic itself seemed to press pause on life, as millions were forced to stay at home, shops were shut and roads, rails, and even the air emptied of nonvital travel and commerce. In many senses it was a time that was supposed to show our shared humanity and interdependence, but rather revealed and entrenched the divisions that were already there: the quest to go back to the "old normal" was in fact a drive to return to old forms of discrimination and privilege: Western, wealthy, white society most likely to receive care and vaccines; Black, Indigenous, People of Color (BIPOC) communities, minorities and the poor faring the worst, and domestic abuse hugely increasing—the UK reported a rise of 33 percent (MSI 2020) which was on top of the already high rate of one in three women worldwide being the victims abuse at home (UN Women n.d.). As ever, women seemed to bear the brunt of whatever ills were facing society as a whole—a situation equally seen during the recent conflicts across the world where rape and abuse of women has been shown once again to be integral to "modern" warfare. Alongside this, and as the waves of Covid-19 have become increasingly less deadly (for the vaccinated) and ignored by governments, the return to the "old normal" has become integral to politically fueled culture wars around anti-wokeness and the supposed eroding of the rights of white, privileged, heteronormative males. Much of this has taken the form of a return to an imagined time when people were "not so sensitive"—i.e., when those that were the focus of abuse and discrimination were not allowed a voice to call such acts out—and a backlash to possible changes initiated by the aforementioned BLM and #MeToo (though it should be noted that many related issues involving disenfranchised groups such as indigenous communities, the poor, BIPOC, and immigrant communities—both legal and nonlegal—have remained consistently unaddressed throughout this time). Women's rights in particular have been brought back into focus through two high-profile instances in the United States, that of the Amber Heard–Johnny Depp defamation case and the overruling of Roe vs Wade by the Supreme Court.

A celebrity couple involved in a big-profile court case following their breakup would seem more the fare of the gossip columns than a possibly important turning point in the battle for women's rights in the 2020s, yet the media and popular attention it garnered has made it so. The most immediate result of #MeToo was the number of cases of historical sexual and physical abuse on women brought against powerful, white males in the entertainment industry. Harvey Weinstein being probably the most well known, but it also brought to light the kinds of sexual violence that was endemic to nearly all workplaces. While the case of Depp and Heard centers around domestic abuse and the power dynamics within that—Depp being a substantially more powerful figure in the film industry than Heard—are reflective of the issues at stake in the Weinstein issue. Amber Heard and Johnny Depp divorced in 2016 after being married for less than a year. Stories soon began to emerge of domestic abuse in the relationship, but the subsequent trial involved a story in *The Washington Post* (December 2018) where Heard, although not naming Depp, said she was "a public figure representing domestic abuse" (Heard 2018). Prior to this Depp had sued the UK newspaper *The Sun* in June 2018 for libel after they cited Heard's claims of domestic abuse and lost with the judgment finding that the allegations of abuse were "substantially true" (Maddeus 2022). However, unwilling to accept that, Depp then brought a defamation case against Heard herself back in the United States in Fairfax County, Virginia in April 2022. Depp claimed that Heard's "untrue" statements had caused damage to his career losing him large amounts of money. Unlike the earlier trial, this one was largely live-streamed and quickly became as much about public performance as it was about ascertaining the truth. The atmosphere around the case, and particularly on social media—something that is normally purposely kept separate from trials in progress—was of a scale that meant it was impossible to be ignored by anyone involved with the trial and it quickly devolved into patriarchal stereotypes of the lovable, if foolish, old rogue (Depp) being taken advantage of by a gold-digging younger woman (Heard). Consequently Depp, a long-term substance abuser who suffers from blackouts, documented aggressive behavior while under the influence, and a growing reputation as a "problem" on set, was shown as an undeserving victim of Heard's conniving and money-grabbing behavior. Heard had already been in many high-grossing films herself by this stage and had even turned down money in the couple's divorce proceedings; so this was not an issue and much of her perceived "bad behaviors" were the purposeful misreading of what women need to do to be successful in a male-dominated industry. Ultimately the final judgment of the court was obviously based on their valuation of each party's performance rather than any facts that were presented—subsequent reports have shown large amounts of material showing Depp lost work due to his own behavior and not Heard's accusations (Stern 2022). Unlike the earlier trial, Depp, who was obviously "clean" of drugs throughout, effectively "gaslighted" the jury into ignoring his abusive behavior and alleging that Heard's was worse, also hiding the fact that his constant pursuit of his ex-wife in court until his story became the dominant is classic abusive behavior. Possibly even more importantly it cast further doubt on one of the tenets of #MeToo in that the victim should be believed, and that if such a high-profile figure as Amber Heard could be repeatedly taken back to court by her abuser and forced to recount and re-live her abuse over and over again, what hope was there for other unknown and "unseen" women—the Bill Cosby case of historical and repeated sexual abuse of multiple female victims tells a similar story (Savage 2021). If the Depp vs Heard case is a step backwards in the fight for women and victims everywhere to be heard and believed, Roe vs Wade being revoked is a far more existential threat on women's rights and the ownership of their own bodies.

The case of Roe vs Wade in 1973 saw the Supreme Court rule that the US Constitution conferred the right to have an abortion, a decision that has rankled pro-lifers, evangelical groups, and many conservatives ever since. The ruling had remained upheld until 2022 after new conservative nominees to the Supreme Court, Brett Kavanaugh and Amy Coney Barratt,[1] nominated during the Trump administration, overturned it citing that the right to abortion was not "deeply rooted in this Nation's history or tradition" (Blake 2022), despite examples to the contrary. This ruling returned judgment over abortion to the State level meaning individual jurisdictions could rule on whether it was allowable or not, ultimately meaning that they (the State) had control over the bodies of women living within

---

[1] Brett Kavanaugh was a controversial nomination as he was accused of the sexual abuse of Christine Blassey Ford, among others, while a freshman at college, an event he claimed to have no recollection of and which the FBI were later accused of insufficiently investigating (see Guardian Staff 2021). Amy Coney Barrett was a nominee rushed through by the Trump Administration, who claimed impartiality despite connections to a deeply conservative evangelical group the People of Praise (see Graham and LaFraniere 2020).

their borders—some states have even passed laws to allow for the prosecution of companies and individuals outside of their state who assist women seeking help with getting an abortion. As usual with such decisions those most affected are women of color, the poor, immigrant communities, and unregistered workers, but also speaks to a push toward more conservative values that limit the role of women within the workplace and positions of power. These repercussions inherently prioritize women as only mothers and homemakers whether they want to assume those roles or not—unsurprisingly this immediately resonated with popular dystopian series *The Handmaid's Tale* (see below) and a wry comment from the author Margaret Atwood herself (Willingham 2022). It should be noted that while Roe vs Wade was overruled following the weighting of the Supreme Court with conservative judges by a Republican President, previous Democrat administrations had done nothing to pass the original ruling into law guaranteeing that the right to abortion would always remain in place. What it does reflect though is the wider agenda of populist and conservative governments around the world that are increasingly denying women access to abortion—the European Union does not enforce it across its members states and countries such as Poland reintroduced an abortion ban as recently as 2021.[2]

What is of further importance within this in terms of the wider political and cultural climate of 2022 is the continued use of "the culture wars" as a means to garner popular support. While often making little rational sense, it constitutes a reaction to seeming "wokeness" in relation to willfully misinterpreted terms such as "freedom of speech" and a "return to traditional values" which in practical terms means continued, if not increased, discrimination of minority groups and the erosion of rights of women, BIPOC, immigrants, and the disenfranchised. This does not mean there have not been points of hope within all this with women continuing to be voted in as presidents and prime ministers—though as noted at the recent G7 meeting of the most powerful world leaders it is once again a "boys club" (Ghitis 2022). With Kamala Harris as the first Black American and Asian American woman as vice president and Ketanji Brown Jackson as the first Black American woman voted onto the Supreme Court, there is still hope. However, not unlike Persephone, it seems for every emergence into the sunlight and the promise of a new Spring, there is the inevitable return to darkness. At least for a while.

---

[2] Unsurprisingly, such bans are always linked to a strong connection between church and state in the respective countries involved.

Introduction

Simon Bacon

With the ongoing draw of populism, conservatism, and isolationism in world politics in the early twenty-first century, one could be forgiven for thinking that the values of inclusion and equality offered by neoliberal globalism have drifted into a purgatorial stasis with little sign of returning. The recent return to a form of excessive conservatism in many regions of the world, and in American politics in particular, seems to have moved the hopes of a re-emergent #MeToo into a parallel dimension within which time appears to have regressed. It might not be so surprising then that parallel purgatorial worlds seem to currently proliferate within popular culture: *Us* (Peele 2018), *The Umbrella Academy* (Blackman 2019–), *Watchmen* (Lindelof 2019), *Insidious* (Wan 2010), *NOS4R2* (Hill 2019–), and maybe more obviously *The Handmaid's Tale* (Miller 2017–). This last is of interest as although the hugely popular television series began in 2017 the novel by Margaret Atwood was published in 1985 suggesting, as the author has noted herself, that the kinds of observations she made about society thirty-plus years ago—and all the events described in the book were actually happening somewhere in the world in the 1980s—are not only relevant today but being realized.

The 1980s marked something of a new era, or consolidation of conservatism and one which would continue both overtly and covertly, virtually uninterrupted up until the present day. Starting with Ronald Reagan becoming president of the United States (1981–9), and to a lesser extent Margaret Thatcher as prime minister of Britain (1979–90), the promise of a continuation of the ground won in terms of women's rights during the 1960s and 1970s soon began to fade. Reagan in particular, while appointing the first woman to serve on the Supreme Court (Sandra Day O'Connor 1981–2006), was a staunch opponent of abortion and reproduction rights and even had the Equal Rights Amendment removed from the Republican platform in 1980—it had been part of their platform since

1940. More so, the conservative promotion of "family values" saw women further vilified as single mothers on benefits and disadvantaged in the workforce by a refusal to raise the minimum wage (women and single mothers forming the biggest proportion of those) and halving the funds of the Equal Employment Opportunities Commission.

The presidency of George Bush Sr. (1989–93) that followed continued much in the same vein and while promoting women's rights abroad, in the United States it tore down "the progress that women and other disenfranchised groups have made over the past 35 years" (Gaag 2004: 17). Bill Clinton, becoming president (1993–2001) on a wave of female support, seemed to offer a change in what had gone before, but his stance relied more on reproductive rights and not much else—it should be noted that during both Bush Sr.'s and Clinton's administrations increased funds were put toward abstinence education than sex education for children resulting in a rise in teenage pregnancies and sexually transmitted infections. Further Clinton signed the Personal Responsibility and Work Opportunity Reconciliation Act promoting childbirth in marriage by controlling the distribution of state welfare payments and effectively controlling women's sexual choices and stigmatizing nonconformism (Feldt 2004: 57), and not to mention his own predatory sexual nature and allegations of coercion and rape that undermined any positive messaging he made. George W. Bush (2001–9) presented a determined turn to the past, with a slow and steady refutation of women's rights returning them to a time when abortion was illegal and reproductive labor was a woman's destiny (Feldt 2004: 172)—it is possibly unsurprising then that it was during Bush's term in office that the phrase "Me Too" was first used on social media in 2006 by Tarana Burke.

Barack Obama becoming president (2009–17) seemed to offer so much more, and indeed much was done to further the cause of women in terms of equality in the workforce, reproductive rights, and personal safety. However, in part due to a Republican majority in Congress, more could have been done in regard to challenging laws already in place regarding the personal and sexual choices open to low-income women. In contrast of course it is the presidency of Donald Trump who sought to dismantle all of the positives forced through by the Obama administration, with a return to the pro-life stance of the Evangelical church and a right-wing base that simultaneously overlooks and finds affirmation in his sexual and misogynistic abuse of women. In many ways then, the present evangelical conservatism has gone full circle, creating its own purgatorial loop where the rights given to women are threatened with returning to what they were forty years ago. Obviously, things are not as straightforward as they often superficially seem, and while the impetus provided by the #MeToo Movement has allowed women to be able to speak out about the violence, inequality, and injustice enacted upon them, this still requires court appearances, appeals, and counterclaims (see the Depp vs Heard case described above) that demand the continual re-living and re-experiencing of the original abuse. It appears that while more women have been "allowed" to speak, meaningful and systemic change is still a distant goal.

Since the Reagan administration then, conservatism and particularly its almost evangelical imperative to regulate and control the female body have been the remit of the GOP, though as noted the Democratic Party, whether purposely or through outside prevention, has not necessarily accomplished as much to reverse that process as they might have. In fact, almost continually it is those women that are the most disenfranchised within American society whose bodies are most under threat from governmental regulation: BIPOC, immigrants, the unregistered, single mothers, low income, disability and physical or mental health issues. The distribution of federal funding toward things such as abortion (The Gag Rule), and relatedly the (non) access to medical insurance for such procedures have all seen women locked in a cycle of poverty and dependence that has seemed inescapable regardless of the party affiliation of the sitting president—many state-level legislators have made it illegal for their citizens to gain access to abortions both in and out-of-state.

That is not to say that there have not been moments when change, even if not legislatively, has seemed possible and some improvements made. The Violence against Women Act was passed in 1994 and in 2013 the American Military lifted a ban of women taking part in active combat. Aside from these it has been rather a list of individual firsts, such as Sally Ride (1983) becoming the first woman in space, Geraldine Ferraro (1984) becoming the first vice president nominee from a major party, Janet Reno (1993) the first woman attorney general, Madeleine Albright (1997) the first female Secretary of State, Nancy Pelosi (2007) the first female Speaker of the House, which she was again in 2019, and Hilary Clinton (2016) the first woman to win the presidential nomination for a major party, which have, potentially, opened the way for other women to follow. Of further note, especially in terms of individual courage, which is a point that recurs within the essays later, are those that came forward in regard to sexual harassment and abuse such as Tarana Burke (2006 and mentioned above), Ambra Gutierrez (2015), and Alyssa Milano (2017) in relation to both the Harvey Weinstein case and Christine Blasey Ford (2019) in regard to Supreme Court nominee Brett Kavanaugh. All of which have energized the #MeToo Movement though often with still undetermined and uncertain outcomes—the founding of #TimesUp in 2018 by a group of Hollywood celebrities was meant to be more action based and provided access to funds for legal action in workplace sexual assault and discrimination cases (see Langone 2018), but subsequently ran into difficulties after it came to light that its leaders had been involved in covering up sexual assault allegations against New York Governor Andrew Cuomo in 2021 (see Maddeus 2021).

In many ways then while there has been change, it has been a continual struggle against backlashes and the conservative, patriarchal system reclaiming what they thought they had lost. Even when there are times when things should have improved, as under Clinton, real change was thin on the ground and the president's treatment of women around him, and his obvious use of his position of power effectively reaffirms the patriarchal "traditionalism" that underpins conservatism.

Making direct correlations between real world, political struggles and cultural artifacts such as films or books can be problematic at best, unless the latter directly cites the former, and maybe even more so in terms of horror-orientated texts that are inherently configured around excess and exaggeration. While this might not make for realistic or balanced interpretations of actual events—not that these do not include scenes of excessive physical or psychological violence—horror, and indeed fantasy, is perfectly situated to represent the affective results of such situations and often posit modes and strategies of resistance. In this sense then such narratives simultaneously describe the purgatorial nature of women's lives within a heteropatriarchal and traditionally conservative society—tradition often being a term used by the Evangelical and Catholic Church to deny change and maintain their own authority—as well as offering possible strategies for coping and even resisting.

Consequently, this collection approximately spans the forty years of conservatism with a focus on the ongoing, seemingly, purgatorial, struggle of women to gain control over their bodies and their futures. And although the narratives considered here lean toward an emphasis on recent texts, they also include earlier historical examples in relation to historical and mythical conceptions of "Underworlds" and purgatorial type-spaces, and also figures such as La Llorona, which is of particular importance here to understanding the ongoing experience of life for women on the Mexican–US borders. In terms of contemporary popular culture the first seminal film in this lineage, and also in terms of the framework of this study, is *Silent Hill*, that first appeared as a game in 1998, but was made into a film by Christophe Gans in 2006. Coming out during George W. Bush's presidency the film constructs a very different purgatorial space. If earlier films like *Hellraiser* (Barker, 1987) posit the dangers of neo-liberalism, then *Silent Hill* reveals the monstrosity of extreme conservatism. Although George W. Bush himself campaigned as pro-women—"W stands for Women" (Finlay 2006: 4)—it quickly became apparent this was not the case since he was engaged in something of a war on women, slowly and methodically eroding much of the progress made under Clinton. More problematically, largely due to Bush's combative approach to foreign relations and the ongoing war on terror, equality and women's rights were not viewed as serious topics to discuss or resolve—this is rather interesting in its literal representation in *Silent Hill* when the female protagonist is standing in front of her husband, but he literally cannot see or hear her as she has become invisible in his world.

The film itself sees a family ripped apart by a monstrous child that was created by evangelical conservatism in a town so extreme that it exists in a parallel dimension that overlays itself in the real world. Once in this purgatorial realm its victims can never leave; however, this does not prevent all three main female characters from creating a sense of self-hood and autonomy within the horror-filled space of the town—coincidentally 2006 is the same year the #MeToo Movement began via the parallel world of social media. None of the women, the daughter Sharon/Alessa (Jodelle Ferland), the mother Rosa (Radha Mitchell), or the policewoman Cybil (Laurie Holden), has transgressed any rules to be where they are, but rather their trapped state reflects their everyday roles within the real patriarchal world beyond the town. Subsequently, in the town of Silent Hill being a mother is a role one is never allowed to leave and no matter how Rosa tries to leave it and return to the real world as herself she is not allowed to. Similarly, being a daughter is fully proscribed and trying to be other than that monsterizes the child as almost demonic in nature. What is of special note is that even though Rosa and Alessa are trapped, they still find ways to be themselves beyond the strict confines of the world in which they find themselves. This theme of resistance and agency by female characters even in spaces within which they are trapped runs throughout the films considered here. Consequently, the narratives looked at in this volume can be seen to often resonate with Deleuze and Guattari's ideas around becoming (2004), and the stultifying nature of patriarchal identity positions where women and girls are uniquely placed to escape and create their own trajectories away from that.

The construction of the parallel purgatorial worlds here often divides into being either a space that mirrors normative patriarchal roles, as seen in *Silent Hill*, or one within which one can escape them, like *Pan's Labyrinth* (del Toro

2006)—curiously both of these see the real world as the truly purgatorial stultifying space that allows no opportunities for individual female identity positions. This is not a unique tactical approach to such real-world situations which find expression in and through popular culture and there are some examples going back as far as the late nineteenth century—Ann Radcliffe the vampire slayer travels between dimensions in *Vampire City* (1867) by Paul Féval. Indeed, the fantasy genre in general is often predicated on the idea of alternate worlds and/or histories, and as noted by Elbar-Aviram (2021), among others, such worlds are often directly linked to and influenced by real-world events and locations—as dramatically seen in Atwood's *The Handmaid's Tale* as mentioned earlier. More so, as she continues, they are often created to comment upon or critique the world/location/political situation of the location that they are mirroring or parallel to. With the introduction of the idea of fantasy and the fantastic it is worth clarifying just how the concept of purgatorial worlds, in the context of this collection, both aligns with and differentiates itself within such a categorization. In relation to such worlds, one immediately thinks of Dante's *Inferno* in terms of levels of interminable pain and suffering, though we should not forget that it was followed by the *Purgatorio* (early fourteenth century). Here, the penitential could work their way out of purgatory, as illustrated by the climb of Dante, guided by Virgil, up the Mount of Purgatory to enter Earthly Paradise.[1] Dante's tale is an example of an immersive world, but Farah Mendelsohn describes the three other types of narrative approach within fantasy worlds and how we as readers/audience engage with them. In total the four types are: portal quest, where we are invited to enter; intrusion fantasy, where the fantastic forces its way into ours; liminal fantasy, where it seems imminent but just out of view; and immersive fantasy, where we have no escape (Mendlesohn 2008: xiv). Most of these types are seen in the worlds considered here; however, their purgatorial nature shapes and often restricts the ways with which they can be interacted.

Of paramount importance here is that the two worlds must be kept apart, after all purgatory is only that if one is trapped there. That is not to say that doorways or portals cannot connect the two worlds/dimensions, or that representatives from the other side cannot intrude into our world. Of note here is the exception to the rule in which momentarily the two worlds become porous, which is always locational and tends to infer that the parallel world occupies the same space

---

[1] The *Chilling Adventures of Sabrina* (Aguirre-Sacasa: 2018–present), season 2, episode 4 "Dante's Inferno" uses the idea of purgatory in its plot. Also their concept of The Weird could fall under a purgatorial space.

as the real one but just in a different dimension. There is also the sense here that though the purgatorial space is a domain to which women are banished or exiled from the patriarchally controlled "real" world, it is also a space that they have some control over. Unlike the other examples this involves a "shimmer" or falling mass, such as snow or ash, that indicates the changing nature of the space one is occupying which compounds both the ideas of a portal and immersion; there is an invite from the other world and/or a need of the occupant of this world which allows the "victims" to be immersed (trapped) in the purgatorial dimension.

The exact nature of the purgatorial world within the texts chosen here often varies in appearance in being almost an exact copy of the real world to something more otherworldly or hell-like, though it often functions in a similar way in being a place for its female protagonists to develop an identity position that was denied them in the real world. In a curious way then the purgatorial space seems to offer opportunities to change or evolve in ways that the real world seems not to. In part this could be explained by the often irrational and/or unfamiliar nature of the purgatorial space which allows for behavior that would be deemed inappropriate in the real world. Equally, the purgatorial world oftentimes announces that it is just that from the start, whereas the real world often hides this fact from those that live there and it means harm to certain groups living there—thereby forestalling acts of rebellion and resistance. Alongside this is the more religious idea around purgatory which requires a passing, if only symbolically, from life to death and, occasionally, back. In this regard Rebecca Reinof's work around the Victorian novel and specifically the "Belly of Sheol" is of use here. Reinof talks of the narrative lull which by unnamed critics is likened to Jonah's sojourn in the belly of the whale, and which she in turn correlates to a journey to Sheol, Hades, or the land of the dead. Jonah's time in this subterranean world is both an escape from the world and a space of "recessive action" which the author further describes as "growth and development" (Reinof 2015: 1–3). Returning to purgatorial worlds and parallel dimensions can then be seen as places beyond or other to the real world (i.e., life) which allow for more focused time on individual growth and/or the development of new or previously unthought of identity positions. The belly of the fish becomes a useful analogy in this sense: being in the world but also outside it—a place of stasis yet also one in which the individual can grow. Maybe more interestingly it is a place where Jonah goes to escape God, and the law of the father. Although he returns to the world he left, largely as noted by Deleuze and Guattari because as a man his trajectory cannot take him anywhere else, the girls and women focused on here have other possibilities in front of them, though none of them come without some form of significant personal sacrifice.

Many of the texts referred to here purposely create their purgatorial worlds as spaces that resemble our own—*Hellraiser* and *Insidious* (Wan, 2010) are two examples that purposely do not do this seeing the other, purgatorial space, as completely alien to our everyday experience and obviously dangerous because of that fact—though they might vary from spaces that could be from our world yet do not appear familiar or to follow the expected norms/laws (*Watchmen*, *We Are What We Are* [Mickle 2013], *Slade House* [Mitchell 2015]) to those which copy Earthly locations but are shown as diseased, decrepit, or overgrown (*Silent Hill*, *Stranger Things* [Duffer Brothers 2016–present], *Triangle* [Smith 2009], *Coraline* [Selick 2009]). The effect of this is twofold in that, firstly, it directly links such stories to our own world and our lived experience of it and which necessarily implies the political realities that inform and shape our relationship to that environment. Secondly, it upsets that sense of the familiar and the known revealing them to be alien, unknown, and often existentially dangerous. This creates a sense of the uncanny, Freud's notion of the unexpected change between the "homely" and the "unhomely" that sees not only a shift in how we are able to interact with this new space but also adapt to a world whose purpose (narrative) has very different goals to our own (Kranc 2014: 143). This is actually an important feature of parallel environments as while we are used to what we think is the purpose of the real world (via religion, evolutionary imperative, ideological, and/or cultural expectation), the proximity of purgatorial space changes this or more often accentuates that of the real world so that one aspect of it becomes existential in its nature—in *Silent Hill* for example what was a tense mother/adoptive daughter relationship in the real world becomes not just a fight for individual survival but a potentially cataclysmic struggle between good and evil. As such this aspect helps to affirm the direct linkage between the texts used here, which feature such copies/doppelgängers of the real world, and the specific cultural context from which they emerged. The uncanny invoked by supernatural copies of the world, the above as it is below trope, often brings the domestic and the familiar in direct conjunction with the spectral, horror, and violence. Consequently, the purgatorial dimension/supernatural realm can be seen to "enhance, threaten, reaffirm" (Robinson 2009: 253) the bonds that existed between character, mothers/children, wives/partners, sisters/brothers, in the real world. This in part begins to explain why parallel worlds which enforce complete immersion upon those in them act as an impetus to change, this time away from reality becomes a space of accentuated and increased emotional states which necessarily initiate a state of psychic fight or flight—either one battles to gain individual agency and resists being consumed by the alien environment or one complies, and identity is lost. Indeed, in many ways it is the nature of the purgatorial space itself that creates the environment that potentializes the women within it, literally forcing the female characters trapped within them to create identity positions that can not only navigate that space but mirror tactics of opposition and occupation that can then be utilized within our own world.

The Levels of Purgatory

The collection is divided into sections which focus on the four main areas identified above: (1) the nature of the purgatorial spaces created as a place that is created as an excess of the real-world situation, or as an escape from it; (2) the main female familial identity positions and relationships, such as wife, mother, and daughter and the subsequent traumas that are enacted between such reified identity positions within excessively conservative societies; (3) the kinds of growth and personal change that are enacted by women and girls within purgatorial spaces and which can also be seen as potentializing possible trajectories away from the conservative world that holds them down; and (4) the idea of tactics of resistance into ways to become both individually and collectively beyond the systems of conservatism and inequality that has previously sought to define them.

"Part One: Purgatorial Space" establishes types and qualities of purgatorial environments and how they are denoted within narrative texts. It begins with Jeffrey Andrew Weinstock discussing "Particulate Matter: Miasma Theory and Modern Horror" which looks at miasma theory, a belief that lasted into the nineteenth century that certain kinds of air carried disease creating a pestilential environment. Cinematic purgatorial spaces often use particulate matter then as a shorthand to represent a dangerous or hostile space, and often one that humanity itself is responsible for in someway. Weinstock then looks at examples of such miasmic spaces as seen in *Silent Hill*, *Penny Dreadful* (Logan 2014–16), and *Stranger Things* (Duffer Brothers 2016–present) to show how society has created ecological and political environments that have become increasingly antithetical to human life. The next chapter, "Between Hell and Hel: Gender, History, and Nature in Subterranean Spaces" by Elana Gomel looks at the creation of a feminine purgatorial space underground, a *hel* of rebirth and growth in contrast to the masculine *hell* of violence and destruction. Looking at

Jeff Long's *The Descent* (2001) and *Deeper* (2007), and Adam Nevill's *Reddening* (2019) Gomel considers ways in which environments of patriarchal conservative containment can be re-envisioned as spaces of change and evolution. The section ends with "La Llorona Hauntings: Storytelling Feminicide at the Purgatorial Mexico/US Border" by Cristina Santos and Sarah Revilla that focuses on the historical beginnings and contemporary retellings of the tragic figure of the "weeping women." La Llorona's grief and never-ending search for her children and her future embodies the plight of Chicana women trapped in the purgatorial space of the Mexican–US border. Indeed, the over-familiarization and comedic use of the figure more recently points less toward recognition of the plight of La Llorona and contemporary weeping women but a forgetting of what and who she represents.

"Part Two: Daughters, Mothers, Trauma" looks more closely at the roles imposed on women by the conservative environment around them. The first chapter in this section "'I Lost All Hope of Going up the Hill': *Silent Hill* as a Female Specific Inferno" by Dawn Stobbart looks at *Silent Hill* but with a slightly different reading of its purgatorial space. Here, it is the trauma and abuse of the child by the extreme and religiously conservative society around her that creates a space of all consuming monstrosity. As argued by Stobbart, the film in particular highlights the kinds of purposeful misrecognition and mistreatment of mental illness in such societies and the inescapable hell they produce for their "daughters." Catherine Pugh's chapter "'Mother Is God in the Eyes of a Child': Doppelgängers, Punishment, and Maternal Otherworlds in *Silent Hill* and *Triangle*" similarly focuses on the nature of the purgatorial world in *Silent Hill* but reads it as one constructed by maternal guilt and trauma that is caused by the ideologically enforced modes of acceptable motherhood created by an ultra conservative society. Further, this guilt is often constructed around the idea of the lost or abandoned child, as seen in texts such as *Poltergeist* (Hooper 1982); *Aliens* (Cameron 1986); *Resident Evil: Apocalypse* (Witt 2004), where the societal reification of family and childhood means that the "mother" must sacrifice everything to always be "there" for the future of the nation. Lastly, "Pray and Obey: The Horror (and Purgatory) of Religious Fundamentalism" by Nicola Tyrell looks at the films *Silent Hill* (Gans 2006), *Silent Hill: Revelation* (Bassett 2012), and *We Are What We Are* (Mickle 2013). All three films feature forms of fundamentalist religion, all constructed as oppositional to the world around them yet equally distilling an excessive conservatism that rigidly defines the roles and behavior of the women who are part of them. Yet, as Tyrell argues, the purgatorial spaces they produce critique the absolute authority of men within them, allowing for an unexpected level of self-determination for those daring to subvert the norms around them.

"Part Three: Female Development in Purgatorial Spaces" looks more explicitly at the ways in which women who are trapped in purgatorial spaces utilize the monstrosity of the environment around them to fashion tactics of resistance and agency to produce often transgressive identity positions in opposition to the all-consuming conservatism around them. The section opens with "The New Eden? The Female-Centered Purgatorial Space of *Dollhouse*" by Erin Giannini with a study of those often worst affected by conservatism, and certainly since Reagan, poor, low-waged woman. Citing an act from 1980 that supposedly protected such women from the exploitation of large corporations, and which appears to have had no lasting effect, Giannini uses the series *Dollhouse* as an example of the kind of purgatorial space created in such circumstances. Here identities are erased and with seemingly little hope to resist or ever escape. The next chapter "The Vampire in the Attic: Constructing Monstrous Female Identities in Liminal, Purgatorial Spaces" by Taryn Tavener-Smith continues something of this, though with a form of hope, in the purgatorial space of *Slade House*. The females trapped within its walls have become monstrous, feeding upon those that come into their orbit but also possessing them, turning others into what they themselves are. However, even in this monstrous space, which is itself a synecdoche of the monstrous restrictive world around it, the vampiric women create their own unique selves in relation to the environment within which they are trapped. "'Into the Further We Go': Exploring Gender, World-building, and the Return of the Fantastic in the *Insidious* Franchise" by Mark Richard Adams looks at the often-forgotten figure of the older woman. In contrast to the traditional trend of having aged men as a demon or ghost hunter, as seen in the figure of Van Helsing from Bram Stoker's *Dracula*, the *Insidious* franchise uses the figure of Elise, a gray-haired woman who treats both the world of monsters and world of men with the same air of authority and assuredness. Indeed, the series approach to time and storytelling, with the past and future being constantly intermingled in a temporal nexus nominally denoted as the present, reveals Elise as never fully in or removed from her world. As such, her ongoing battles with the forces of extremism, often conservative in nature, are simultaneously ones that will never end but also battles which she has already won. In the concluding chapter in this section "Coded Outcry: Margaret Atwood's *The Handmaid's Tale* (1985 and 2017–Present) and *The Testaments* (2019)," Gina Wisker explores the world beyond Atwood's original story, a world that is thirty-five years older but oddly the same. Looking particularly at the television adaptation of the novel (2017–present) and the book's long-awaited sequel *The Testaments* (Atwood 2019), Wisker uncovers that history is never quite what we think it is, and that female resistance, even in the most purgatorial of places, hope springs eternal. As such, the dystopian tale gives renewed belief in the accumulation of small acts of subversion and agency, that might, after great sacrifice, bring about eventual change.

"Part Four: Spaces of Female Resistance" continues the argument from the previous section into ways of more obvious resistance and possible escape for those caught in a conservative purgatorial space. The section begins with "Of Monstrous Spaces: Female Identity in *American Horror Story: Murder House* and *American Horror Story: Hotel*" by Pembe Gözde Erdogan and starts with a more general overview of family and the relationships between its various members: father, mother, and daughter. In particular, it highlights the monstrosity of enforcing such roles as unchanging and transhistorical rather than fluid and evolving. More so, within the purgatorial realms created, it reveals the possibility of deterritorializing and reconstructing the nature of family and familial bonds beyond societal constraints. Following this is "'This Time I'll Get It Right': Female Coming-of-Age within Purgatorial Time Loops" by Shawn Edrei who looks at a very particular kind of purgatorial space, the time loop. The idea of an ever-recurring period of time—typically restarting from a specific morning the protagonist woke up—constructs an inescapable regime of repetition and regulation where the same politicized environment remains in place forever. However, as Edrei explains in narratives such as *Puella Magi Madoka Magica* (manga-to-anime), *X-Men* (comics-to-television-to-film), and *Elsinore* (theater-to-videogame), the young female protagonists enact a form of maturation through this process allowing them to eventually escape this toxic repetition. In "The Trauma We Inherit: Sister Night, Black Female Identity and the Parallel Racial Purgatory of *Watchmen*," Kevin J. Wetmore Jr. examines the parallel world created in the television series *Watchmen* (Jefferson 2019). In this world the two main protagonists are both women, one African American and the other Vietnamese American with the latter being the criminal nemesis of the former, who is a policewoman. Wetmore explores why each has chosen the path they have in relation to the extreme conservatism around them and how they have constructed their respective identities in relation to the systemic racism of the worlds around them. In a related manner, the final chapter in this collection "'We're Human Too, You Know': Tethered Journeys and Shadowed Struggles in Jordan Peele's *Us*" (2019), by Nancy Johnson-Hunt, talks of change over time.

In fact, a very similar amount of time as although *Us* is set in the United States of 2019, the events within it began in 1986 when a small African American girl wanders into a fun fair and literally comes out a different person. While the film focuses largely on events in the real world, it is the accumulating act of resistance by the girl left down below that brings the narrative to its denouement as the gates of purgatory open spilling its contents over into "real" America. The borders between worlds have gone and the conservative society that segregated the unwanted, the othered, and the feminized—see Gomel's chapter—will finally need to recognize those it previously refused to see.

Even as the film *Us* comes to an end, the potential for change has only been proposed, and nothing has substantially altered at films end. Indeed, this is a state which, arguably, America and many multicultural societies have remained in for much of their recent histories. One can hope, as seen with some of the examples here, how one individual woman can stand for the collective and that the sacrifices, resistance, and rebellion of one individual (woman) can bring about change for a "sisterhood," or collective. This volume closes with a similar sense of possibility still to be realized and a belief that in spite of continual setbacks and a portion of the population still finding solace in the privilege offered by conservative traditionalism, the purgatory that it provides for the many will come to an end, soon and irrevocably.

Works Cited

Blake, A. (2022), "The Supreme Court's Draft Opinion on Overturning Roe v. Wade, Annotated," May 3. https://www.washingtonpost.com/politics/interactive/2022/dobbs-alito-draft-annotated/.

Deleuze, G. and F. Guattari (2004), *A Thousand Plateaus: Capitalism and Schizophrenia*, Brian Massumi (trans.), London: Continuum.

Feldt, G. (2004), *The War on Choice: The Right-Wing Attack on Women's Rights and How to Fight Back*, New York: Bantam.

Finlay, B. (2006), *George W. Bush and the War on Women: Turning Back the Clock on Women's Progress*, London: Zed Books.

Ghitis, Frida, "Opinion: 'Show Them Our Pecs!' The G7 'Boys Club' Is Back," *CNN*, June 29, 2022. https://edition.cnn.com/2022/06/28/opinions/g7-boys-club-leaders-women-ghitis/index.html. Accessed August 5, 2022.

Graham, R. and S. LeFraniere (2020), "Inside the People of Praise, the Tight-Knit Faith Community of Amy Coney Barrett," October 8. https://www.nytimes.com/2020/10/08/us/people-of-praise-amy-coney-barrett.html.

Guardian Staff (2021), "FBI Failed to Fully Investigate Kavanaugh Allegations, Say Democrats," July 22. https://www.theguardian.com/us-news/2021/jul/22/brett-kavanaugh-sexual-misconduct-allegations-fbi-senators.

Heard, A. (2018), "Opinion Amber Heard: I Spoke up against Sexual Violence—and Faced Our Culture's Wrath. That Has to Change," *The Washington Post*, 18 December. https://www.washingtonpost.com/opinions/ive-seen-how-institutions-protect-men-accused-of-abuse-heres-what-we-can-do/2018/12/18/71fd876a-02ed-11e9-b5df-5d3874f1ac36_story.html.

Kranc, J. H. (2014), "'You Don't Even Need the Island to Be Weird': J. J. Abrams and the Weirding of the Small Screen," in T. R. Cochran, S. Gina and P. Zinder (eds), *The Multiple Worlds of Fringe: Essays on the J.J. Abrams Science Fiction Series*, 139–54, Jefferson: McFarland & Company, Inc.

Longone, A. (2018), "#MeToo and Time's Up Founders Explain the Difference between the 2 Movements—And How They're Alike," *Time Magazine*, March 22. https://time.com/5189945/whats-the-difference-between-the-metoo-and-times-up-movements/.

Maddeus, G. (2021), "Time's Up Dissolves Advisory Board That Included Natalie Portman, Jessica Chastain and Reese Witherspoon," Variety, September 9. https://variety.com/2021/film/news/times-up-advisory-board-natalie-portman-jessica-chastain-reese-witherspoon-1235060159/.

Maddeus, G. (2022), "Johnny Depp's Second Defamation Trial Gets Underway in Virginia," April 11. https://variety.com/2022/film/news/johnny-depp-amber-heard-virginia-trial-1235229579/.

Mendelsohn, F. (2008), *Rhetorics of Fantasy*, Middletown: Wesleyan University Press.

MSI (2020), "Welcome to MSI Reproductive Choices UK," n.d. https://www.msichoices.org.uk/#.

Reinof, R. (2015), *The Victorian Novel of Adulthood: Plot and Purgatory in Fictions of Maturity*, Athens: Ohio University Press.

Robinson, C. (2009), "Mommy, Baby, Ghost: The Technological Chain Letter and the Nuclear Family in the *Ring*," in L. M. DeTora (ed.), *Heroes of Film, Comics and American Culture: Essays on Real and Fictional Defenders of Home*, 253–68, Jefferson: McFarland & Company Inc.

Savage, Charles (2021), "Bill Cosby's Release from Prison, Explained," October 14. https://www.nytimes.com/2021/07/01/arts/television/bill-cosby-conviction-overturned-why.html.

Stern, M. (2022), "More Than 6,000 Pages of Docs Were Unsealed in the Depp v. Heard Defamation Saga, Including Heard's Worry that Depp Would Use Her Nude Pics and the Exclusion of Marilyn Manson," *The Daily Beast*, August 1. https://www.thedailybeast.com/unsealed-docs-from-johnny-depp-v-amber-heard-defamation-trial-contain-shocking-new-claims.

UN Women (n.d.), "The Shadow Pandemic: Violence against Women during COVID-19." https://www.unwomen.org/en/news/in-focus/in-focus-gender-equality-in-covid-19-response/violence-against-women-during-covid-19.

van der Gaag, N. (2004), *The No-Nonsense Guide to Women's Rights*. Oxford: New Internationalist Publications Limited.

Willingham, A. J. (2022), "'Handmaid's Tale' Author Has a Message about Roe v. Wade," *CNN*, July 12. https://edition.cnn.com/2022/07/12/entertainment/margaret-atwood-handmaids-tale-roe-wade-instagram-cec/index.html.

Part One

Purgatorial Space

1

Miasma Theory, Particulate Matter and Modern Horror

Jeffrey Andrew Weinstock

In the fourth episode of the final season of the Showtime/Sky Atlantic series *Penny Dreadful* (2014–16), the character Dracula (Christian Camargo) tries to entice series protagonist Vanessa Ives (Ava Green) to give herself over to him and thus bring about the apocalypse: "Give me your flesh. Give me your blood. Be my bride," he tells her, "[a]nd then all light will end and the world will live in darkness. The very air will be pestilence to mankind. And then our brethren, the Night Creatures, will emerge and feed."

And, indeed, in the final episodes of the series, as our updated crew of light seeks to thwart Dracula's dark designs, the air becomes pestilential (see Figure 1.1). Making use of what has now become a common visual motif in contemporary horror, *Penny Dreadful* depicts pestilential air as fog and particulate matter floating in the air, signifying environmental despoliation, a carcinogenic atmosphere, and the presence of disease. In this, it joins other horror vehicles such as *Silent Hill* (2006) in which the air is filled with ash from an endlessly burning coal fire beneath the town; *Stranger Things* (2016–) in which the "Upside Down," the lair of the monster, is marked by particulate matter; and even *Get Out* (2017) in which the blackness of "the Sunken Place" into which protagonist Chris (Daniel Kuluuya) is thrust is interrupted by bits of detritus floating like stars in the dark.

Contemporary horror cinema and television in this way offers an updated version of "miasma theory"—the belief that existed up through the nineteenth century that diseases were caused by "bad air" and the presence of miasma, a "poisonous vapour in which [are] suspended particles of decaying matter that

Figure 1.1 Pestilential air surrounds werewolf Ethan Chandler (Josh Hartnett) in *Penny Dreadful,* created by John Logan © Showtime Networks 2014–16.

was characterized by its foul smell" ("Miasma Versus Contagion"). Miasma theory found its way into a good deal of nineteenth-century Gothic writing—Charles Brockden Brown's two novels dealing with yellow fever, *Arthur Mervyn* (1799) and *Ormond* (1799), for example, correlate the disease with bad air; Edgar Allan Poe makes much of the "rank miasma of the tarn" in "The Fall of the House of Usher" (1839); the plague in Mary Shelley's apocalyptic *The Last Man* (1826) is carried on the winds, as is death in M. P. Shiel's later *The Purple Cloud* (1901). The twenty-first-century updating of miasma theory uses visual markers of bad air—dust motes, ash, floating particles, poisonous fog—as shorthand for a hostile environment. In modern horror, the bad air is essentially the milieu of the beast and an emanation of evil. But this recurring visual motif is arguably also a product of twenty-first-century ecological concerns as reflected by the snow-like radioactive fallout in the HBO/Sky UK series *Chernobyl* (2019). This convergence of real-world concerns with horror suggests an important way in which twenty-first-century horror is inevitably marked by the anxieties of the Anthropocene as human beings contend with horrors of our own making: modern miasma channels our awareness of environmental despoliation and ecological disaster and reflects our despair over human avarice and cruelty.

Miasma Theory

Miasma theory, the belief that disease is spread by "bad air," has a long history. As Carl S. Sterner summarizes in his overview of "Miasmic" theory, the assumption that bad air is the cause of pestilence can be traced back at least to ancient Greece. "Hippocrates," writes Sterner,

> believed bad air to be the cause of pestilence—or, more accurately, believed bad air was equivalent to pestilence. Vitruvius, in his *Ten Books on Architecture*, warns of the dangers of various kinds of bad air—exhalations from marshes, pestilential air, and unhealthy vapors .... Greco-Roman physician Galen ... expanded upon the theory of bad air, tracing individual susceptibility to the balance of humors in the body.
>
> (Sterner 2007: 1)

"The concept of bad air," continues Sterner, "was the primary explanation for disease in general, and the plague in particular, during the Middle Ages and into the Renaissance" (2007: 2). By the nineteenth century, as Daniela Blei notes, the belief that disease is caused by bad air was so firmly entrenched in conventional thinking that it was simply accepted as common sense (Blei 2020: n.p.).

The correlation between bad air and disease, already well established, was then strengthened further at the start of the nineteenth century by science on the one hand and daily existence on the other. Concerning science, Blei observes that late-eighteenth-century researchers discovered that the air exhaled by human beings is, in fact, deadly. "Experimenters such as Joseph Priestley," explains Blei, "put mice in airtight bell jars and observed that the mice died when alone, but lived longer if there was a plant inside. These experiments led doctors to warn against inhaling 'carbonic acid gas' (today we call it carbon dioxide) by breathing in air that others had exhaled—a common occurrence in crowded urban spaces like theaters, schools, and churches" (Blei 2020; see also Kiechle 2017: 26–7). And, where daily life is concerned, industrialization and urbanization resulted in polluted air that smelled bad and resulted in or triggered respiratory diseases. Blei puts it this way concerning nineteenth-century America:

> [U]rban environments were olfactory nightmares: Chicago reeked of its slaughterhouses, New Orleans smelled like its gasworks, fertilizer factories dumped stinking heaps of waste in the middle of Manhattan, and animal carcasses rotted in the filthy canals of Providence, Rhode Island. For the first time in history, large numbers of Americans lived in overcrowded cities, many

in poorly ventilated apartments, and killers such as cholera, tuberculosis, yellow fever, and typhus could strike at any moment, and often did.

(Blei 2020: n.p.)

Wietske Smeele explains that the "filth [of] growing urban centers" amplified the miasma theory of disease:

> With so many people packed into increasingly cramped spaces that were not adequately equipped with the sanitation measures necessary for such large populations, foul air became the norm of the urban landscape, as did infectious disease. Miasmatists, with social reformer Edwin Chadwick and nurse Florence Nightingale as their most famous proponents, believed that disease was created and carried by foul air emanating from sewage, polluted waters, and putrefying organic matter ... Air ... was seen as the primary threat to health in the first two-thirds of the [nineteenth] century.
>
> (Smeele 2016: 17)

London's Edwin Chadwick, who was instrumental in reforming England's Poor Laws and who led the charge in instituting sanitation and public health reforms, told a parliamentary committee in 1846 that "[a]ll smell is, if it be intense, immediate acute disease; and eventually we may say that, by depressing the system and rendering it susceptible to the action of other causes, *all smell is disease*" (Halliday 2001, emphasis mine). Florence Nightingale, for her part, believed that "cholera, smallpox, measles, and scarlet fever were all miasmatic in nature" and, as explained by Steven Johnson, advocated that schools, homes, and hospitals employ a particular "air test" to detect organic matter in the air (Johnson 2006: 124).

This belief that foul air caused or carried disease, promulgated by scientists and physicians, was repeated and reinforced across the nineteenth century by authors, philosophers, and political theorists in both literal and figurative ways—and, as Melanie A. Kiechle explains in her study *Smell Detectives: An Olfactory History of Nineteenth-Century Urban America*, "before germ theory explained that microscopic germs, microbes, bacteria, and viruses cause illnesses, miasma theory rationalized ill health ranging from headaches, nausea, diarrhea, and slight fevers to deadly outbreaks of cholera, yellow fever, and typhus as a result of inhaling bad air" (2017: 5). In the literature of the period, the association between foul air and disease is so ubiquitous as to be virtually inescapable. Yellow fever, which plagued eastern and southern American cities during the summer, was associated by American novelists with the air—this is the case in both of Charles Brockden Brown's novels involving yellow fever in Philadelphia, *Arthur Mervyn* (1799) and *Ormond* (1799). William Wells Brown's *Clotel or The President's Daughter: A Narrative of Slave Life in the United States* (1853) depicts the horrific outcome of a yellow fever outbreak in New Orleans as follows:

> The disorder spread alarm and confusion throughout the city. On an average, more than 400 died daily. In the midst of disorder and confusion, death heaped victims on victims. Friend followed friend in quick succession. The sick were avoided from the fear of contagion, and for the same reason the dead were left unburied. Nearly 2000 dead bodies lay uncovered in the burial-ground, with only here and there a little lime thrown over them, *to prevent the air becoming infected*.
>
> (Brown 1853: n.p., emphasis mine)

More generally, Edgar Allan Poe's "The Fall of the House of Usher" (1839) foregrounds atmospheric effects from start to finish, highlighting the "pestilent and mystic vapour" and "rank miasma of the tarn," and both Poe and Melville foreground the pestilential nature of the air in ships' holds. Cynthia Harris notes that "miasmatic thinking" undergirds Charles Dickens's *Bleak House* (1852–3) in which disease is associated with particular places, notably tenements and cemeteries, such as "a hemmed-in churchyard, pestiferous and obscene, whence malignant diseases are communicated to the bodies of our dear brothers and sisters who have not departed" (Harris 2018: n.p.). This same belief is repeated in a literal way in Frederick Engels's *The Condition of the Working-Class in English in 1844*, which notes the pernicious effects of "miasmatic gas" and "miasmatic vapours" (n.p.) in depressed economic areas. The naïve American Daisy Miller in Henry James's early 1878 novel of the same name succumbs to "Roman Fever" (Malaria), associated with the air, after an ill-advised evening trip to the Colosseum.

The list here of nineteenth-century literary texts that associate bad air with disease and decay is long indeed—one could add that Dracula appears to Renfield in the form of fog in Stoker's novel and that bad or poisonous air is recurring motif of decadent poetry. At its most virulent, bad air in literature is presented as having apocalyptic consequences—this is the case in Mary Shelley's *The Last Man* (1826) and then again in M. P. Shiel's *The Purple Cloud* (1901). In philosophy, Nietzsche privileges the use of bad air as a broad metaphor for the decay of European morality and religion in *Beyond Good and Evil* (1886) and *On the Genealogy of Morals* (1887). "Bad air," in the nineteenth century, was thus shorthand for diseased conditions, both physical and moral.

It is important to note that miasma theorists were not altogether wrong; they, however, generally mistook correlation for causation. Rank odor can certainly signal unhealthy conditions and poor ventilation helps disease to propagate—and, in the case of carbon monoxide poisoning, associated in the nineteenth century with illuminated gas lighting and coal fires, or heavily polluted air triggering asthma and other respiratory conditions, the air itself can, in fact, be deadly. In most cases, however, it is not the air that kills; as concerns cholera, the cause was usually bacterial contamination of water rather than air. In the case of yellow fever, the cause is a virus spread by mosquito bites. Typhoid fever is a bacterial infection spread via contaminated water or food, and so on. Nevertheless, for much of human history up through the nineteenth century, foul odors and "bad air" "were not merely clues that air was unhealthy; they were the substance of ill health itself" (Sutter in Kiechle 2017: xi). "In the 1800s," writes Kiechle, "scientists and physicians, politicians and reformers, housewives and day laborers"—and we might add artists and authors—"shared common sense as well as environmental knowledge that foul odors directly harmed health and caused illness" (2017: 15).

Miasma Theory Revisited

On Saturday April 26, 1986, the core of the No. 4 reactor at the Chernobyl Nuclear Power Plant near the Ukrainian city of Pripyat ruptured, leading to an open-air reactor core fire. Contaminated air then carried radioactive particles across Asia and Europe. The sequence of events leading up to the disaster and its aftermath are dramatized in the 2019 HBO/Sky Atlantic miniseries *Chernobyl*—and among the most memorable images from this powerful series is of onlookers to the meltdown being showered with radioactive contamination, with children playing in it as though it were snow (see Figure 1.2).

This image of poisonous particulate matter falling from the sky is emblematic of what we might consider the "miasmatic turn" of modern horror media. Although miasma theory began to be superseded in the second half of the nineteenth century by germ theory as science and medicine gained a better understanding of the etiology of various diseases, the visual register of contemporary film and television—finding a basis in twentieth- and now twenty-first-century anxieties related to nuclear fallout, climate change, global pandemics, vast wildfires, and other catastrophes with greatly extended geographic disbursement—has allowed for a reformulation of miasma theory in which fog and particulate

Figure 1.2 Children playing in the radioactive ash from Chernobyl in *Chernobyl*, created by Craig Mazin © HBO 2019.

matter serve as shorthand for toxicity, monstrosity, desolation, and decay. The recurring visual motif of bad air is arguably now a staple of contemporary horror and functions as a condensed marker of an alien environment antagonistic both to human life and to conventional neo-liberal values. A privileged avatar of the modern eco-Gothic, twenty-first-century bad air returns us to nineteenth-century miasma theory, often illustrating the consequences of human greed, negligence, or hubris. Bad air in this respect is the "object correlative" of cosmic indifferentism or moral debasement. However, contemporary representations of bad air also are tied to specially Anthropocene anxieties related to nuclear energy, environmental despoliation, and climate change. In twenty-first-century horror, the air is again pestilential, and the modern miasma of bad air reflects Anthropocenic dread over uncontrollable forces that imperil human existence.

Mist and fog are, of course, stock features of the Gothic and horror that elicit anxiety primarily by circumscribing vision. Protagonists become vulnerable as a consequence of being unable to locate the source of threat and to negotiate their surroundings. Mistiness also functions in both horror and fantasy as a conventional marker of the thinning of boundaries between worlds. As the world of conventional reality dissolves into mist, conveyance between worlds becomes possible. Protagonists often wander accidentally into different worlds or creatures from other realities may emerge from the mist into ours, as in John Carpenter's *The Fog* (1980) and Stephen King's "The Mist" (first published in 1980 and then memorably adapted for film by Frank Darabont in 2007). Steam, smoke, or fog is, indeed, almost obligatory in visual representations of supernatural horror, marking the milieu of the monster and the inhospitableness of the environment: the smoke that surrounds the demon in *Night of the Demon* (Jacques Tourneur, 1957), the fog on the moors of *American Werewolf in London* (John Landis, 1981), Freddy Kruger's hellish boiler room from *A Nightmare on Elm Street* (various, 1983–present), the thin layer of mist that obscures the alien pods in *Alien* (Ridley Scott, 1979), and so on.

There is, however, a distinction to be made between the Gothic or fantasy trope of fog and mist as natural phenomena that presage or accompany the emergence of the beast or the dissolution of boundaries, and particulate matter as a marker of toxicity—the latter of which is the recurring conceit of twenty-first-century horror and clearly reflects contemporary anxieties concerning environmental collapse and calamity; put differently, the conceit itself of bad air is Gothicized in modern media. It does not just accompany and/or obscure the threat; it itself *is* part of the threat—both to the lives of the protagonists and, often, to the world at large.

The nuclear fallout of Chernobyl—and the subsequent desolation of the surrounding area—finds its reflection, for example, in Christophe Gans's 2006 horror film *Silent Hill*—itself a transmedial adaptation of the 1999 Konomi videogame of the same name. Within the film, Rose da Silva (Radha Mitchell) travels with her adopted daughter, Sharon (Jodelle Ferland), to the abandoned town of Silent Hill, West Virginia, hoping to address her daughter's sleepwalking by returning with her to the place she is from. Following a car accident on the periphery of the town, Rose discovers Sharon is gone and enters Silent Hill after her. What initially engages her attention is ash that falls from the sky like snow (see Figure 1.3), blanketing the town—the product of a coal-seam fire that has been smoldering for thirty years and that was the cause of the town's abandonment. A gas station attendant later warns Rose's husband, Christopher (Sean Bean), "Breathe enough of them fumes, oh, bound to kill ya." The ash and fog that Rose encounters on the outskirts of the town presage the desolation she will find within (see Figure 1.4). Like the abandoned city of Pripyat near Chernobyl, Silent Hill—at least on the surface—is a ghost town. As Rose enters, she encounters empty buildings, rusted cars, trash-strewn streets, and dust and ash everywhere—and a huge chasm in the heart of the town. Indeed, perhaps the most impressive aspect of Gans's cinematic adaptation of the videogame is the rendering of the town's post-apocalyptic desolation, including the haunting interiors of crumbling buildings such as a school and a hotel.

However, the ash and fog in *Silent Hill* are not just the toxic aftermath of an eco-disaster; as is now conventional in fantasy and horror, they mark the

Figure 1.3 Rose considers the falling ash in *Silent Hill*, directed by Christophe Gans © TriStar Pictures 2006. All rights reserved.

Figure 1.4 Rose entering the abandoned town of Silent Hill in *Silent Hill*, directed by Christophe Gans © TriStar Pictures 2006. All rights reserved.

town's liminal status as a place caught between dimensions. What Rose discovers through her exploration of Silent Hill is that the town cycles between two dimensions—at times, it is a part of our recognizable world; at other times, it shifts into a nightmarish alternate dimension of mutated humans and monstrous being's hostile to human life. Unlike the mutations caused by radiation, Silent Hill's monsters are not directly the product of the fallout from the coal-seam fire—they instead result from the unleashed psychic powers of a persecuted little girl; however, darkness, ash, and decay are their poisonous milieu. As in the culmination of *Penny Dreadful*, the pestilential nature of the air in Silent Hill reflects the toxic nature of its monstrous inhabitants.

The cyclical interdimensional nature of Silent Hill finds its corollary in the "Upside Down" of the Netflix series *Stranger Things*; within *Stranger Things*, the Upside Down is an alternate dimension existing in parallel with or as the flipside of our dimension. The breach between dimensions, viewers learn, was opened by a test subject named Eleven (Millie Bobby Brown) while immersed in a sensory deprivation tank. During scenes of her experiences within such tanks, Eleven's consciousness is represented as projected into an empty, unbounded black space. Unlike the other spaces discussed here, however, this space of psychic projection is presented as a sterile point of contact. This, too, has become a kind of stylized visual shorthand for an alien dimension. Finding its roots in films such as *Dreamscape* (Joseph Ruben, 1984) and *Altered States* (Ken Russell, 1980)—and sharing a strikingly similar aesthetic with Jonathan Glazer's 2013 *Under the Skin*—the absence of particulate matter and detritus signals that this is a form of astral projection—outward rather than in—and the space is not "real" in a physical sense. It is rather a liminal zone between worlds where the real world meets the "Upside Down"—that this is a point of contact is suggested by the inverted mirror reflection of Eleven in the polished surface of the floor (see Figure 1.5).

Figure 1.5 Eleven (Millie Bobby Brown) in *Stranger Things,* created by The Duffer Brothers © Netflix 2016–.

In marked contrast to the emptiness and sterility of Eleven's psychic projections are the actual incursions into the Upside Down in *Stranger Things* where the toxicity of the air is foregrounded by the presence of particulate matter. In season 1, Sheriff Hopper (David Harbour) and Joyce Byers (Winona Ryder) wear hazmat suits as protection as they enter the alternate dimension to retrieve the kidnapped Will Byers (Noah Schnapp) (see Figure 1.6). The alternate dimension of the eerily post-apocalyptic Upside Down with its fog and particulate matter greatly resembles Gans's Silent Hill. In season 2, tunnels beneath the town of Hawkins that originate from the breach between worlds similarly are marked by pestilential particulate matter, against which the boys, Mike (Finn Wolfhard), Dustin (Gaten Materazzo), and Lucas (Caleb McLaughlin), protect themselves with makeshift bandana masks and goggles.

The breach between worlds, the viewer discovers, was the consequence of hubristic scientific exploration conducted at the Hawkins National Laboratory, apparently under the auspices of either the CIA or NSA, and interestingly finds its roots in the Cold War as Eleven's powers were originally used by the Hawkins research center director Dr. Martin Brenner (Matthew Modine) to track a Russian agent and thus gain a strategic advantage in the contest against the Soviet Union. As Jason Landrum notes, the Cold War thus acts like "a repressed historical referent" in the first season (2017: 142). Season 3 of *Stranger Things* then foregrounds this Cold War context directly by introducing Soviet scientists attempting to access the Upside Down on their own, and then a Soviet base improbably located beneath the Hawkins mall. Although the events in the

Figure 1.6 Sheriff Hopper (David Harbour) and Joyce Byers (Winona Ryder) in the hazmat suits in *Stranger Things,* created by The Duffer Brothers © Netflix 2016–.

Stranger Things seasons released at the time of this writing are set just prior to the Chernobyl disaster (season 1 takes place in 1983; season 4 in 1984; and season 5 in 1985), *Stranger Things* by way of this Soviet subplot arguably triangulates Chernobyl through images of toxic fallout brought about through reckless scientific endeavor—and possibly through the mushroom cloud resonances of the Upside Down's big bad, the Mind Flayer, a monstrous entity that extends itself upward like smoke before Will Byer's terrified eyes and seems to create its own weather as it is often depicted surrounded by a red thunderstorm (see Figure 1.7). Ludovic A. Sourdot adds that November of 1983—the historical setting for the first season of *Stranger Things*—was the month in which ABC television broadcast the TV movie *The Day After* that represented a nuclear attack on the United States and its apocalyptic aftermath. The movie attracted a viewing audience of some 100 million Americans (Sourdot 2018: 208). It is arguably not just the Cold War that serves as a structuring historical referent for the series, but anxiety of the atomic age as well.

In *Stranger Things*, the presence of particulate matter in the air signals a transition between and into another dimension. The barrier between this world and the Upside Down having been breached by hubristic scientific exploration, our world has been "contaminated." Monsters have gained access and, with them, the bad air that is their milieu. The Upside Down, particularly in season 1, is presented as a zone inhospitable to human existence—the

Figure 1.7 The Big Bad, the Mind Flayer, creating its own weather in *Stranger Things*, created by The Duffer Brothers © Netflix 2016–.

inversion of our world—and our possible future—is a dark, empty zone of decay marked consistently by particulate matter in the air. The conceit has become so prominent that it is now just "common sense." The miasma does not just mark the encroachment of the monstrous; it is itself toxic, and it shows us where we could be headed.

In Jordan Peele's 2017 allegory of American race relations, *Get Out*, the Upside Down is internalized as the Sunken Place, the interior space into which Chris (Daniel Kaluuya) sinks at the command of his hypnotist, Missy (Catherine Keener), leaving his body available for usurpation. Produced by the most intrusive use of special effects in the film, the Sunken Place is a liminal zone of helplessness and incapacitation. Chris is simultaneously floating in space and submerged in the depths of the ocean, and the only interruption of the seamless blackness is bits of particulate matter that float, like Chris, in the endless darkness, and suggest eventual decay. In the void of his interior prison, Chris himself floats like a bit of particulate matter, unable to alter his course (see Figure 1.8).

Importantly, the Sunken Place in *Get Out* obviously differs from the post-apocalyptic settings of *Silent Hill* and the Upside Down in *Stranger Things* in that it functions symbolically as part of the film's allegory of modern race relations. Suggestive of the Middle Passage from Africa to America during the slavery period and of the bodies of the kidnapped Africans who died and were tossed overboard, it more generally symbolizes Black incapacitation and disenfranchisement within racist white culture as Chris's mind and body are

Figure 1.8 Chris (Daniel Kaluuya) in "the Sunken Place" in *Get Out*, directed by Jordan Peele © Universal Pictures 2017. All rights reserved.

colonized by the mercenary Armitage family. As Sarah Juliet Lauro puts it, the visual space of the Sunken Place "signifies the usurpation of Chris's body" (2020: 154). Sarah Ilott adds that the Sunken Place "functions as metaphor for the literal and system silencing of minorities fighting to make their oppression heard" (2020: 124). "In the Sunken Place," writes Adam Lowenstein, "you become a spectator to your own body, your own life, your own words and actions now beyond your control" (2020: 109). Unlike Eleven's excursions into the dark space of psychic projection, Chris's submersion is deep within himself and not of his own volition.

The Sunken Place then is a different kind of catastrophe, one in which the viewer is submerged along with Chris in an alien interior space. The self becomes a prison marked by darkness and decay. Peele could have rendered this space as entirely black—like the space of psychic projection in *Stranger Things*. However, the image is marked by bits of particulate matter through which Chris floats. While in one sense suggestive of stars, the idea of Chris being submerged in a "Sunken Place" suggests we read the bits as decayed matter. Echoed by Chris's own white outfit (note that he is not dressed in white in the "real world" of his encounter with Missy—the white perhaps to make him stand out against the darkness better, while also suggestive of a space suit), the particles in the water thus serve as eerie foreshadowing of Chris's own eventual fate if not released from his psychic confinement. In the Sunken Place, any sense of self eventually disintegrates, leaving only bits of floating matter.

The visual register of the Sunken Place thus aligns it with other representations of inhospitable or toxic atmospheres present in contemporary horror. The correspondence, however, goes beyond that as the Sunken Place, like Silent Hill and the Upside Down, is a place of torture and imprisonment that becomes accessible as a consequence of human avarice and cruelty. Silent Hill's environment is poisonous due to both coal mining and the torture of a little girl by the town's fanatical cult. The opening of the Upside Down on *Stranger Things* is accomplished by a young girl taken from her mother and forced to be a test subject in the pursuit of Cold War military advantage. The Sunken Place is, as Alex Svensson explains, a "metaphor for slavery and other insidious forms of corporeal regulation and dehumanization" (226). The particulate matter in the air of all three is the residue of cruelty and abuse that humans inflict upon one another and the world. It is the literalized detritus of environmental despoliation, rape, child abuse, xenophobia, militarization, and slavery.

The eco-conscious protest of human avarice and cruelty at the heart of contemporary miasma theory in horror media is perhaps best illustrated by the spectacular and much-acclaimed episode 8 of David Lynch and Mark Frost's *Twin Peaks: The Return* ("Gotta Light?" first broadcast on June 25, 2017). In this episode, Lynch and Mark Frost take us back in time to the first detonation of a nuclear device by the United States Army in the New Mexico desert. Following the explosion, in one of the most audacious sequences in modern television, *Twin Peaks* takes us into the swirling heart of the mushroom cloud with Krzysztof Penderecki's 8:37 composition *Threnody to the Victims of Hiroshima* (1960) played in its entirety as the music bed. As we fly through the storm (see Figure 1.9)—into the heart of the mushroom cloud, the Mind Flayer, the center of the nuclear reactor at Chernobyl—we witness the birth of Bob, *Twin Peak*'s resident evil spirit, unleashed upon humanity as a consequence of human manipulation of immense natural forces. As Sam Adams puts it for *Slate*, "The detonation of the atomic bomb, an instrument of mass death and potential human extinction, brings Bob into the world" (Adams 2017: n.p.).

Commentary about this episode has tended to focus on the "sin" of nuclear weapons (Metz 2017). For Metz, for example, the episode is about acknowledging American "atomic culpability" in relation to the bombing of Hiroshima and Nagasaki (Metz 2017). Seitz, similarly, reads the episode—what he refers to as the "most startling flashback in the history of American television," as about "reckoning with boomer indulgence and American moral and imperial decline" (Seitz 2017). Lindsay Stamhuis expresses this point concisely: "the use of the atomic bomb brought evil into this world" (Stamhuis 2017). She then adds concerning *Twin Peaks* creators Lynch and Frost, "given that both of its

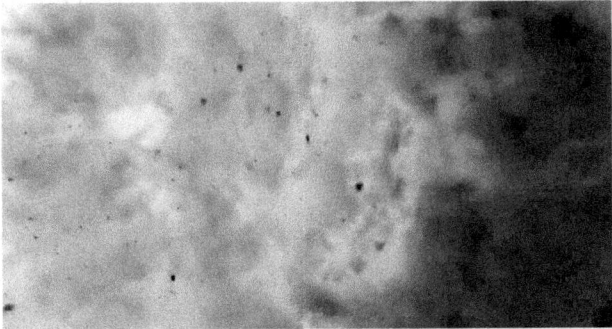

Figure 1.9 Into the heart of the maelstrom in *Twin Peaks: The Return,* created by David Lynch © Showtime 2017. (Compare with *Stranger Things*' Mind Flayer above [Figure 1.7]).

creators grew up in the shadow of the Cold War, with the (literal and figurative) fallout of test projects like Trinity raining down on the American psyche, it's not surprising that this would be the natural place for them to turn in order to explain the origins of their fictional monsters" (Stamhuis 2017). Ashlee Joyce extends the ramifications into the present, writing, "[t]hrough the symbolism of the bomb offered in Part 8, the series turns into meditation on the evils wrought by nuclear technology that brings political and artistic anxieties latent since the Cold War into sudden and urgent dialogue with 21st century neoliberal America" (2019: 14).

In keeping with Joyce, I would like to suggest that the dust, ash, and debris of the Trinity Test scene are not simply a flashback to a specific moment. As the camera flies into the mushroom cloud and the filming vacillates between black and white and color, we become unhinged in time. The scene condenses Hiroshima and Nagasaki with Chernobyl—and Bikini Atoll and Three Mile Island and Fukushima and other sites of nuclear tests and disasters. The intense violence of the swirling matter and debris acts as a nightmarish Rorschach test of contemporary nuclear—and, more broadly, environmental—anxieties, and its fallout rains down across contemporary horror media. In *Twin Peaks*, Lynch and Frost suggest that nuclear testing is what somehow created passage between the alternate spirit of world of the Black Lodge and our own world. Similarly, in *Stranger Things*, Cold War experiments created the breach between our world and the Upside Down, letting the monsters in. In *Silent Hill*, trauma and pain find expression in perpetually falling ash while in *Get Out*, the Sunken Place is a tomb created by racism, with decay marked by floating bits of particulate matter. What the insistent recurrence of particulate matter in modern horror finally makes clear is that these other places are not spaces apart but rather a world of our making just around the corner.

Works Cited

Adams, S. (2017), "With a Surreal Flashback, *Twin Peaks* Rewrote the Rules of TV, Again," *Slate*, July 26. https://slate.com/culture/2017/06/twin-peaks-part-8-is-one-of-the-most-radical-hours-of-tv-ever.html.

Blei, D. (2020), "In 19th-Century America, Fighting Disease Meant Battling Bad Smells," *Atlas Obscura*, April 8. https://www.atlasobscura.com/articles/public-health-bad-smells-miasma.

Brown, W. W. (n.d.), *Clotel; Or, The President's Daughter* [1853]. http://www.gutenberg.org/ebooks/2046.

Engels, F. (n.d.), *The Conditions of the Working-Class in England in 1844*. http://www.gutenberg.org/ebooks/17306.

Halliday, S. (2001), "Death and Miasma in Victorian London: An Obstinate Belief," *British Medical Journal*, 323(7327), December 22, 1469–71, doi: 10.1136/bmj.323.7327.1469.

Harris, C. (2018), "Miasmatic Thinking in Charles Dickens's *Bleak House*," *Synapsis*, February 12. https://medicalhealthhumanities.com/2018/02/12/miasmatic-thinking-in-charles-dickens-bleak-house/.

Ilott, S. (2020), "Racism that Grins: African American Gothic Realism and Systemic Critique," in D. Keetley (ed.), *Jordan Peele's* Get Out: *Political Horror*, 114–30, Columbus: The Ohio State University Press.

Johnson, S. (2006), *The Ghost Map: The Story of London's Most Terrifying Epidemic—and How It Changed Science, Cities, and the Modern World*, New York: Riverhead Books.

Joyce, A. (2019), "The Nuclear Anxiety of *Twin Peaks: The Return*," in Amanda DiPaolo and Jamie Gillies (eds), *The Politics of Twin Peaks*, 11–34, Washington, DC: Lexington Books.

Kiechle, M. A. (2017), *Smell Detectives: An Olfactory History of Nineteenth-Century Urban America*, Seattle: University of Washington Press.

Landrum, J. (2017), "Nostalgia, Fantasy, and Loss: *Stranger Things* and the Digital Gothic," *Intertexts*, 21(1–2), Spring–Fall: 136–58.

Lauro, S. J. (2020), "Specters of Slave Revolt," in D. Keetley (ed.), *Jordan Peele's* Get Out: *Political Horror*, 147–59, Columbus: The Ohio State University Press.

Lowenstein, A. "Jordan Peele and Ira Levin Go to the Movies: The Black/Jewish Genealogy of Modern Horror's Minority Vocabulary," in D. Keetley (ed.), *Jordan Peele's* Get Out: *Political Horror*, 101–13, Columbus: The Ohio State University Press.

Metz, W. (2017), "The Atomic Gambit of *Twin Peaks: The Return*," *Reviews*, 41(3), Fall. https://quod.lib.umich.edu/f/fc/13761232.0041.324/-atomic-gambit-of-twin-peaks-the-return?rgn=main;view=fulltext.

"Miasma Versus Contagion" (2019), "Cholera in Victorian London," *Science Museum*, July 30. https://www.sciencemuseum.org.uk/objects-and-stories/medicine/cholera-victorian-london#miasmas-versus-contagions.

Poe, E. A. (n.d.), "The Fall of the House of Usher" [1839]. https://www.eapoe.org/works/tales/ushera.htm.

Seitz, M. Z. (2017), "The Eight Episode of *Twin Peaks: The Return* Is Horrifyingly Beautiful," *Vulture*, June 26. https://www.vulture.com/2017/06/twin-peaks-the-return-part-8-atom-bomb-flashback.html.

Smeele, W. (2016), "Grounding Miasma, or Anticipating the Germ Theory of Disease in Victorian Cholera Satire," *The Journal of the Midwest Modern Language Association*, 49(2), Fall: 15–27.

Sourdot, L. A. (2018), "The Upside Down of Education Reform during the Reagan Era: A Re-Examination of Education Policies through *Stranger Things*," in Kevin J. Wetmore, Jr., (ed.), *Uncovering Stranger Things: Essays on Eighties Nostalgia, Cynicism and Innocence in the Series*, 205–14, Jefferson: McFarland & Co., Inc.

Stamhuis, L. (2017), "Destroyer of Worlds: Nuclear Fallout in the World of Twin Peaks," *25yearslater*, June 30. https://25yearslatersite.com/2017/06/30/destroyer-of-worlds-nuclear-fallout-in-the-world-of-twin-peaks/.

Sterner, C. S. (2007), "A Brief History of Miasmic Theory." http://www.carlsterner.com/research/files/History_of_Miasmic_Theory_2007.pdf.

Svensson, A. (2020), "'Do You Belong in This Neighborhood?' *Get Out*'s Paratexts," in D. Keetley (ed.), *Jordan Peele's* Get Out*: Political Horror*, 223–36, Columbus: The Ohio State University.

2

Between Hell and Hel: Gender, History, and Nature in Subterranean Spaces

Elana Gomel

No Hell below Us?

Most mythologies locate the kingdom of the dead underground. The "vertical thinking" that envisions the universe as composed of separate and discrete layers piled on top of each other—hell below, heavens above, our world in the middle—goes to the very beginning of human history and still has a powerful emotional resonance. As Stallybrass and White described it in their classic *The Politics and Poetics of Transgression*, "the high-low opposition in each of our four symbolic domains—psychic forms, the human body, geographical space, and the social order—is a fundamental basis to mechanisms of ordering and sense-making in European cultures" (1986: 3). In other words, the dark subterranean space in mythology corresponds to the nether regions of the human body and to the repressed and/or disavowed fantasies, fears, and desires of the human psyche. And it also corresponds to what Freud famously (or infamously) called "the dark continent" of femininity.[1]

The subterranean is the domain of darkness, impurity, and female monstrosity. The connection between the underground and femaleness is very old, going back to the Neolithic cults of fertility goddesses that presided over the cyclical patterns of death and rebirth. The very word "hell" derives from the old Germanic word for "hidden," which is also the name of the goddess of the underworld in Nordic mythology: Hel. In Milton's *Paradise Lost*, Hell is the abode of "darkness visible" where dwells the deformed female monstrosity of Sin, beautiful above the waist but serpentine below, with hellhounds infesting her womb—a graphic illustration of Stallybrass's and White's vertical symbology.

---

[1] In his essay "The Question of Lay Analysis" (1926).

But with the rise of industrial cities, subterranean spaces became assimilated to a whole new discourse of the technological sublime, based on the "exclusion of nature" (Williams 2008: 20). Multiple studies of "underground cities" in literature and cinema emphasize their role as repositories of complex fears about social unrest, urban collapse, and economic inequality. The representation of underground cities in speculative literature and cinema tends to deploy the symbolic vocabulary of masculinity: technology, violence, and conquest. From the cannibalistic, machinery-operating, subterranean Morlocks in H. G. Wells's *The Time Machine* (1895), to the underground Roman state in Joseph O'Neill's *Land under England* (1935), and to the Tube serial killers of *C.H.U.D.* (1984) and *Creep* (2004) movies, the technological underground has become the stage for playing out the fear of violent unhinged masculinity and runaway progress. Hell has been redefined as a torture-chamber of technology. In James Blish's *Black Easter* (1980), the infernal city of Dis, borrowed from Dante's *Divine Comedy*, is a contemporary metropolis, with bored demons in police uniforms directing bad traffic.

But alongside the industrial sublime of underground cities, there persists in speculative literature the older strand of representing the subterranean as a liminal, feminine space of death and rebirth. A new distinct subgenre of *subterranean horror* has emerged, both in writing and onscreen. Represented by such novels as *Reddening* (2019) by Adam Nevill, *The Cavern* by Alister Hodge (2019), *To the Center of the Earth* (2020) by Greig Beck, and such movies as *The Cave* (2005) and *The Descent* (2005), subterranean horror has its own distinctive set of narrative tropes whose history goes back to the Imperial Gothic of the lost world novel and its exploration of the literal and metaphorical dark continents.

In this chapter, I want to consider this history and the modern deployment of subterranean horror, especially in its gender vocabulary and the connection between femininity and political power. I will argue that subterranean horror treats underground spaces as pockets of "deep time," living fossils of archaic antiquity, populated by extinct beasts and harkening back to the pre-technological age. Rather than the mechanical Hell of technological cities, the underground becomes the domain of Hel: of dark, pagan, natural forces, where female characters struggle with the archetypal monsters of chaotic devouring femininity.

The tension between Hell and Hel, between the dark cavern and the underground city, complicates the Stallybrass and White scheme of vertical high-low opposition. I will argue that in subterranean horror it is supplanted by the horizontal opposition between rivaling inscriptions of gender and power. The subterranean chronotope encompasses both time and space, both femininity and masculinity, both nature and culture, and holds them in an uneasy balance that reflects the ongoing crisis of historicity. The rise of the Anthropocene has reawakened old myths of Mother Nature as a deadly and punitive force and has tied these myths to the revolt against technology. And since psychological experiences of gender have always been inflected by social, cultural, and religious forces, contemporary femininity, as reflected in subterranean horror, is uneasily situated between technology and nature, between Hell and Hel.

In what follows, I will provide a brief history of subterranean horror before focusing on representative contemporary examples. For reasons of length, I will only discuss novels, though some of my conclusions would apply to cinematic representation as well.

"We Must Go Deeper into Greater Pain"

Subterranean horror, as I define it here, has some specific narrative features, which remain relatively invariant through its history. It depicts the descent of a protagonist into an underground realm; it involves a profound transformative experience; and it is intertextually linked with the mythical depictions of Hell, especially Dante's *Inferno*.[2] The subtitle comes from the 1982 novel by Dante Aleghieri *Canto VI.I*. It is not to say that every subterranean horror novel or movie explicitly quotes *The Divine Comedy* but rather that there is an inevitable carryover from the Christian imagery of darkness, suffering, and evil underground to contemporary popular culture.

However, the real birth of subterranean horror owes as much to science as it does to religion. Early precursors of the genre, Ludwig Holberg's *Niels Klim's Underground Travels* (1714) and Edgar Allen Poe's *The Narrative of Arthur Gordon Pym* (1838), exploit the pseudo-scientific theory of the hollow Earth, which still crops up in recent movies such as *Iron Sky: The Coming Race* (2019) (see Standish 2007). The title of the latter comes from the 1871 novel by Edward Bulwer-Lytton's *The Coming Race* (1871). This novel marks the watershed in the development of subterranean horror: introduction of evolutionary fears and anxieties in the wake of the Darwinian revolution. The underground is no longer merely a place of the dead; it becomes a repository of the dead—and yet living—past.

---

[2] Dante Aleghieri (1982), "Canto VII," *Inferno* [1308–20], John Ciardi (trans.), https://infernobydante.wordpress.com/2013/10/23/canto-vii/.

In the second half of the nineteenth century, subterranean worlds become populated with "living fossils" of prehistoric animals and archaic cultures. Descent into the underworld is a journey into the geological past in Jules Verne's *Journey to the Center of the Earth* (1864), in which the protagonists encounter prehistoric creatures in underground caves. A whole zoo of prehistory roams the subterranean realm, popularizing the Darwinian notion of deep geological time and displaying to the curious public the new discoveries of paleontology: from cave bears (Arthur Conan Doyle's "The Terror of Blue John Gap," 1910) to mammoths and dinosaurs (Vladimir Obruchev's *Plutonia*, 1924).

But Darwinism had another offshoot besides growing interest in prehistoric fauna. It gave rise to progressionist theories of history, which, in turn, merged with imperialism and racism to animate the Imperial Gothic (Brantlinger 1988). The obverse side of the triumphalist discourse of imperial expansion, the Imperial Gothic expresses the profound unease over the return of the socially and psychologically repressed, and the rebellion of the past against the present. A specific subgenre of the Imperial Gothic is the lost world novel, in which the European protagonist penetrates what Nadia Khouri memorably called the "invaginated world" filled with ancient and barbaric civilizations, prehistoric animals, and conspicuous treasure (1983: 172). Most people connect the lost world novel with Arthur Conan Doyle's eponymous 1912 novel but in my discussion of the genre I made the case for it being far more widespread in fin-de-siècle literature, including such modernist classics as Joseph Conrad's *Heart of Darkness* (Gomel 2007).

Not all lost world novels are subterranean horror but all fin-de-siècle subterranean horror is related to the lost world novel. Notable examples include the *Pellucidar* cycle of Edgar Rice Burroughs (1914–63), Abraham Merritt's *The Moon Pool* (1919), and H. P. Lovecraft's *The Mound* (1929). All these texts conflate the fears of degeneration, monstrous femininity, and "inferior" races. They develop a series of tropes that evoke the ancient imagery of Hell to articulate modern misogyny and racism.

In these texts, the underground becomes a chronotope in Bakhtin's sense of the word: literally "spacetime" or the space of time, the haunted house of evolution. And yet, as cave bears, dinosaurs, and "primitive" men are lurking under the surface of European civilization, the underground, paradoxically, is also imagined as a space of technological progress. In Bulwer-Lytton's novel, the "coming race" of the Vril-ya, inhabiting the underworld, are no throwbacks to the past but rather harbingers of the horrifying future. Highly technological and endowed with telepathic powers, these creatures threaten humanity by their very existence. In *Pellucidar* and *The Moon Pool*, the underground "natives" possess technologies unknown to the West.

The subterranean Hell is where the fear of the past meets the fear of the future. H. G. Wells's *The Time Machine* (1895) and *The First Men in the Moon* (1901) conflate the two through the vivid imagery of primordial savagery entwined with soulless machinery. Raw meat on the metal table in the Morlocks' dark caverns and the eugenic monstrosity of Selenites in their sub-lunar labyrinth reflect the anxiety of the age poised between progressivism and dystopia.

In the liminal space of the underground, the vocabulary of gender is used to articulate the uneasy vacillation between escaping the past and rejecting the future. Central to this vocabulary is the gendering of the protagonist versus the subterranean world itself. In the classic nineteenth- and twentieth-century novels of subterranean horror, the protagonist/explorer is always male, while the world he encounters is replete with feminine symbolism, from the scantily clad princesses of *Pellucidar* to the Freudian undertones of Lovecraft's tentacled monstrosities. But even as this convention persists well until the turn of the millennium, it is being gradually subverted both by the rise of feminism and by the revelation of the connection between toxic masculinity and dystopian violence. Thus, already by the mid-twentieth century, the misogyny of the Imperial Gothic gives way to more complex interrogations of the relationship between time, power, and gender.

Mothers in Fatherland

Joseph O'Neill's *Land under England* (1935) has been named one of the best science-fiction horror novels ever written, and it is arguably one of the most unusual ones.[3] While ostensibly following the conventional template in having a male protagonist descend into the underground hell of darkness, it reverses the gender valuation of both the vertical hierarchy of high/low and the archetypal opposition of light/dark. A bold anti-fascist allegory, it prefigures gender reversals of contemporary subterranean horror.

The novel depicts the quest of a son for his father that, like Orpheus's quest for Eurydice, leads him to Hell. Anthony Julian follows his father, an embittered soldier of the Great War, lost in dreams of "Roman glory," to an underground

---

[3] By Karl Edward Wagner. See N. G. Christakos (2007), "Three By Thirteen: The Karl Edward Wagner Lists," in Benjamin Szumskyj (ed.), *Black Prometheus: A Critical Study of Karl Edward Wagner*, Gothic Press.

realm populated by the descendants of Roman legionaries. The first part of his descent follows the conventional plot trajectory of the infernal journey. The cave system is a darker and more Gothic version of Verne's volcanic tubes, illuminated by the fitful gleams of electric auroras and populated by carnivorous monsters. In his quest for his father, Anthony navigates the "ghastly valleys of blackness," where spiderish creatures recall the mythical archetypes of feminine evil, such as Arachne, and look forward to Tolkien's Shelob (O'Neill 1978: 40).

But when Anthony finally reaches the deepest chasm, where even auroras give out, he finds not the maternal abyss but the paternal torture chamber, not the primordial past but the barbaric future. The underground Romans have developed telepathic powers that allow them to cohere into a unified body politic, in which individuals are stripped of their minds and turned into unconscious automata. The rulers of this new Roman State who are called Masters of Will and Knowledge are part of the social machinery that leaves no place for agency, choice, or desire. In this new Roman State, telepathy achieves the same result as violent brainwashing does in Orwell's 1949 novel, *Nineteen-Eighty Four*.

> This hypnotic calm was the result of the most profound form of hysteria, a hysteria so deep and compelling that it had drowned the personality. The thing that was invading me and oppressing me, compelling me to conform to it— this force that was emanating from the group was a wave of feeling that was welling up from depths of fear; the panic, not of individual, but of a whole race, a permanent dread that had seized the depth of its life. It was through this that rulers, driven mad by themselves, had been able to hypnotise a nation.
>
> (O'Neill 1935: 155)

It is impossible not to see in the descriptions of the Roman State a not-so-veiled reference to fascism, especially to Mussolini who deliberately embraced the symbolic paraphernalia of Imperial Rome. In some ways, O'Neill's analysis of the totalitarian mindset is more astute than that of Orwell because he clearly shows the profound difference between the fascist New Man and the liberal humanist subject. Without self-consciousness, the Romans have literally become a collective organism like a coral reef or a beehive:

> I saw this underworld State clearly as the monstrous machine that it was—a blind thing, with no vision, no pity, no understanding … It saw that I was the only human being left in this world outside the machine …. a world in which man, as we know him, had ceased to exist.
>
> (O'Neill 1935: 243–4)

In the last sections of the novel, Anthony is subjected to a mental rape by his father who cannot accept his son's revulsion from the idea of being "absorbed" into the Roman State. The father is a frighteningly real image of the fascist male, traumatized by the Great War and eager to get a payback by leading the Roman legions back to "seize back again the lands of the upper earth from the barbarians" (O'Neill 1935: 244).

But the father does not win because Anthony also has a mother. His memory of her is Anthony's mental bulwark against his father's telepathic assault. He denounces his previous self-identification with his father and embraces his mother's gentle and nurturing femininity: "My mother, who had cared for him and me, she had been left outside … I would kill him, if I had to" (O'Neill 1935: 260–1). He does not have to at the end, as a giant spider performs this Oedipal act for him. But the last words of the novel are "Yes, mother," as Anthony finds his way to the surface (286). In choosing between his two parents, Anthony makes a political decision. Democracy in the novel is gendered as feminine, while totalitarianism is identified with masculinity.

The gender dynamics of *Land under England*, unusual in its time, prefigures gender reversals of modern subterranean horror. Even though Anthony is a man, his strange odyssey resonates with contemporary heroines who explore the liminal spaces of the abyss, in which they confront and/or embrace archetypal femininity, and struggle with the technological sublime.

Deep, Deeper, Deepest

Jeff Long's *The Descent* (1999) was hailed as a masterpiece by some reviewers and dismissed by others as being not "quite as good as it thinks it is."[4] The book is an ambitious exercise in subterranean horror, referencing everything from *The Divine Comedy* to fin-de-siècle lost world novels. But it is particularly interesting in its representation of a new gender dynamics against the background of globalism and what Francis Fukuyama in the celebrated book published not long before *The Descent* called "the end of history" (Fukuyama 1992).

The novel, narrated from multiple points of view and covering multiple locales from Himalayas to New Mexico, from Galapagos to China, depicts the discovery of a new subterranean hominin species, *Homo hadalis*, or hadals. The hadals are supposed to be an inherently evil breed, practicing cannibalism, torture, and

---

[4] http://www.infinityplus.co.uk/nonfiction/descent.htm.

enslavement, and abducting humans for their own nefarious purposes. Much like Lovecraft, Long superimposes supernatural overtones on an ostensibly rationalistic world-building. The hadals are almost never described at any length; they are only glimpsed in horrifying encounters as when they emerge to feed on the bodies in a mass grave in Srebrenica. Despite the fact that they are merely another branch on the evolutionary tree, they are consistently represented as demonic, beyond the capacity of human language to come to grips with:

> Survivors began trickling upward. Suddenly the military hospitals were taking in bloodied soldiers raving childishly about beasts, vampires, ghouls, gargoyles. Lacking in vocabulary for the dark monstrosity below, they tapped into the Bible legends, horror novels, and childhood fantasies. Chinese soldiers saw dragons and Buddhist demons. Kids from Arkansas saw Beelzebub and Alien.
>
> (Long 1999: 115)

Hadals inhabit a global subterranean domain, which stretches under all of Earth's landmasses and oceans, ignoring geographical, political, and national boundaries. The cross-cultural myths of Inferno are the result of the knowledge of this domain percolating to the surface. Hell is real and literal, and it even has a literal Satan. It turns out that the murderous hadals are led by a deified leader. There is a secret group of scientists and religious figures dedicated to tracking him down. One of them, Father Thomas, explains the existence of Satan in a way which purposefully conflates natural and supernatural: "The term Satan signified a historical character. A missing link between our fairy tale of hell and the geological fact of it" (Long 1999: 181). The chasm between "the fairy tale" and "the geological fact" is bridged by the "real and not accidental" evil of the hadals (180). It seems that in his description of the hadals Long is resurrecting the racist imaginary of the Imperial Gothic, which is based precisely on the conflation of biological difference and moral opposition. In the fin-de-siècle evolutionary fantasies, other races are not merely different or even inferior; they are inherently evil. It is startling to find this trope resurrected in a novel published at the *fin de millénaire*. But a closer look reveals that Long utilizes what seems to be a racist narrative convention for different ideological ends. His problematic is neither imperialism nor fascism. Rather, it is globalization.

Hell is both limitless and timeless. The evil of the hadals is simply another way to state that they have no history. Their murderous interactions with humanity follow the same pattern whether they happen at the dawn of the Neolithic or yesterday. Disregarding national boundaries and geopolitical divisions, hadal tunnels devour space, just as the monotony of hadal violence ignores time. Hell is the "flat world" of Thomas Friedman's celebrated book of the same title (2005), published in the heady days of neoliberalism when the collapse of the USSR seemed to promise the eternal triumph of democracy, or as Fukuyama put it in 1992, "the end of history." If the lost world chronotope preserves the past as a sort of museum exhibit populated by living fossils, in Long's novel neither past nor future really exists. There is only the eternal "now." Hell is the machinery of global capitalism devouring space and time.

Not unexpectedly, when the novel finally reaches its climax of displaying the real Satan (after 600 pages of turgid prose), he turns out to be a human being: a Jesuit who claims to be a reincarnation of various historical and mythical characters, including Moses.[5] Father Thomas is "the hadal rex, or mahdi, or king of kings"—or perhaps merely a deified cult leader (Long 1999: 554). But this would-be godling is only a side-show. The real power in the new global world belongs to a multinational corporation called Helios which colonizes Hell, turning it into a high-tech transportation hub, and wiping out the demonic hadals in the process. Interestingly enough, Helios's genocide of the subterranean natives is not even deliberate but rather a side-effect of their modernization drive. In relation to Helios, the posturing Satan/God, with his barbaric armor and quotes from *Paradise Lost*, is an irrelevant remnant of the pre-capitalist past. In Hell, history has been reduced to a heap of discounted trinkets.

There is a new Dante in the Inferno of globalization, and she is female. The protagonist of the novel is the nun Ali von Schade from Texas, a linguist, and a humanitarian. Recruited by Father Thomas, she joins a group of male adventurers and mercenaries as they descent into the heart of darkness. Thomas hopes that her extraordinary linguistic abilities will "restore [his] memory": through her, I'll remember all the things time has stolen from me (Long 1999: 558).

Ali is supposed to balance the violent masculinity of Satan and the sexual cruelty of the hadals and humans alike. She is depicted as an embodiment of the *shekinah*, which is the feminine aspect of God in Judaism, and Thomas's failed attempt to steal her power represents his unsuccessful bid to "reign in Hell." Ali's odyssey charts her progress to maturity and full embrace of her femininity (she eventually marries one of her fellow explorers and becomes pregnant). And yet, this nod to the feminism of the 1990s feels curiously irrelevant. Global power is as genderless as it is timeless. Helios's conquest of Hell is not ideological and,

---

[5] The plot twist is borrowed from Karel Capek's *War with the Newts* (1936), in which the leader of the sentient newts who have declared war on humanity turns out to be a human being with the same initials as Adolf Hitler.

therefore, not gendered in the same way in which imperialism and fascism are. The vertical symbology of power has been flattened into a network of business alliances, bids, and acquisitions. Ali's supposedly feminist bildungsroman is a sideshow; her confrontation with Thomas makes no difference to the techno-conquest of Hell. At the end, the underground is neither the dark abyss of femaleness nor the violence-infested masculine lair of Satan but only a new marketplace.

Mothers and Other Monsters

In many contemporary subterranean horror novels, female protagonists become the norm, and the monstrosity infesting the underground realm is explicitly gendered as feminine. However, the chasm between the two only grows, as popular texts uneasily navigate the new calculus of power which dispenses with the older gendered symbology of the lost world novel. In fact, subterranean horror often inadvertently displays a sort of gender muddle, in which femaleness and femininity work at cross purposes. Instead of finding their identity in the liminal space of the underground, women explorers lose their lives to archaic images of archetypal female power.

In Alister Hodge's *The Cavern* (2019), a brother-and-sister team hunt a monster in abandoned mines in the Australian outback. The monster is called the Miner's Mother. A female creature with the unlimited capacity for reproduction, this giant four-eyed carnivorous newt with a chameleonic ability to blend with her surroundings threatens the people of a small township and perhaps humanity as a whole. The relationships between the women characters and this alien "matriarch" range from surrender to fight. Kaz, living in an impoverished mining town, offers human sacrifices to the Miner's Mother. Elli, coming from the rich metropolis, tries to kill her. In either case, class counts for more than gender. Whether as a supplicant or a gun-toting hunter, twenty-first-century women do not recognize themselves in the devouring mother-goddess.

Adam Nevill's *The Reddening* (2019) is a much more accomplished and self-aware novel of subterranean horror. Replete with intertextual references to classic British horror writers, especially H. G. Wells and Arthur Machen, the novel sets out to explore the meaning of Hell in the context of long British history, covering the period from the Neolithic to the 1980s to today. And as opposed to *The Cavern*, it is quite aware of the gendered symbology of the underground and explicitly engages the mythology of fertility cults and prehistoric mother-goddesses. And yet, it comes to the same impasse as *The Cavern* and *The Descent*: real power is no longer religion, ideology, or even violence. It is celebrity and money. And neither has gender.

The Reddening stands out in not trying to disguise its supernatural elements under the veneer of a quasi-scientific discourse. Evolutionary theories no longer matter in the global world where the cachet of science has been eroded by the fragmentation of the field of knowledge, conspiracy theories, and fake news. The cave system discovered under Devon is infested by pagan demons, Paleolithic Venuses with animal heads: "The creature's torso suggested a heavily-breasted woman with wide hips … But if that was a head then it was the head of an animal" (Nevill 2019: 16).

This "black mother with her white pups," a hyena-human hybrid, has been worshipped by the locals for centuries in cannibalistic ceremonies where participants painted themselves with red ochre—an ancient ritual going back to Neanderthals (Nevill 2019: 297). The caves are the burial place of nine "red queens"—prehistoric matriarchs buried with animal skulls and embodying the ancient power of female magic.

A disillusioned and burned-out journalist Kat is drawn into a long investigation of various murders and disappearances in Devon that ultimately lead her to the confrontation with the monstrous goddess and her canine brood. She has a vision of "cyclical time," in which the "red" violence of prehistory seeps into, and contaminates, the supposed march of progress.

> the past was red and the future was red for certain … She'd seen how red the world was at its end, which wasn't too far away, and she'd learned that even though much could conceal the red in every heart, those that didn't abide by the red were never saved.
>
> (Nevill 2019: 300)

Instead of fighting against "the red," Kat identifies with it. She embraces her gender identity as rooted in the fertility-and-violence-infused pagan past. At the end of the novel, she is putting on red lipstick to her entire face—a modern equivalent of the Neanderthal red ochre: "The colour of the lipstick must have excited her imagination because when she closed her eyes, she acknowledged a now familiar idea that another red face existed behind her own" (Nevill 2019: 332). But it turns out that this "red face" is yet another mask beneath which lies the real face of power: a celebrity glamor shot. The entire pagan cult is a charade, a disguise of a criminal enterprise of drug-trafficking. While the hyena goddess is real, the people involved in the "reddening" are simply a bunch of illegal cannabis-growers. What started as a neo-pagan society founded by a famous folk-rock musician of the 1980s has, by 2019, devolved into a sordid drug-trafficking network involving bent policemen, "a stream of electricians and builders, assorted tradesmen, every employee at a food distribution center, the owners of four large yachts and even a headmaster" (Nevill 2019: 326). This pathetic roster of local corruption are the priests of the Mother Goddess, and her caves are their warehouses. Their appropriation of the terrain of the past is not an imperialist conquest but a capitalist acquisition.

In this world, gender is only another tool of reinventing oneself as a commodity. Kat's acceptance of the reddening is a return to her former lucrative journalistic position. Her glimpses of the prehistoric past, "a long pale place, so open and so wild," are framed by police raids and drug traffickers' jostling for power (Nevill 2019: 333). The past has been subsumed into the eternal present of global capitalism.

But paradoxically, the difference between *The Descent* and *The Reddening* shows that history still matters. *The Descent* reflects the triumphalist moment of liberal democracy in the 1990s. Twenty years later, the end of history has come and gone, and the UK is caught in the doldrums of post-Brexit uncertainty: "unemployment, a collapsing health system, the price of food, the terrible economy, a plummeting pound, the unpredictable climate, the strikes, unrest" (Nevill 2019: 16). While Helios in Long's novel is a legitimate multinational company with an almost godlike reach (as its symbolic name indicates), the drug cartel of *The Reddening* is not only illegal but almost comically inept, its use of the "reddening" ceremony on a par with gang-identifying tattoos. Eventually as its hippie founders die or are killed, a more up-do-date group of businessmen take over, intent on bringing paganism in line with new managerial practices. Before killing the 1980s matriarch, one of them explains: "The red has taken its toll. I know, I know. We've all watched it happen and it's been sad to see. But we've another queen. All will be well under new management" (Nevill 2019: 321). The red queen is a trademark; the caves are a Disneyland; and the monstrous past is subsumed into the depressing present.

Infernal Rides

The vicissitudes of subterranean horror chart the development of a fictional genre along the axes of gender, political power, and the changing concepts of space and time. It came into being as a subset of the Imperial Gothic, reflecting the fin-de-siècle anxieties about race and gender, while absorbing much or the traditional vertical imagery of Hell derived from pre-Christian and Christian sources. It became a means to explore the last century's struggle between democracy and fascism. And it has evolved (or perhaps devolved) into an entertainment empire that recycles the older templates of infernal journeys and resurrects the ancient archetypes of the devouring Mother Goddess to deliver thrills and chills to the growing global horror audience. The female characters in these novels and movies tap into the generic tradition that has become increasingly nostalgic and self-referential. No matter how many monstrous Mothers lurk underground and how many modern women succumb to their lure and/or fight off their cannibalistic femininity, the real source of horror lies elsewhere: in the "flattening" affect of global capitalism that harnesses Stallybrass's and White's hierarchy of transgression to the strategies of marketing. Gender becomes irrelevant to the calculus of consumerism. There is no longer Hell or Hel but only a techno-ride in which darkness and its monstrous denizens are just another special effect.

Works Cited

Blish, J. (1980), *Black Easter and Day after Judgment*, New York: Arrow Books.
Brantlinger, P. (1988), *Rule of Darkness: British Literature and Imperialism, 1830–2014*, Ithaca, NY: Cornell University Press.
Friedman, T. (2005), *The World Is Flat*, New York: Farrar, Straus and Ciroux.
Fukuyama, F. (1992), *The End of History and the Last Man*, New York: Free Press.
Gomel, E. (Spring/Summer 2007), "Lost and Found: The Lost World Novel and the Shape of the Past," *Genre*, 60: 103–27.
Hodge, A. (2019), *The Cavern*, North Hobart: Severed Press.
Khouri, N. (1983), "Lost Worlds and the Revenge of Realism," *Science-Fiction Studies*. (No.30. Vol. 10, Part 2): 170–90.
Long, J. (1999), *The Descent*, New York: Crown Publishers.
Nevill, A. L. (2019), *The Reddening*, Devon, England: Ritual Limited.
O'Neill, J. (1978), *Land under England [1935]*, London: New English Library.
Stallybrass, P. and A. White (1986), *The Politics and Poetics of Transgression*, Ithaca, N.Y.: Cornell University Press.
Standish, D. (2007), *Hollow Earth*, Boston: Da Capo Press.
Williams, R. (2008), *Notes on the Underground*, Princeton: MIT Press.

3

La Llorona Hauntings: Storytelling Feminicide at the Purgatorial Mexico/US Border

Cristina Santos and Sarah Revilla-Sanchez

The ghost of La Llorona has haunted Mexican and Chicanx sociocultural imaginary for over five hundred years. In the well-known, colonial version of this legend, it is said La Llorona wanders the earth, wailing, in search of the children she drowned in a river. Even earlier colonial versions link La Llorona to the Aztec goddess who foretold the fall of Moctezuma's empire to the Spaniards as a mother losing her children. Though La Llorona is best known as the epitome of female monstrosity—given that she murders her children and renounces motherhood—postcolonial and colonial versions also represent her as a victim of colonization, racism, sexism, and classism. Moreover, the specter of La Llorona is not confined to a specific geographical location, but rather wanders across cultures and across time, trapped in an in-betweenness, a type of ghostly purgatory. La Llorona has made recurrent appearances in North American and Latin American popular culture (*Kilometer 31* 2006; *Grimm* 2011–17; *Riverdale* 2017–23; *The Curse of La Llorona* 2019), some of which aim to challenge our perceptions of this ghostly and "evil" woman (*Woman Hollering Creek* 1991; *Mamá* 2013; and even Disney's *Coco* 2017). Drawing from Avery F. Gordon's *Ghostly Matters* (2008), who posits that ghosts are signifiers of larger hauntings that take place, we question what the ghost of La Llorona reveals about Mexico's haunting feminicides at Ciudad Juárez (*Narcos: México* 2018–21).

The focus of this chapter is to investigate recent refigurations of La Llorona in the cultural imaginary as an embodiment of a borderland purgatory that tells the stories of feminicide (missing and murdered girls and women) at the Juárez/El Paso border and the purgatorial space they occupy both in life and in death.

This research is supported by an Insight Grant from Canada's Social Sciences and Humanities Research Council.

Though the term *femicide* is more widely used in Anglo-American literature to refer to the murder of women by men because of their gender, Mexican scholar Marcela Lagarde translated this term as *feminicidio* ["feminicide"]. Furthermore, *feminicidio* implies the State's complicity in these gendered murders and the structural violence that underlines this phenomenon, through impunity and discriminatory access to legal justice (Lagarde 2006).[1] Since the early 1990s, over five hundred girls and women have been murdered and disappeared along the Mexico/US border (Gaspar de Alba and Guzmán 2010: 3).[2] Similar to the historical roots of the legend of La Llorona, the racialized bodies of the missing and murdered women are "more or less dead"—in life they are denied a political existence and, in their disappearance and/or death, are lost to an eternal anonymity (Driver 2015: 23). The border takes on a haunted funeral-like geographical space[3] where girls and women experience not only a corporal vulnerability but also a precariousness of life. Much like La Llorona, these missing girls and women endure a spectral space of purgatory—stripped of their names, identities, and, most of all, their humanity.[4] Similar to the historical iterations of La Llorona, the women and girls at the Juárez/El Paso border occupy a racialized and gendered vulnerability that, within the frames of violence, it increases the precariousness of their personhood and, as a result, opens them to the threat of violence and human degradation (Butler 2016: 1). When the bodies of dead girls and women are reduced to their mutilated body parts and their personhood denied, the borderland dumping grounds become a purgatorial space of their ungrievable lives—a dehumanization (or as Butler states, the derealization) of bodies who are not considered (political) subjects (Butler 2004: 72). Furthermore, these predominantly "brown" female bodies are not only marginalized bodies, but they also make up a conveniently invisible workforce—a "living dead" because they are a dehumanized labor force, not to mention usable and disposable sexual objects. It is from this purgatorial existence where the ghost of La Llorona emerges reviving the very sociohistorical forces that subjugated La Llorona: an unrelenting conquest, colonization, and disposal of the racialized female other.

---

[1] In this chapter, we use the term feminicide unless we are quoting someone's work.
[2] This number refers to official murders and disappearances, but there are many which have not been recorded.
[3] Orozco describes the *funeralization* of Ciudad Juárez's landscape through the public display of memorialization of disappeared and murdered women that also seeks to "decolonize gender relations that produce zones of female death" (2019: 134).
[4] See Judith Butler *Precarious Life: The Powers of Mourning and Justice* (2004) and *Frames of War: When Is Life Grievable* (2016).

Beyond the Legend: La Llorona, Feminicides, and the Purgatorial Borderlands

La Llorona is the ghost figure of the wailing woman dressed in white doomed to roam the earth as punishment for her past sins. From its earliest sources the legend of La Llorona finds its roots in powerful mythological Aztec warrior goddesses only to be consumed by colonization and systemic racism, classism, misogyny, and sexism. The figure of La Llorona has proven to move beyond geographic, cultural, and historical boundaries—it has demonstrated to have a cross-cultural and trans-historical persistence since it remains a conclusive representation of the various ways that women, especially racialized and poor women, continue to be victimized. The pre-colonial roots for La Llorona's legend are linked to the indigenous mythological figures of Coatlicue and Cihuacoatl.[5] Indeed, the colonial discourse exemplifies the role of the European male's gaze that views the female indigenous body as an extension of the "savage" land they have "discovered" that also needs to be dominated and conquered.[6] Most importantly, Coatlicue and Cihuacoatl prophesize the fall of the Aztec Empire to the Spanish and establish foundational narratives of the relationship between women dressed in white and a mother's wailing for their lost children: "Dear children, soon I am going to abandon you! We are going to leave" (Read and González 2000: 149). This wail is also associated with the legend of La Llorona and is refigured as the mothers' raised voices for justice for their lost daughters at the Juárez border, a point to which we shall return.

While the wails of La Llorona have often been associated with pain and grieving—like grieving mothers—in literary fiction, her cries have also been resignified as hollers. In her short story "Woman Hollering Creek" (1991) Chicana writer Sandra Cisneros reimagines La Llorona's wails as screams, embodied by the short story's creek named "La Gritona." Regarding her own revision of this legend *Prietita and the Ghost Woman/Prietita y la Llorona* (1995), Gloria Anzaldúa posits: "I've recuperated la Llorona to trace how we go from victimhood to active resistance, from the wailing of suffering and grief to the grito ['scream'] of resistance, and on to the grito ['scream'] of celebration and joy" (Anzaldúa cited in Rebolledo 2006: 280). Thus, feminist retellings of La Llorona have recuperated the precolonial roots of this legend, and with it,

---

[5] See Santos (2017: 64–9) for a discussion of the Aztec mytho-history of these indigenous warrior goddesses.
[6] See Octavio Paz's discussion of the dualism *chingón/chingada* as part of the colonial colonizer/colonized dialectic (1961: 76).

the wailing woman can be heard beyond her attributed grief and sin—a wail echoed in the shouts of mothers calling for justice for their missing/murdered *maquiladora* daughters.[7]

As marginalized identities—often regarded as the living dead (Driver 2015: 25)—these missing and murdered women at the purgatorial space of the Juárez/El Paso borderlands also echo La Llorona figures who no longer mourn in silence. Similarly, Carbonell notes that "La Llorona's ancient weeping may testify to women's pain, but in these tales of maternal resistance this pain-filled wail also embodies a battle cry-a holler prompted by the continuing presence of Coatlicue who demands confrontation and resistance" (1999: 71). In addition to literature and film, these sounds of resistance are often heard in popular music. In March 2019, La Llorona appeared among anti-feminicide protests in a new version of the Mexican popular song "La Llorona", performed by Snowapple in collaboration with writer Pedro Miguel and animation studio La Furia.[8] This music video depicts a woman as she walks across empty streets at night and factories—reminiscent of maquiladora assembly plants in Ciudad Juárez—can be seen in the background. After being presumably murdered, she walks along the desert until she reaches a forest seemingly submerged under water and disappears. Soon after, the murdered woman (re)appears as a ghostly woman dressed in black—a La Llorona refiguration that resonates with victims of feminicide. Along with the lyrics, which are cries against impunity and silence, La Llorona's laments for her missing and murdered daughters are rendered audible. However, when vocalized from the purgatorial space of the Juárez/El Paso borderlands this lament brings much-needed attention and acknowledgment to the unchanging undead/phantasmal nonexistence of these disappeared and murdered women and girls.

In November 2020, during the Day of the Dead[9] festivities in Mexico, a group of women placed an altar in memory of murdered women in the city of Puebla (*Periódico Central* 2020). These women also evoked La Llorona in a rewriting of the lyrics of the popular song: "Todos me dicen feminazi, Llorona, feminazi porque yo lucho" ["Everyone calls me feminazi, Llorona,

---

[7] See Revilla-Sanchez (2021) for a discussion of La Llorona's wails and sounds of resistance in anti-gendered violence protests in Mexico.
[8] The folklore song "La Llorona" has been interpreted by multiple artists, among them, Chavela Vargas and Lila Downs. The song "La Llorona-Ser Mujer" ["La Llorona-Being a Woman"] is part of an interdisciplinary art project.
[9] Day of the Dead is celebrated on November 1 and 2 each year to commemorate family and friends who have passed away. A common practice includes placing altars in memory of deceased people.

feminazi because I fight"].¹⁰ Through an act of public mourning, these women conjured La Llorona and raised their voices together: "ayer tomaste mi mano, Llorona, y ahora marchamos juntas" ["yesterday you held my hand, Llorona, and now we march together"]. In 2021, La Llorona was echoed once again during massive anti-violence protests in Mexico carried out on International Women's Day through the voices of La Catrina Son System, Nana Mendoza, and Vivir Quintana with the song "Llora, llora" ["Cry, cry"].¹¹ These songs reinforce a connection between La Llorona and the voices of grieving mothers and activists who mourn their murdered children and raise awareness of the ongoing violence in Mexico and the Mexico–US borderland. Drawing from Jacques Derrida and Achille Mbembe, Gloria Godínez (2017) traces a connection between La Llorona, mourning mothers, and the politics of death. Echoing the precolonial version of the legend and *neobarroco* art, she explores La Llorona as a grieving mother whose grief is perceived as the search for her missing children to properly mourn them. Godínez argues that *madres dolientes* ["grieving mothers"], who manifest in the streets and public squares, cry for their disappeared children and thus make visible their ghosts (152). That is, recalling Gordon's language of haunting, La Llorona is a ghost who not only reveals a haunting is taking place, but her active wails simultaneously carry messages of pained, grieving mothers and serve to make visible and palpable the affects that resonate with both grieving mothers and murdered women. But what does it mean to conjure La Llorona now in the context of feminicide? As Domino Renee Perez (2010) notes, the dynamism of the legend of La Llorona allows it to transcend generations and to reflect the concerns of her era, what Alicia Gaspar de Alba et al. (2010) call "an epidemic of femicides" (8). Gaspar de Alba also explores "the poor brown women … as expendable as pennies in the border economy" in her fictional detective novel *Desert Blood: The Juárez Murders* (2005) while also stating in the "Disclaimer" that "the victims are a composite of real-life victims" (v). La Llorona's haunting during the past five centuries not only hints toward a repressed past of injustices against racialized and poor women since colonial times, but, through her resurfacing, she also denounces the present patriarchal society and the politics of death that rules the borderland purgatory.

---

[10] Pejorative term (feminist + nazi) originated in the United States but has been widely used in Mexico to refer to feminists. See Lamas (2021) for a discussion of this term.
[11] Vivir Quintana is a Mexican composer, singer, and activist, notably known for the 2020 "Canción sin miedo" ("Song without fear").

The legend of La Llorona also embodies the virgin/whore paradigm, which is not pre-Hispanic in origin but part of the evangelization process of the Spanish conquest. That is, Spanish colonial discourse demonizes the female body and transposes a patriarchal discourse onto indigenous and mestiza women—not only as an additional process of colonialization but also gender oppression via control of the female body and sexuality. Drawing from her fieldwork at the Mexico/US border in the early twenty-first century, Schmidt Camacho traces the resurfacing of the legend of La Llorona as a cautionary tale within the contexts of maquiladoras, NAFTA, and capitalism. According to Schmidt Camacho (2004):

> La Llorona's legend exacts a double punishment: she loses both her children and her partner. The story chillingly prefigures the dominant discourse about the victims of the feminicidio, the Mexican government's cynical claim that the murdered girls and women courted their own deaths as sexual deviates and prostitutes.
>
> (Camacho 2004: 29)

Similar to La Llorona, victims of feminicide are often framed as sexually, socially, and culturally transgressive. As working, single, independent women, maquiladora workers are often perceived as deviant (from the heteronormative, patriarchal, and *machista*[12] structures) and thus punishable. In this cautionary tales, a parallel can be made between La Llorona, condemned to roam the earth for her sins, and victims of feminicide, whose murders are usually unresolved. We argue that in these purgatorial borderlands, these women's absence evokes what Gordon calls "a sense of the ghostly" (2008), that is, they unsettle the border space by affectively making the social structures of classism, misogyny, racism, and sexism felt in everyday life. The dominant discourse underlying the various iterations of La Llorona figures depicts the colonial inheritance of indigenous or mestiza women being used by Spanish males, having their children only to be disowned and never given legal recognition of their relationship. These women find themselves abandoned, ignored, silenced, and disposed of in life, so in death they roam the streets at night dressed in white crying out for their

---

[12] In *Desert Blood*, Alicia Gaspar de Alba illustrates the economic, political, and social tensions of *machismo*. She writes that "Juárez is not ready for the liberated woman, at least not in the lower classes. Their traditions are being disrupted in complete disproportion to changes in their economic status. They are expected to alter their value system, to operate within the cultural and political economy of the First World, at the same time that they do not move up on the social ladder. The Mexican gender system cannot accommodate the First World division of labor or the First World freedoms given to women" (2010: 252). She also sheds light on *machismo* and gender expectations with her comment that "women are being sacrificed to redeem the men for their inability to provide for their families, their social emasculation, if you will, at the hands of the American corporations" (2010).

dead children—haunted by their murderous actions and haunting the living as a reminder of their own sad stories. Feminicide's purgatorial borderlands resonate with Rivera Garza's words, "Impunity cemented the deadly contract that kept women in their places—the kitchen or the coffin. Silence sealed the patriarchal pact that kept men on top" (2020: 52). Not only is the purgatorial space of the borderlands a hunting ground—an in-between space that seems to be lawless where the girls/women are dehumanized, devalued, and disposable—it also embodies how "horror [is] an inherent element of humanity" (Driver 2015: 59).

By using these refigurations of La Llorona from colonial roots to contemporary representations in popular culture, the following section will consider conflicting representations of female "brown bodies" in American crime drama *Narcos: México* (2018–21; Gaumont International Television). Since, as Butler explains, it is the lack of representation that increases the risk of being dehumanized, it is by using the power of the image that one can convey the reality of suffering and of lives lost (2004: 141, 144, 146). By reading the television series *Narcos: Mexico* as a popular culture representation of the Mexico/US borderland in parallel with recurrent La Llorona figures in cultural imagination, we argue that this specter continues to haunt society because she is a disembodied ghostly marker, not only of her own victimization but also the mistreatment of her children: the purgatorial space that brown bodies occupy as living citizens but also as the missing and murdered women of Ciudad Juárez. It is from within this purgatory—which we define as culturally, socially, and racially transgressive—that a new adaptation of La Llorona emerges, as the victimized poor "brown" female but also as a mobilized motherhood searching for her missing daughters/children.

Deaths and Disappearances at the Mexico/US Border in Popular Culture

Season three of the television series *Narcos: Mexico* includes a sub-plot that explores the purgatorial space of the rising numbers of missing and murdered girls and women on the Juárez border as a backdrop to its main focus on the drug trade narrative and the rise of the Guadalajara cartel in the 1980s. The story is set at a time when little was known about feminicide in the Mexico/US border, and before the Juárez murders became known as the "black legend of the border" (Gaspar de Alba and Guzmán 2010: 2). This series exemplifies what Schmidt Camacho has called "the masculinist order of the border space" (2004: 42): when the girls' dead bodies are found, the comments made by the coroner and the police focus on the victims' perceived behavioral transgression—they shouldn't be out late at night; they are whores. This discourse of victim blaming includes views of the disposability of these girls' lives and bodies as confirmed by the coroner who does not even bother to file reports of the deaths. When a conscientious police officer attempts to find a missing girl and asks his commanding police official for permission, he is told to mind his business because he is entering a situation that does not correspond to him (season 3, episode 3). The following episode (season 3, episode 4) makes the connection of the missing and murdered girls and the fact that they tend to be workers that cross the border to El Paso to work: maquiladoras victimized because of their ethnicity and poverty while on La Ruta ["The Route"], the bus taking girls to the factories (season 3, episode 5). It is only in season 3, episode 10 that the term "femicide" is mentioned in the television series when they depict the discovery of various dismembered bodies dumped in the desert (see Figure 3.1).

Figure 3.1 illustrates how corpses and missing bodies have become part of the Mexico/US purgatorial space where *Narcos: Mexico* takes place. This purgatorial space is embodied by what Mariana Berlanga Gayón (2015) calls a "spectacle of violence" where mass graves and mutilated corpses are made visible and missing bodies are rendered invisible and unrecognizable. Yet, their absence must not be understood as passive because "their empty spaces constitute the black hole of a nation gone awry" (Rivera Garza 2020: 51). However, as Nuala Finnegan notes in her book *Cultural Representations of Feminicidio at the US-Mexico Border*, the

Figure 3.1 Shot of desert dumping ground for victims of feminicide in *Narcos: Mexico*, season 3, episode 10, created by Carlo Bernard, Chris Brancato, and Doug Miro © Gaumont International Television 2018–21.

murders of Juárez must not be studied as an isolated emergent phenomenon but rather as "a continuum of gender violence that has simply taken a terrifying new turn" (2019: 23). The examination of these La Llorona/"brown female bodies" departs from the essential recognition of racial, social, and sexual prefiguratives that expect a certain code of behavior that solidifies a social condemnation of a woman who does not know "her place" in her familial or social environment. Thus, the legend of La Llorona is tri-fold for our discussion of the missing/murdered women at the Juárez border as represented in *Narcos: México*: (1) these victims are mirrors of various figurations of La Llorona that depict a victimization of the racialized poor female[13] at the hands of a perceived socially and racially superior male (European via colonialization) vs American (via globalization/NAFTA); (2) the persistence of sociocultural gendered scripts that deem noncompliant females as deviant "bad women" and whose non-conforming behavior is punishable; and (3) as the symbol of the grieving mother looking for her lost/murdered daughters.

Based on the victim-blaming comments made by the coroner and the police in *Narcos: Mexico*, La Llorona mirrors missing and murdered women in that they are configured as "bad women" because, as stated by Alicia Gaspar de Alba in *(Un)Framing the Bad Woman*, they are "confrontational to a patriarchal world view" and one that is ultimately punished for her noncompliance with abuse, torture, and rape—that is, a "ritual destruction of the female body" (2014: 7–9, 161).[14] A ritualized destruction of the female body not only devalues and dehumanizes the female body by dismembering/fragmenting it and positing the Mexican female body as "bodies made for violence" (Schmidt Camacho 2004: 22). It is a dismembering of the deviant female body that also has its roots in Aztec mythohistory in the story of Huitzilopochtli decapitating and dismembering his sister Coyolxauhqui and throwing her body parts tumbling down the temple steps because he feared her power—an act that some critics associate with the cultural disempowerment of women (Lara 2008: 105; Gaspar de Alba 2014: 190–4; Orozco 2019: 143). By murdering the goddess, the Christian patriarchal ideologies eliminate the source of female power—in dismembering Coyolxauhqui's body this same colonial power achieves a dis-articulation of female body and speech (Gaspar de Alba 2014: 17).

Set in the 1980s, *Narcos: Mexico* brings to light many of the drawbacks of capitalism—embodied by women's incorporation into the workforce and

---

[13] See Santos (2017: 68–78).
[14] In her detective novel, *Desert Blood*, Gaspar de Alba includes nonfictional information that has circulated with respect to the treatment of *maquiladoras* such as mandatory birth control, proof of menstrual cycles, and even sterilization (2005: 90, 95).

their perceived social transgression—exacerbated in the 1990s through the North American Free Trade Agreement (NAFTA). The economic and political dimensions of the murders of Juárez reveal a connection between gender and neoliberalism (see Schmidt Camacho 2004; Krasna and Deva 2019; Segato 2019), especially in relation to manifestations of violence (see Valencia 2012) and impunity (see González Rodríguez 2012). The latter is even more pertinent when considering the bodies upon which violence is inflicted. As retold in *Narcos: Mexico*, the missing and murdered girls are associated with crossing the border to work. As usually single, working, poor, disenfranchised, racialized women in the Mexico/US borderlands, these women tend to be framed as socially, racially, sexually, and culturally transgressive. This transgression resonates with La Llorona since she too inhabits a similar state of precarity, a sort of purgatory that threatens to silence women—both as victims and those left behind to see justice for their missing/murdered daughters. This echoes Wright's (2011) argument about their disrupting presence as working bodies and murdered corpses. In these purgatorial borderlands, their presence disrupts the social order, and their removal (by murder) signifies an urban cleansing. It is in this state that La Llorona emerges and mourns her murdered children.

In Figure 3.2 the image of a mother hanging a sign for her missing daughter on a light pole echoes a common thread of these murdered women to the

Figure 3.2 The search for the disappeared girls at the Juárez border in *Narcos: Mexico*, season 3, episode 10, created by Carlo Bernard, Chris Brancato, and Doug Miro © Gaumont International Television 2018–21.

figuration of La Llorona, and that is the role of the mother grieving for her lost child/ren. In Ciudad Juárez, *desaparecidas* ["disappeared women"] are commemorated with light poles painted black with pink crosses to mark the place where they were last seen. These crosses are usually painted by mothers of the disappeared where "[t]he cross itself is a physical marker of memory! it materializes and personifies the victims of femicide, giving their deaths a presence" (Orozco 2019: 147). It is a mother's politicized grieving as a way to reclaim her daughter's identity to rescue their humanity from the mutilated body parts or disappeared bodies. In their activism these mothers revert to politicized acts such as those used by the Mothers of Plaza de Mayo in Argentina, to speak the names of their missing and murdered daughters. Judith Butler explains, "lives remain unnameable and ungrievable" (2004: 150) and to be retrieved from the purgatorial space of their death/disappearance is to return their humanity by restoring the integrity of their bodies, and by extension, their lives. In fact, La Llorona's historical passive wailing has transformed into a holler, a voice that seeks justice for these missing and murdered women in recent cultural artifacts and social activism such as: murals (*La Llorona's Sacred Waters* 2004); plays (*Braided Sorrow* 2008); new versions of the popular Mexican "La Llorona" song (Snowapple 2019; La Catrina Son System ft. Quintana 2021); and of dismembered and disappeared bodies (*Narcos: Mexico*). La Llorona's unrelenting presence in contemporary stories demonstrates the persistence of a colonial inheritance of a purgatorial haunting that continues to exist since colonial times and emphasizes a vulnerability of brown bodies that have been figuratively and literally displaced into purgatorial spaces. This purgatorial existence is rendered possible by the "collapse of law or its replacement with new forms of social control that render racialized migrant women vulnerable to torture, sexual abuse, murder, and disappearance" (Schmidt Camacho 2004: 23).

Institutionalized religion has also been a dominant factor in casting the role of women and prompting situations in which La Llorona figures in history have found themselves defined and limited to their positions as mothers and wives—social roles that have been traditionally used to silence and/or censor women's voices within private domesticated spaces. While the *madres dolientes* ["grieving mothers"] denounce social injustices, in this series their voices are trapped inside the purgatorial borderlands, unable to shatter the necropolitical logic that rules the purgatory. In fact, as Schmidt Camacho notes, "[j]ust as La Llorona's complaint is heard as a wail, the demands of mothers for the truth and justice for their missing daughters have fallen outside the grammar of normative political speech" (2004: 31). As fiction illustrates, the wails of La Llorona have often been associated with pain and grieving, but her cries have also been resignified as hollers in feminist retellings of this legend (Carbonell 1999). Through these hollers of resistance and memory, as well as visual markers, the ghosts of murdered girls and women are conjured in these borderlands.

Within this borderland purgatory, the colonial inheritance of La Llorona's gendered and racialized victimization is revised to include now a dialectic of NAFTA, capitalism, and xenophobia under the forty-fifth president of the United States (POTUS). In this sociocultural context La Llorona's search for her missing and murdered children mirrors not only the vulnerability of brown bodies as the missing and murdered women at the Juárez/El Paso border but also those imprisoned brown bodies held at ICE (US Immigration and Customs Enforcement) detention centres—of parents separated from their children due to immigration and citizenship policies. The complexities of existing as a "brown body" under the forty-fifth POTUS are depicted in the reboot of *Party of Five* (2020). In the pilot episode a Mexican American family is separated when the parents are taken to an ICE detention centre[15] and returned to Mexico and the older son is left to care for his siblings. In this episode of *Party of Five*, purgatory is the very real caged spaces of the ICE detention centres and the cries of families being forcibly separated—a new version of La Llorona's purgatorial space and a mourning for her children that are missing, imprisoned, and/or murdered. In re-examining representations of Mexican and Mexican American bodies in popular culture, we have shown that the current reimagining of La Llorona is more than a monster or ghost; she is the signifier of a larger haunting purgatorial space that points to racism and gendered violence that has persisted since the Spanish colonization and endures into contemporary gendered discourses of power and dominant patriarchal ideologies.

---

[15] While the focus of this chapter is on Mexican and Mexican American bodies at the Mexico/US border, ICE detention centers affect immigrants from multiple nationalities. The American series *Superstore* (2015–21) follows the storyline of Mateo, an undocumented Filipino employee who is detained by ICE in season 4. *The Cleaning Lady* (2022–present) also includes a storyline depicting the repercussions of ICE detention centres and forced deportations: in S01.E05 the main character is saved from deportation whereas her friend is not so lucky and is sent back to Mexico and separated from her young children who remain in the United States.

Works Cited

Berlanga Gayón, M. (2015), "El espectáculo de la violencia en el México actual: del feminicidio al juvenicidio," *Athenea Digital*, 15(4): 105–28.
Braided Sorrow (2008), [Play] directed by A. J. García.
Butler, J. (2004), *Precarious Life: The Powers of Mourning and Justice*, New York: Verso.
Butler, J. ([2009] 2016), *Frames of War: When Is Life Grievable?* New York: Verso.
Carbonell, A. M. (1999), "From Llorona to Gritona: Coatlicue in Feminist Tales by Viramontes and Cisneros," *Melus*, 24(2): 53–74.
Cisneros, S. (1991), "Woman Hollering Creek," in *Woman Hollering Creek*, 43–56, New York: Vintage Contemporaries.
Cleaning Lady, The (2022–present), developed by Miranda Kwok, Chicago: Shadow Dance Pictures.
Coco (2017), directed by Lee Unkrich, USA: Walt Disney Studios.
Curse of La Llorona, The (2019), directed by Michael Chaves, Burbank: Warner Bros.
Driver, A. (2015) *More or Less Dead: Feminicide, Haunting, and the Ethics of Representation in Mexico*, Tucson: University of Arizona Press.
Finnegan, N. (2019), *Cultural Representations of Feminicidio at the US-Mexico Border*, Milton: Routledge.
Gaspar de Alba, A. (2005), *Desert Blood: The Juárez Murders*, Houston: Arte Público Press.
Gaspar de Alba, A. (2014), *[Un]Framing the "Bad Woman": Sor Juana, Malinche, Coyolxauhqui, and Other Rebels with a Cause*, Austin: University of Texas Press.
Gaspar de Alba, A. and G. Guzmán (eds) (2010), *Making a Killing: Femicide, Free Trade, and La Frontera*, 1st ed., Austin, TX: University of Texas Press.
Godínez, C. (2017), "Lloronas, Mothers, and Ghosts: Necrobaroque in Mexico," *Revista Interdisciplinaria de Estudios de Género de El Colegio de México*, 3(5): 129–63.
González Rodríguez, S. (2012), *The Femicide Machine*, M. Parker-Stainback (trans.), Cambridge, MA: Semiotext(e).
Gordon, A. F. (2008), *Ghostly Matters: Haunting and the Sociological Imagination*, Minneapolis: University of Minnesota Press.
Grimm (2011–17), created by Stephen Carpenter, Jim Kouf, and David Greenwalt, Universal City: Universal Television.
Kilometer 31 (2006), directed by Rigoberto Castañeda, Mexico: Lemon Films.
Krasna, D. and S. Deva (2019), "Neoliberalism, NAFTA, and Dehumanization: The Case of Femicides in Ciudad Juárez," *Fast Capitalism*, 16(1): 31–40.
Lagarde, M. (2006), "Del femicidio al feminicidio," *Desde el Jardín de Freud*, 6: 216–25.
La Llorona-Ser Mujer (2019), [Song] Artist Snowapple.
La Llorona's Sacred Waters (2004), [Mural] Artist J Alicia.
Lamas, M. (2021), *Dolor y política. Sentir, pensar y hablar desde el feminismo*, México: Océano.
Lara, I. (2008), "Goddess of the Américas in the Decolonial Imaginary: Beyond the Virtuous Virgen/Pagan Puta Dichotomy," *Feminist Studies*, 34.1(2): 99–127.

Llora Llora (2021), [Song] Artists La Catrina Son System, Vivir Quintana, and Nana Mendoza.

Mamá (2013), directed by Andy Muschietti, Universal City: Universal Pictures.

Narcos: México (2018–21), created by Carlo Bernard, Chris Brancato, and Doug Miro, Neuilly-sur-Seine: Gaumont International Television.

Orozco, E. F. (2019), "Mapping the Trail of Violence: The Memorialization of Public Space as a Counter-Geography of Violence in Ciudad Juárez," *Journal of Latin American Geography*, 18(3): 132–57.

Party of Five (2020), created by Amy Lippman and Christopher Keyser, Culver City: Sony Pictures Television.

Paz, O. (1961), *The Labyrinth of Solitude: Life and Thought in Mexico* [1950], L Kemp (trans.), New York: Grove Press.

Read, K. A. and J. J. González (2000), *Mesoamerican Mythology: A Guide to Gods, Heroes, Rituals, and Beliefs of Mexico and Central America*, New York: Oxford University Press.

Rebolledo, T. D. (2006), "Prietita y el Otro Lado: Gloria Anzaldúa's Literature for Children," *PMLA*, 12(1): 279–84.

Renee Perez, D. (2010), "Essays: Interludes and Encounters, La Llorona Redux," *Review: Literature and Arts of the Americas*, 43(80): 110–15.

Revilla-Sanchez, S. (2021), "Haunting Murders: Feminicide, Ghosts, and Affects in Contemporary Mexico," MA diss. University of Victoria, Canada.

Rivera Garza, C. (2020), "On Our Toes: Women against the Femicide Machine in Mexico," *World Literature Today* (winter): n.p. https://www.worldliteraturetoday.org/2020/winter/our-toes-women-against-femicide-machine-mexico-cristina-rivera-garza.

Riverdale (2017–2023), created by Roberto Aguirre-Sacasa, Hollywood: Warner Bros and CBS Studios.

Santos, C. (2017), *Unbecoming Female Monsters: Witches, Vampires, and Virgins*, Lanham: Lexington Press.

Schmidt Camacho, A. (2004), "Body Counts on the Mexico-U.S. Border: Feminicidio, Reification, and the Theft of Mexicana Subjectivity," *Chicana/Latina Studies*, 4(1): 22–60.

Segato, R. (2019), "La escritura en el cuerpo de las mujeres asesinadas en Ciudad Juárez," in X. Leyva Solano and R. Icaza (eds), *En Tiempos de Muerte: Cuerpos, Rebeldía, Resistencias*, 67–88, Buenos Aires, Chiapas: Cooperativa Editorial Retos.

Superstore (2015–21), created by Justin Spitzer, Universal City: Universal Television.

Valencia, S. (2012), "Capitalismo gore y necropolítica en México contemporáneo," *Relaciones Internacionales*, 19: 83–102.

Wright, M. W. (2011), "Necropolitics, Narcopolitics, and Femicide: Gendered Violence on the Mexico-U.S. Border," *Signs: Journal of Women in Culture and Society*, 36(3): 707–31.

Part Two

Daughters, Mothers, Trauma

4

"I Lost All Hope of Going up the Hill": *Silent Hill* as a Female Specific *Inferno*

Dawn Stobbart

The film adaptation of *Silent Hill* is one that has divided audiences since its release in April 2006. Based loosely on the videogame of the same name, *Silent Hill* was lauded for its visual effects in release, which Roger Ebert suggests make it "look more like an experimental art film than a horror film" (Ebert 2006: n.p.). However, in the same review, Ebert considers that for newcomers to *Silent Hill* the narrative was convoluted and confusing (Ebert 2006), with knowledge of the videogame franchise being fundamental to understanding the plot, themes, setting, music, and even the cinematography of the film.

Silent Hill is not a direct adaptation of the first videogame, but there are many crossover points that tie the two together. The music was composed by Akira Yamaoka, who was also responsible for the game music, while visually, camerawork is reminiscent of that seen in the videogame series. Crane shots provide a familiar viewpoint for videogame players, and these are combined with "follow" shots that show the protagonist from above and behind as they move through the setting again highlighting a link with the visual elements of the game. As Bordwell and Thompson suggest, this forces an identification with the protagonist by "keeping our attention fastened on the subject of the shot" (Bordwell and Thompson 2008: 199), which allows Gans to keep the aesthetic and "feeling" of the town of *Silent Hill* that the videogame franchise is famed for, and to recreate some of the famous scenes in the game.

The videogame franchise on which the film, *Silent Hill*, is based is iconic in horror gaming. Beginning with *Silent Hill* in 1999 (Konami 1999), the franchise is founded on the concept of a small town named Silent Hill as an abject space (Kirkland 2015b: 163), which protagonist Harry Mason explores in search of his daughter Cheryl—one of many who search the town looking for answers throughout the franchise. As with the videogame series, the film offers a narrative reflection of mental health—with the setting itself representing "trauma, psychological breakdown, repressed memories, perversion and familial disfunction" (Kirkland 2015a: 164). More explicitly however, the film centers on the town of Silent Hill as a supernatural space created in the mind of the child, Alessa Gillespie. After many years of abuse, culminating in sexual assault and immolation Alessa has a psychotic break, which creates an alternate version of the actual town. In presenting this version of events (rather than the original story: that Alessa is impregnated and sacrificed to bring about the birth of a God, with the help of Michael Kaufman, a doctor), Gans offers a specifically female reimagining of *Inferno*, the first book of Dante's *Divine Comedy*, reorienting a masculine ordering of Hell through a female perspective.

The Divine Comedy

The Divine Comedy, by Dante Alighieri, is frequently considered to be one of the great works of Western literature. Written in the early part of the fourteenth century, the narrative traces the journey of Dante from the depths of Hell, through Purgatory, and finally ending as he looks on the Face of God in Heaven. While the *Comedy* encompasses all the soul's journey toward God, *Silent Hill* is concerned with the first Cantica: *Inferno*. In keeping with the structure of *Inferno*, *Silent Hill* shows the journey of one person as they descend into Hell (see Figure 4.1), each "level" accessed from the one before. Rose must navigate

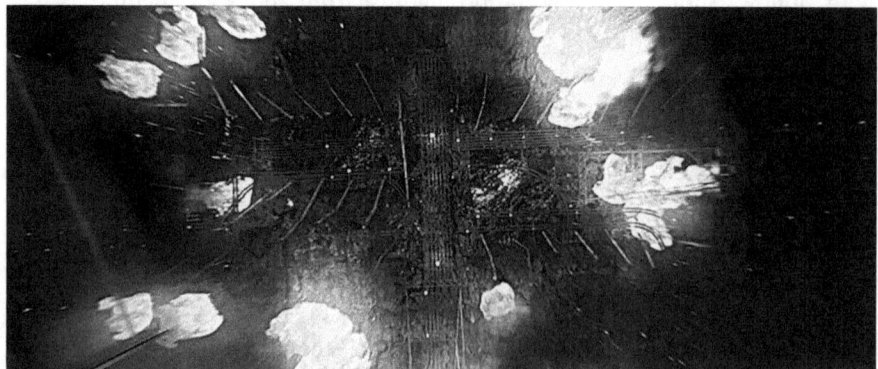

Figure 4.1 Sharon stares into Hell in *Silent Hill*, directed by Christophe Gans © Alliance Atlantis, 2006.

these layers of Hell to escape the town, just as Dante must navigate Inferno, Purgatory, and Heaven to reach the end of his journey.

The viewer is given an initial glimpse of Gans interpretation of Hell during the opening scene of *Silent Hill* as Sharon (Jodelle Ferland) sleepwalks to the edge of a waterfall precipice near her home. The establishing shot moves from above and behind the swaying child to looking down into the darkness of the waterfall, which changes, as the camera drops, into a decayed and industrial landscape with a fiery, burning bottom layer, where a child resembling Sharon can be seen looking upwards: this is Dark Alessa.

Dante situates the Christian Devil, Lucifer, as being at the bottom of the pit of Hell, showing him as a parody of the angelic forms of heaven. Gans tries to reproduce this by positioning a child as the Devil. The Bible is clear that children are considered a gift and reward (Psalm 127:3), that "the kingdom of Heaven belongs to such as these" (Matthew 19:14), and moreover that those who cause children to sin would be better cast into the sea (Luke 17:2). In *Silent Hill* Gans destabilizes this Biblical understanding, creating an entity that looks like a child, but identifies itself as "the dark part of Alessa" (Gans 2006). This is a character who couches their identity in Biblical language, telling Rose "This is the End of Days, and I am the Reaper" (Gans 2006). Known as Dark Alessa, this being was created in 1974 following an event referred to as the Great Fire, when after being immolated Alessa's soul is split in two. Dark Alessa promises Alessa that she can wreak revenge on the cult that killed her and spends the intervening time between the fire and the events in the film hunting and killing the cultists for her. It is Dark Alessa that creates the levels of these worlds, both the Fogworld and the Otherworld, and it is she that can temporarily replace the Fogworld with the Otherworld, until the cult is able to pray Dark Alessa's influence away from them. All the events of the film are at the instigation of Dark Alessa, to bring about revenge for the child. It is she that takes Sharon to the orphanage; she who calls to Sharon in her dreams; and it is she that causes Rose to crash the car upon arrival in *Silent Hill*. Having engineered Sharon and Rose's presence in this limbo, Dark Alessa is able to use them to fulfill her promise to exact revenge on the cultists.

Abandon Every Hope, Ye That Enter

The film incarnates *Silent Hill* as an abandoned town in West Virginia, and as with the videogame series, the town appears to function as a character in its own right (Perron 2018: 35). Based loosely on the town of Centralia (a real US ghost town with a mine burning under it), there has been a fire under the fictional town since 1974, when nine-year-old Alessa Gillespie was immolated by a local cult, The Brethren. When the ritual fire is spilled, it quickly spreads, causing a subterranean inferno that is still burning during the film's temporal setting of 2004, thirty years later. The narrative premise of the film centers on there being another version of Silent Hill that exists alongside, but is distinct from, this reality: unseen and accessible only by those whom Dark Alessa chooses. It is this limboic *Silent Hill* that Gans uses to incorporate a third level of the town, one which explicitly reflects and references the suffering of Alessa. Gans positions the town in layers, each existing "under" the previous one and which can only be accessed from the one above (or below). Here, the viewer can see a relationship between *Silent Hill* and the first inkling of a relationship to the *Comedy* on a structural level. There are three realms to the *Divine Comedy*—Hell, Purgatory, and Heaven—collectively representing the tripartite Other World after death, and we see similarities in *Silent Hill*'s construction. As well as sharing the basic (and now widespread) notion of Hell as being underground, there are three levels, or versions, of *Silent Hill*, one under the other. Whilst these environments are simple by the standards of *The Divine Comedy*, they nevertheless encompass a recognizable Christian vision of Hell, beginning with the "real" town of Silent Hill.

The top layer of the town is the "real" Silent Hill. It is here that Alessa was immolated in 1974. In this incarnation, Silent Hill is an abandoned town where visiting requires Personal Protective Equipment (PPE) to prevent inhaling the toxic fumes that rise to the surface. The long-term decay is evident as Christopher Da Silva (Sean Bean) and Thomas Gucci (Kim Coates) search the town for Rose, Sharon, and Cybil. This is the Silent Hill that the living can visit and interact with, with no evidence of the nightmare that exists below its surface, as hidden as the fire that burns there. Visually, this town is represented as being decayed and empty, but at the same time filled with light and color (as the scenes with Bean and Coates show), the contrast between this and the foggy world beneath clear: sunlight does not reach the hidden levels of the town.

The other levels of *Silent Hill* are part of the nightmare that is Alessa's existence and are populated mainly by women: a female hellscape created by female trauma, visited upon the female child by the female leader of the community. With two specific levels this *Silent Hill* has become incarnate as the result of years of persecution and abuse, and which is populated by those who helped create it, many of whom are female (although there are men in the congregation of the cult). Dark Alessa states: "When you're hurt and scared for so long, the fear and pain turn to hate, and the hate starts to change the world," and the film shows this to be so (Gans 2006). It is the Fog World that takes up most of the film. This is the level that Rose awakens in after crashing her car and finding Sharon missing. Just as Dante woke to find himself in a dark wood, Rose awakens in a place where "death could scarce be bitterer" (Alighieri 2005: Canto 1, 7), enveloped in fog, with ash falling gently her. There is a correlation here to the moment when the Pilgrim's "heart plunged deep in fear" (2005: 15) when looking on the road to Hell; the sense of vulnerability and confusion the viewer sees in Rose is evident in Dante as he begins his tale.

As Dante embarks on his journey through Hell, he is joined by Virgil, who has been sent to guide him. Dante is lost, and it is Virgil's job to get him back on track. Police Officer Cybil Bennet (Laurie Holden) takes on this role in *Silent Hill*, her status as a police officer endowing her with authority and lawfulness from the outset. Her first words, "Hey there, is everything alright?" (Gans 2006), and asking Rose if she needs help position her as a good person, and as with Virgil, she acts in a measured manner, always on the side of justice. Her arrival in the foggy version of *Silent Hill* comes just as Rose asks for assistance and admitting that she is "not okay." Whilst it is the case that Dark Alessa *leads* Rose through *Silent Hill* by leaving clues for her to follow to reach a specific conclusion, Cybil is her guide. Rose knows where she wants to go, and Cybil provides support for her to get there—even placing herself in physical danger to ensure this happens.

The monotonous gray fog that the town is famous for obscures natural light and muffles sound, creating a muted aural atmosphere something akin to *shinshin*—a term for the sound of silence during snowfall (Chen 2020: n.p.). Fog is a common symbol for the supernatural across media, and so its use in *Silent Hill* is no surprise: horror films abound that contain long shots of fog rolling into an area the protagonist is about to enter; its opaqueness makes it perfect for hiding ghosts and other monsters from view. In *Silent Hill*, the fog is an omnipresent symbol of the town existing as a psychological limbo, a nightmare environment created from Alessa's subconscious knowledge of the town, and is colored by her life experiences and is reflected in the foggy ash of the real world. This level is populated mainly by the "Cult of the brethren," having been trapped there by Alessa in 1974. The cult appears to believe that they alone survived an apocalypse, and that they continue to remain alive through prayer, led by Christabella Gillespie (Alice Krige), the leader of the cult. As with those that exist in Dante's Hell, the inhabitants of Silent Hill do not recognize that they have done wrong, and that others are transgressors. This is made clear when Dark Alessa tells Rose, "For over 30 years they've lied to their own souls. For 30 years they denied their own fate," with only two characters seeming to understand the reality of their situation as being in Hell—one being Dahlia Gillespie, Alessa's mother (Gans 2006).

Dahlia is introduced to the viewer soon after Rose arrives in *Silent Hill*, the two coming face-to-face as Rose searches for Sharon. Dahlia is unkempt and dirty; cast out of the "Church of the brethren" she wanders the silent gray streets alone. While Dahlia has been confined to the foggy limbo of *Silent Hill* for her part in the treatment of Alessa, she is protected from harm in a way that no other character is. She is the only resident of *Silent Hill* able to move around the town freely, while all other inhabitants have to return to the sanctuary of the church for safety during the periods that the Otherworld dominates *Silent Hill*.

Whilst Dahlia has been confined to Limbo alongside those who have abused Alessa, Gans takes pains to portray her in a sympathetic light, showing her as caring for Alessa, but unable to prevent the abuse of her daughter, a weak rather than wicked woman. She contacts the police to intervene and save her daughter's life in 1974, although they arrive too late to prevent the immolation. It is Dahlia of all the characters that appears to understand the truth of the special status of the town, telling Rose that "only the dark one opens and closes the door to Silent Hill" (Gans 2006), and later that "it's your sins that hold you here" (Gans 2006); her words are an approximation of Bible verse in their delivery and timbre. In Dahlia, Gans shows a woman broken by guilt, and Alessa as a daughter that cannot harm her mother, despite what happened to her. Dahlia, instead, is snubbed. Her daughter refuses to acknowledge her: even in the film's finale, she is ignored. This is complicated by Gans's further treatment of Dahlia, which sees Alessa protect her mother from harm in arguably one of the best scenes in horror film. Cult member Anna is throwing stones at Dahlia outside the Church as the Otherworld takes over the Fogworld.

As Anna is preparing to throw a rock, Pyramid Head (see figure 4.2), the most famous *Silent Hill* monster, appears and, in a scene to rival any example of body horror, Anna has her clothes ripped from her body and then in an identical movement, her skin is also removed, spattering Rose and Cybil with her blood. The inference here is clear; while Alessa condemns her mother to Hell, she will not allow anyone to physically harm her. This protection can also be seen at the end of the film; Alessa once again spares Dahlia's life when all other members of the cult are destroyed. Dahlia asks Rose why she alone was spared Alessa's wrath, to which Rose responds, "You're her mother. A mother is God in the eyes of a child" (Gans 2006).

Figure 4.2 Pyramid Head in *Silent Hill*, directed by Christophe Gans © Alliance Atlantis, 2006.

The leader of the cult group that inhabits the foggy world of Alessa's trauma is her aunt, Christabella. It is she that keeps the cultists in relative safety; their faith prevents Alessa's entry to the Church where they hide from her revenge. As the antagonist of *Silent Hill*, Christabella is responsible for the Hell that Alessa creates. She encourages the emotional torment of the child, she convinces Dahlia to surrender Alessa, and she burns the child alive, bringing about the extreme psychotic break that creates the town. Furthermore, Christabella creates a parallel for Dante's criticism of the Simonists in the eighth Circle of Hell.

In *Inferno*, Dante puts real-world figures in Hell. Criticizing even the Papal Seat itself, Dante the pilgrim comes across Pope Nicholas III in the eighth Circle of Hell, upside down with his feet on fire, and who calls his predecessors and successors Simonists: those that sold favors and offices for their own profit. Whilst not a Simonist, Christabella, nevertheless, forms a critique of religion in the same vein as Dante's condemnation: her position as leader of the religious group, and her actions against Alessa situate her alongside the religious figures Dante sees as belonging in Hell. Dante offers an opportunity for his reader to recognize dishonesty in public life in calling out the Simonists and suggesting that they will meet an agonizing fate, and this is reflected in the portrayal of Christabella in the town of Silent Hill; her outward demeanor of caring and compassion as a religious leader is belied by her cruelty, and her conscious-less actions to ensure her way of life.

Situated under the foggy limbo is a hellish pit: the Otherworld. In the "real" world, there is a mine that has been on fire for thirty years but is also a literal hell where the adult Alessa resides. Reachable by an elevator that appears to drop several hundred meters—if not kilometers when Rose enters it—this version of *Silent Hill* is causally linked to the trauma she experienced at the hands of the cult that lived in *Silent Hill*, both for her and for those trapped there by her. This level of Alessa's reality is the decayed industrial environment the viewer is shown in the first scene, where an already-moldering world becomes hellish, populated by monstrous creatures bent on the destruction of anything they come across. With a color scheme "that combin[es] red and brown" (Kirkland 2007: 75), and calling to mind the fiery pits of Hell, this aspect of the film can be placed alongside the description of Malebolge in *Inferno*:

> There is a place in Hell called Malebolge
> Cut out of stone the color of iron ore
> Just like the circling cliff that walls it in.
>
> (Alighieri 2005: Canto 18, 1–2)

Dark Alessa can occasionally expand this level of hell to include the Fogworld, gaining a foothold in allowing the Otherworld to overtake the town until the cult are able to pray it back again. The gray monotone landscape is replaced by rusted metal and nightmarish monsters can roam freely and pursue and destroy anyone that is found outside the Church, their time in purgatory ended with destruction, rather than salvation. As Rose rightly tells them, "[y]our faith brings death. You are alone in this limbo and God is not here."

As with the Pilgrim in *Inferno*, the lower down in Silent Hills hellish depths Rose travels, the worse the crimes that have been committed are. However, unlike *Inferno*'s Hell, which punishes all men (and women) for their sins, *Silent Hill* reflects Alessa's inner turmoil; the crimes are those that have been visited on her and the monsters that populate the town are reflections of the trauma that she has suffered. This is how Alessa populates *Silent Hill*'s Hell and punishes those who have wronged her, by turning them into the monsters that roam the Otherworld.

The school janitor (Colin – see figure 4.3) is a sexual pervert who assaults ten-year-old Alessa prior to her immolation. In Alessa's Hell, he is remade, his body bound eye to feet by barbed wire that obstructs his sight. He walks on his hands, pulling his torso behind him across the rancid bathroom floor dragging his genitals beneath him. His hands infect the already-decayed world around him: pustules sprout from the vein-like growth that forms and black fluid leaks from it. Alessa's

Figure 4.3 Colin the Janitor in *Silent Hill*, directed by Christophe Gans © Alliance Atlantis, 2006.

condemnation of Colin is clear: he is a verminous creature, whose touch brings disease with it, and in her Hell, his physical form reflects his actions. In *Inferno* Dante metamorphoses the sinner's forms into a perverted castigation of sin, according to Sophie Stuber in the Stanford Daily, creating a "cruel and twisted form of punishment" (2018), and this is precisely what can be seen in the Colin monster.

Alongside the representation of the Dantean Hell, a major theme of the film is to consider how this Hell is created by Alessa and influenced by those around her at the time of its inception. At its heart, the *Silent Hill* franchise is an exploration of mental health as it might be experienced by the sufferer. While this representation is somewhat problematic as attitudes to mental health representations have changed in the twenty-first century, at the same time the franchise is attempting to portray something that is difficult to visualize: how it feels to be in the throes of a decline in mental health—without trying to narrowly define cause and/or effect.

It is known that horror can be a reflection not of how the world looks, but how it *feels*, and Kirkland writes that for the videogame series:

> [t]here are suggestions that the town of Silent Hill represents a beacon to particularly troubled individuals, for whom the landscape and the creatures

within it assume a reflection of their own inner turmoil. The ways in which these repressed elements manifest as monsters in climactic boss battles suggests a therapeutic process whereby distressing memories take physical form, are confronted, and destroyed. The player participates in such processes, battling these inner demons on the protagonist's behalf, vanquishing these manifestations of their guilt, trauma, and personal conflict.

(2015: 164)

This is also seen in the film, albeit from a simpler perspective. Instead of representing a beacon to many individuals, the town is a beacon to Sharon alone—a child who cries out for the town in her restless dreams. The individual purgatory of the game world or the universal Hell of Dante's *Inferno* is replaced by a personal hellscape created by Alessa, although Gans took pains to present this in the same aesthetic style as the videogame, *Silent Hill*.

A Mother Is God in the Eyes of a Child

The impetus of the film is the journey Rose makes to save Sharon, a journey that itself functions as a test for Rose to prove her worth in the eyes of Alessa. Following the structural template of *Inferno*, Rose leads the viewer down stairways, steps, and an elevator, as she makes her way through Silent Hill and into Alessa's past, each discovery more traumatic than the last. Pilgrim-like, Rose journeys toward the center of this hell with details of Alessa's life being revealed along the way. She is directed to the school where Alessa was bullied by her peers, the bathroom where Alessa was sexually assaulted by the janitor, and the hotel room where she was burned alive to "purify" her mother's sin. Finally, having successfully faced the darkest secrets of Alessa's past, Rose is led to Alessa's physical form: a bed-bound, scarred woman, in the basement of the Brookhaven hospital. Flashbacks are used alongside vocalization to make clear to Rose—and the viewer—the depths of the trauma the child had been subjected to, and which the adult is damaged by. During this scene, Rose is shown that *Silent Hill* is a hellish construction, "a dream of this life" that "must end, and so too must the dreamers within it" (Gans 2006). Successful completion of this journey shows Dark Alessa that Rose is worthy of being a mother, and that she is willing to face any danger for her child—unlike Alessa's birth mother. "Rose, then, transforms from being merely the mother of her adopted daughter Sharon as she traverses Silent Hill, to a figure of righteousness and divine retribution over Christabella." Green remarks adding that Christabella "is herself a false mother preaching a false religion" (2014: 149).

If Rose's trial through *Silent Hill* provides the movement of the film, then the narrative is Alessa's. As Rose navigates *Silent Hill*, the viewer comes to understand her motives and actions, and to empathize with her. Here, some potentially problematic elements of the film come to the fore in relation to mental illness and trauma in how Alessa is presented. It is possible to suggest that Alessa's severe trauma results in her developing a supernatural dissociative disorder, in which she creates a "dark" alternate version of herself, one which becomes physically manifest. Whilst developing a dissociative disorder might be a reasonable reaction for such trauma, within the supernatural context of the film this can result in a problematic understanding of mental suffering and its results. As Jack Yarwood explains in *Mental Illness in Video Games and Why We Must Do Better* (2015), creators do not often want to increase stigma and are merely looking to entertain. However, reusing these tropes perpetuates the stereotype that there is a relationship between people with mental health problems and violent behavior, and to some extent this is what happens with *Silent Hill*. The film does attempt to represent Alessa as a morally complex person, rather than just a villain; as Amy Green notes, "Alessa, even at her most furious and bloodthirsty, never moves past the realm of being sympathetic" after "having been made to suffer at the hands of the adults around her, both those who victimize her and those who fail to save her in time" (Green 2014: 152).

This is most graphically seen at the climax of the film where we the audience are still encouraged to sympathize with Alessa even after she exhibits the most extreme forms of violence seen in the film. The apex of *Silent Hill* comes when Dark Alessa can enter the church, having entered Rose's body in an inversion of the birth motif. Despite having created the foggy world within which the church is situated, Alessa is unable to enter the sacred space of the cult in her own form, and therefore is unable to face her own demon: Christabella. When confronted for her actions by Rose, Christabella stabs her through the heart, the blood dripping onto the floor of the church and the seal of the cult that lies there. This monstrous act destroys the protection that the cult has built against Dark Alessa, allowing her to enter the church and bring in the Otherworld with her. Like an avenging angel, adult Alessa rises from the portal that is created from Rose's blood. Strapped to her bed, only able to move her head, her face scarred by the burns she suffered at the hands of the cult, Alessa is finally able to exact her revenge. The cult is decimated by barbed wire, with Christabella's death being particularly graphic. Dragged aloft in a Christlike pose, with barbed wire constraining her spread-eagled above the church dais, the viewer is shown Christabella's legs being held apart, and as she whispers "help me to stay pure" she is vaginally impaled by strands of wire with barbed ends, the wires erupting from her chest, before tearing her asunder. Her "rape" by the sharpened wire barbs can be seen in relation to the pain that Alessa felt when she was assaulted prior to her burning, and the subsequent bisection is also reminiscent of the division that occurs in Alessa: the birth of Dark Alessa. With the destruction of the cult, Alessa's revenge is complete. It is at this point that the souls of the two parts of Alessa's soul coalesce in Sharon, and the cult is destroyed.

A Happy Ending?

After Alessa's revenge, Rose takes her daughter by the hand and leads her from the church and only Dahlia left in Silent Hill's purgatory, as alone as she always has been. Just as Dante, "passed the point to which all weight from every part is drawn" (Alighieri 2005: Canto 34, 110–11) and can make his way to the next step of his journey, Rose crosses the chasm that separates the town from the real world and retraces their steps home. However, when they arrive there, home is a mental construct just as much as *Silent Hill*, created from Sharon's memories.

Often, throughout media, a return to the family home is an indicator of a return to the previous state, a status quo where "conventional moralities and identities are [often] proclaimed as triumphant," a stance that *Silent Hill* refutes (Hughes and Smith 2009: 1). In a poignant final scene, Rose and the now "whole" Alessa/Sharon enter the front door of their home, slowly crossing the room to a sofa where Rose sits. As the child toward her bedroom the camera pans to show darkness outside and fog all around. In juxtaposition, Christopher awakens on the same sofa, sunlight coming through the window as it rains outside. As the film ends, the viewer is reminded of *Inferno* and Virgil's explanation as to how "when it is morning here, there it is evening" as the distance between them is dignified by Rose remaining in darkness while Chris is in the light (Alighieri 2005: Canto 34, 118). Chris's light comes through his omission from the family home—and by extension, the family—which further suggests a desire for Alessa/Sharon to have her mother all to herself and to experience the love she has been denied so far.

While at first glance there appears to be little relationship between *Inferno* and *Silent Hill*, there is a clear thread joining the two. Christophe Gans's adaptation retains much of the atmosphere of the videogame, uses the basic story of the first game, and interrogates a specifically female Hell. Refigured through Alessa's memories and trauma, Gans uses a broad brush to paint this Hell in the same shades as Dante, whilst reworking the details to show a hell created in the shadow of the mental, sexual, and emotional abuse delivered on the child, Alessa. Both Dante's poem and Gans's film share the same core message for traversing Hell: to have courage and faith in the face of peril and adversity. Just as Dante descends into Hell to gain understanding, so too does Rose, both protagonists being rewarded with truth and understanding when they leave Hell and start on the next stage of their journey the Pilgrim toward Purgatory and Paradise, and Rose toward a fuller understanding of her daughter.

Works Cited

Alighieri, D. (2005), *The Divine Comedy: The Vision of Paradise, Purgatory, and Hell* [1308–20], Rev. H. F. Cary (trans.). https://www.gutenberg.org/files/8800/8800-h/8800-h.htm.

Bordwell, D. and K. Thompson (2008), *Film Art: An Introduction*, 8th ed., New York: McGraw-Hill.

Chen, K. (2020), "It's a Shin Shin Snowfall Day," New York State Writers Institute, December 17. https://www.nyswritersinstitute.org/post/it-s-a-shin-shin-snowfall-day#:~:text=%E6%B7%B1%E3%80%85%E2%80%93%20shin%20shin%20%E2%80%93%20is%20a,a%20sound%20of%20no%20sound.

Ebert, R. (2006), "Where There's Smoke, There's Witches," RogerEbert.com, April 20. https://www.rogerebert.com/reviews/silent-hill-2006.

Green, A. M. (2014), "Mother Is God in the Eyes of a Child:" Mariology, Revelation, and Mothers in Silent Hill, *JCRT*, 14(1), Fall 2014. https://jcrt.org/archives/14.1/green.pdf.

Holy Bible, The, (2022), Authorised King James Version. https://www.kingjamesbibleonline.org/.

Hughes, W. and A. Smith (2009), "Introduction: Queering the Gothic," in W. Hughes and A. Smith (eds), *Queering the Gothic*, 1–10, Manchester: Manchester University Press.

Kirkland, E. (2015a), "Masculinity in Video Games," *Camera Obscura*, 24(71): 161–83.

Kirkland, E. (2015b), "Restless Dreams and Shattered Memories: Psychoanalysis and Silent Hill," *Brumal: Research Journal of the Fantastic*, 3(1): 161–82.

Kirkland, E. (2016), "Team Silent Hill," in E. McCarthy and B. M. Murphy (eds), *Lost Souls of Horror and the Gothic: Fifty-Four Neglected Authors, Actors, Artists, and Others*, 212–14, Jefferson: McFarland & Co., Inc.

Kirkland, E. (2007), "The Self-Reflexive Funhouse of Silent Hill," *Convergence: The International Journal of Research into New Media Technologies*, 13: 403–15.

Perron, B. (2012), *Silent Hill: The Terror Engine*, Ann Arbor: University of Michigan Press.

Perron, B. (2018), *The World of Scary Video Games*, London: Bloomsbury Academic.

Silent Hill (1999), created by Konami Computer Entertainment, Konami.

Silent Hill 2 (2001), created by Konami Computer Entertainment, Konami.

Silent Hill (2006), directed by Gans, Christophe, Culver City: TriStar Pictures.

Stuber, S. (2018), "*Reading Dante as a Feminist*," *The Stanford Daily*, June 4. https://stanforddaily.com/2018/06/04/reading-dante-as-a-feminist/.

Yarwood, J. (2015), "Mental Illness in Video Games and Why We Must Do Better," *alphr.com*, December 21. *https://www.alphr.com/games/1002271/mental-illness-in-video-games-and-why-we-must-do-better/*.

5

"Mother Is God in the Eyes of a Child": Doppelgängers, Punishment, and Maternal Otherworlds in *Silent Hill* and *Triangle*

Catherine Pugh

The foggy, gray, and obscure otherworlds of *Silent Hill* (2006) and *Triangle* (2009) swallow up those who transgress their borders, twisting spatial and temporal rules to create a kind of maternal heterotopia. It is here, like in *The Others* (2001), that unwanted truths must be acknowledged, where the Good Mother is questioned, and often found wanting. These liminal spaces trap their characters in a limbo-like nonspace, a waiting room somewhere between life and death, reality and fantasy, where identity is temporarily put on hold. In these spaces, the mother is held in stasis; dissociated from the truth, she can remain the self-sacrificing, caring Good Mother with no consequences or acknowledgment for her sins. The purgatorial otherworld itself, however, is filled with indications that something is wrong, hints and references that a transgression has been committed. It is only when the purgatorial world is broken and the truth revealed that the punishment can be completed, leaving the Bad Mother to either acknowledge her actions or deny them and perish. There is, however, no true escape from these closed-off heterotopias, with both *Silent Hill*'s Good Mother Rose (Radha Mitchell) and *Triangle*'s Bad Mother Jess (Melissa George) remaining trapped as the films draw to a close.

Silent Hill, based on the 1999 videogame of the same name,[1] follows Rose DeWitt, whose adopted child Sharon (Jodelle Ferland) begins to mention "Silent Hill" while sleepwalking. Concerned for her daughter, Rose takes the girl to visit Silent Hill, an isolated town covered in fog and ash since a devastating fire

---

[1] In the original game, it is a male protagonist called Harry Mason that searches the eponymous town for his missing daughter.

destroyed it in 1974. After swerving her car to avoid a doppelgänger of Sharon in the middle of the road, Rose wakes up to discover her daughter missing and the road out of town collapsed, making escape impossible. Joined by another outsider, police officer Cybil Bennett (Laurie Holden), Rose searches Silent Hill for Sharon, attempting to solve the mystery of the town's ghostly origins while avoiding periodic incidents where the landscapes transitions to become dark, rust-covered and filled with nightmarish monsters. In the sunny "real" world, however, Rose's husband/Sharon's father Chris DeWitt (Sean Bean) fruitlessly searches for them in the abandoned Silent Hill with the help of the evasive Inspector Gucci (Kim Coates). Eventually, Rose discovers the story of Alessa Gillespie (Jodelle Ferland), a young girl immolated as a witch during a "purification" ritual in 1974 that went wrong and ultimately burned down the entire town. Alessa's pain and anger caused her to split, creating the doppelgängers of Sharon (her remaining goodness and innocence) and Dark Alessa (responsible for the shifts in reality throughout Silent Hill). Rose ultimately joins with Dark Alessa to rescue Sharon from the townspeople, who are attempting to repeat the "purification" ritual with her, but on returning home they find that they are still a part of the foggy otherworld. While Rose is the primary mother in the film, there are other mothers that appear, notably Dahlia (Deborah Kara Unger)—Alessa's biological mother—who is left a traumatized outcast after Alessa's burning and Christabella (Alice Krige), the matriarch of the town who orchestrated Alessa's "purification."

Triangle is the story of exhausted single mother Jess, who joins recent acquaintance and potential romantic interest Greg (Michael Dorman) and his friends on his yacht for the day, only for the boat to capsize in a mysterious storm. The group finds shelter on abandoned ocean liner *Aeolus*, where it appears that temporal laws do not apply. One by one, all are murdered by a masked killer until only Jess remains. Desperate to get home to her autistic son, Tommy (Joshua McIvor), Jess defeats the masked assailant and pushes them overboard, before an identical group of the friends—including a doppelgänger of Jess—suddenly arrive. When her attempts to change the outcome of the second loop fail, Jess realizes that the only escape is for all her friends to die, thereby summoning the yacht that she can use to get home. For the third loop, the original Jess dons the killer's clothing and murders the others before being knocked into the sea. She wakes up sometime later and rushes home to find yet another doppelgänger yelling at, and hitting, her son. In a fit of rage and denial, original Jess brutally beats her violent doppelgänger to death. Snippets of Jess getting ready for her trip from the opening of the film are revealed to be part of this loop, her actions taking on a new and ominous meaning (the paint-splattered dress she packs into a suitcase is actually the body of her doppelgänger, for example). As Jess drives her and Tommy away from the house, she accidentally hits a bird and, distracted by her son's crying, crashes the car. The camera pans across the scene of the accident, revealing Jess dead and Tommy dying as a mysterious taxi driver tells her that there is little chance of saving the boy. Jess asks to be taken to the docks, willingly reboarding the yacht in a repeat of the opening scene, thereby loop once more.

The supernatural Gothic otherworlds of *Silent Hill* and *Triangle* form what Michel Foucault calls heterotopias: contradictory, ritualistic spaces that are essentially worlds within worlds. Similar to the nonspace (and often incorporating them), heterotopias are parallel spaces; disturbing and transformative, intended to either generate an image of a utopian space (gardens, fairs) or remove undesirable bodies (prisons) in order to create a "real" utopia. The spaces featured in *Silent Hill* and *Triangle* act as a holding ground for these undesirable bodies, removing them—"them" primarily being the Bad Mothers of Jess, Christabella, and the townspeople of Silent Hill—from the real world. The spaces are self-enclosed, functioning on a system of rituals and doubling that offers introspection without the benefit of resolution. Punishments meted out by these worlds do not tend to come with the opportunities for forgiveness, appeal, or escape. Foucault explains that heterotopic spaces "presuppose a system of opening and closing that both isolates them and makes them penetrable … the heterotopic site is not freely accessible … the individual has to submit to rites and purifications. To get in one must have a certain permission and make certain gestures" (1986: 28). The otherworlds of both *Silent Hill* and *Triangle* require death to enter and ritual to leave. Jess cannot leave the *Aeolus* without repeating the various rituals required in the loop (primarily, killing her friends and a version of herself), but chooses to return by asking the taxi driver to take her to the docks. Rose and Sharon are only able to leave *Silent Hill* once Alessa has her final revenge on the townspeople, which is only achieved through a ritualistic sacrifice. However, although they can leave the town, they cannot return to the world they left.

The Good Mother versus the Bad Mother

Sarah Arnold speaks of the Good Mother, an archetype of an "idealised form of mothering" that is constantly adapted by sociological values, yet nonetheless "valorises self-sacrifice, selflessness and nurturance" (2013: 37). Arnold notes that the Good Mother is often overshadowed by a powerful father (whether he is a protective or destructive force), while the "maternal horror film struggles to find an alternative position from which she can speak" (2013: 37–8)—something that is found in these films through the maternal space of the otherworld landscape. The Good Mother is an example of what Patricia DiQuinzio calls "essential motherhood": an ideology of idealized motherhood involving selflessness, self-sacrifice, empathy, and an innate awareness of the needs and care of others. It also positions motherhood as "natural and inevitable" for women, meaning that "women's desires are orientated to mothering and women's psychological development and emotional satisfaction require mothering" (DiQuinzio 1999: xiii). Essential or Good Motherhood therefore becomes a masochistic role, with the mother experiencing pleasure and self-worth from suffering (Arnold 39–40). Jess is seemingly an example of the self-sacrificing Good Mother and other characters reassure her of that. She expresses to Greg that she feels guilty when she is not with Tommy, to which he replies, "That's because you're a good mother. But you can't be everywhere all of the time." She is seen as a Good Mother primarily because of her self-sacrifice, yet when the spectator actually sees examples of her mothering, she is revealed to be far from ideal, swearing at, berating, and hitting her child while demanding "one fucking day off" and for Tommy to be a "normal kid." Jess also uses her supposed role as the Good Mother to excuse homicide, flatly telling Downey (Henry Nixon), "Sorry, but I love my son" as she kills him. Despite Greg's attempts to comfort her by saying that Tommy will be safe and cared for until she returns, Jess puts her role and desires as a mother over the safety of everyone else in the group. By the third loop, she has become dismissive about their lives, simultaneously seeing them as real people—she comforts Sally (Rachel Caprini) as she dies—and objects, as she knows they will return to life. Despite insisting to the others that she is trying to save them, she is nonetheless responsible for every death aboard the *Aeolus*; by trying to invoke the Good Mother, she in fact becomes the obsessive, overpowering Bad Mother.

Much of the criticism on the Bad Mother revolves around the mother as monster (see Julia Kristeva 1982; and Barbara Creed 1993), usually as a literal or figurative castrator whose obsessive actions cultivate psycho-sexual deviant behavior in the child and/or stops them from entering the Symbolic. Arnold, however, challenges this discourse by applying a melodramatic framework to the Bad Mother, acknowledging both the fears of and the unconscious desire for the monstrous mother in horror. Both Kimberly Jackson (2016) and Arnold speak of the potential appeal of the bad mother, arguing that, rather than some evil monster, she is a complex figure simultaneously invoking desire and repulsion. Arnold suggests that melancholia reframes the Bad Mother as a negative relationship rather than the embodiment of monstrous desires, writing

> [i]nstead of going through abjection (in the horror film this is represented as confronting the horrific and confirming its status as outside of the Symbolic universe), the subject/child regresses to the maternal. In other words, the horror of the film is not found in the monstrous maternal, rather horror is evoked in the child's melancholia for the mother.
>
> (2013: 100)

Arnold goes on to explain melancholia as the denial of the separation between mother and child. Melancholia can be alleviated when the child can accept and mourn the loss of the mother; abjection here refers "to the encounter with that which is already lost; in a sense, a desire for this which is known to be lost" (2013: 100). While the child must abject the mother with the support of father figures and substitutes, there is no capable father figure in either *Triangle* or *Silent Hill*, with potential candidates either killed or separated from mother and child. Alessa and Tommy cannot successfully abject the obsessive matriarch who swallowed them up with the authority of the archaic mother (Christabella and Jess respectively), and so become stuck in a stagnated, repetitive liminal space.

Dahlia from *Silent Hill* is shown to be nurturing toward her daughter and nonviolent toward her enemies, choosing to avoid weapons and confrontation. Dahlia is portrayed as weak, timid, and naive, easily bullied into handing Alessa over to Christabella for "purification" and realizing the reality of her actions far too late. She tries to invoke the Law of the Father for protection by fetching the police, but they do not arrive in time to stop Alessa from being burned. In contrast to the more action-orientated Rose, Dahlia is more akin to the mothers from the family horror films of the 1970s and 1980s, where passivity and compliance to the Law of the Father increase the risk for both her and her children (Arnold 2013: 46). Obedience and conformity do not guarantee safety, just as unconditional love and care can still result in the archetypal evil child. Devotion to her children is not enough; the true Good Mother must take action. Dahlia initially rejects the Law of the Father by refuting the strict social rules of Silent Hill and refusing to name her illegitimate child's father. For this, her daughter Sharon is branded a witch and forcibly "purified" by being burned alive. When she attempts to call on patriarchal authorities, they are practically powerless, arriving late and unable to save the child or the townspeople that burned alongside her when the fire raged out of control. Dahlia is left as a symbol of the dangerous, ugly feminine—the mad crone—unkempt and elderly.

In contrast, Rose is forced to defend herself against the monsters of Silent Hill. Her only tool is a flashlight she obtains toward the end of the film, which she uses as a distraction rather than for attack. However, she invites violence in to the towns-people's safehouse by allowing Dark Alessa to use her as a vehicle to get inside the church, which has so far repelled her. Rose confronts the townspeople with what they did to Alessa but rejects phallic authority (weapons; law enforcement; the Father) for storytelling and in doing so allows both Alessa and Dark Alessa to enter the church and obliterate all within. Rose may be an agent of violence, but she does not commit aggressive actions herself, refusing to legitimize the brutality taking place around her by instructing Sharon not to look as Alessa takes her revenge. Rose takes her place as the archetypal Good Mother, protecting her child rather than taking revenge—nurturing her rather than committing violence for her. As she and Sharon go to leave the church, Dahlia (the only other survivor of the massacre) asks Alessa why she let her live. "Mother is God in the eyes of a child," Rose replies, echoing something Cybil said to her earlier. Alessa still loves Dahlia, but Rose is Sharon's mother, with Rose firmly stating that "I'm her mother. I knew that from the moment I first laid eyes on her." Dahlia is left shaken but alive, yet only Rose—the true Good Mother—is allowed to leave, although it is later revealed that she is still trapped in an otherworld, where the father (both literally and figuratively) cannot follow.

Triangle's Jess, on the other hand, is obsessed by her devotion to Tommy— her supposed role as the Good Mother driving her actions as she commits increasingly violent acts in her attempts to be reunited with her son. She sees herself as only Mother, with no real friends or romantic interests. Almost all her conversations revolve around Tommy and his needs. Even before events take a horrific turn, she frequently speaks of her determination to get back to him, while a charged exchange with Greg shows how she prioritizes her role as mother over the other characters' desires and fears:

> **Greg**: Don't you see that this is all just in your mind? Jess! Ships don't magically appear out of nowhere. They have skippers. I mean, in your world, right now, maybe they don't.
> **Jess**: My world is waiting outside school for his mother to pick him up. Don't talk to me about my world.

The importance of this exchange is underlined as it is repeated several times over the course of the film as the original Jess moves through the various loops, seeing the conversation play out from different perspectives. Jess appears to have little life or identity outside of her son, compounding the shock and horror felt when her violent side is revealed. Suddenly, the film's introductory snippets of Tommy painting and Jess getting ready are developed into a full story, instantly changing the domestic scene (albeit with stressful events such as the paint being spilled and Tommy crying) into a murderous one as original Jess beats her counterpart to death with a hammer. Original Jess, however, still sees herself as the Good Mother; she kills her counterpart both to protect her son and to obliterate a part of herself that she despises. Despite the potential for her role being revised, the horror mother is still based in essential motherhood. As much as Jess attempts to confirm the bond with her son, she cannot avoid the violence that is part of her; as much as she insists to Tommy "that wasn't mommy" because "mommy's nice," she cannot erase the fact that she has been violent (both to Tommy and to others) and therefore cannot return to a state of essential mothering.

Purgatorial Worlds and Maternal Space

The otherworlds of *Silent Hill* and *Triangle* are gray, inescapable spaces packed with symbolism. Similar to haunted house narratives, they punish transgressors by forcing them to confront horrific and unacknowledged traumas. Realizing these unwanted truths or untold stories appears to be the key to leaving the otherworld, yet, as proven in both these films, they are almost impossible to escape from once crossed into. It is either outright stated or heavily implied that the characters who exist in these spaces have previously died, underlining the impossibility of their return to the real world. These liminal spaces rest somewhere between life and death, forcing those trapped within to acknowledge their transgressions in a gothic and ghostly landscape of psychological torture.

Gothic texts are structured as theatrical and sublime, interested in power, pain, and manipulation. The liminal landscapes of *Silent Hill* and *Triangle* act as sites of Gothic punishment, imprisoning their inhabitants in a purgatorial limbo where their fears are continually manipulated in a cycle of psychological torture. Richard Davenport-Hines writes that "in the nineteenth century the gothic imagination was enlisted to express new ideas about suffering, punishment and redemption" (1998: 195), and manifestations of this can be found within supernatural otherworlds that expressly punish the Bad Mother. The town of Silent Hill was destroyed in the fire that was intended to kill only Alessa—the townspeople's attempt to purify the witch/illegitimate child resulting in their own demise. Rose chastises them for their propensity to "[b]urn anything you're afraid of. Burn anything you can't control." The burning of Alessa led to instant punishment when the fire got out of control and devastated the entire town (or, as Dark Alessa puts it, "Your weapons can turn back on you"). But for the crime of "darken[ing] the heart of an innocent" (Silent Hill 2006)[2] they are caught in a thirty-year limbo before being ripped apart by Alessa's metallic razor-sharp tendrils.

While exploring the empty *Aeolus*, the group of friends in *Triangle* discuss the name of the ship, reciting the story of Sisyphus (the son of Aeolus), who the gods condemned to push a rock up a mountain only for it to roll down again when he reached the top. The story of Sisyphus foreshadows Jess's punishment, where she is condemned to repeat the same tasks only to end up where she began. One of the Group, Sally, notes that Sisyphus was being punished because he either cheated death or made a promise to death he did not keep. If god(s) are involved in the creation of these purgatorial worlds, then they are there to cultivate helplessness through demonstrations of power and cruelty rather than redemption through suffering. As Silent Hill's Rose says to Christabella, "You are alone in this limbo ... and God is not here." The terrifying beauty of the sublime be found despite the despair of these purgatorial otherworlds, but the landscapes themselves are sites of punishment, not salvation or enlightenment.

Once inside the otherworld heterotopia, strange spatial and temporal events begin to take place. Dutch angles are employed in both films alongside uncanny camera placements to create a sense of unease and disorientation. Rose's first exploration of Silent Hill includes shots similar to the original videogame, with the camera placed at higher or lower angles than expected, and unusual framing, such as the camera peering out from within a broken pram. Rose's initial examination of the town often positions her in the background, her small figure becoming lost in the vast and grey environment. Similarly, *Triangle* utilizes discomforting spatial logic to create a sense of confusion and powerlessness. For instance, upon the group first boarding the ship, the camera looks down at a partially obscured Downey and Sally as they walk past the stairs, later revealed to be a point-of-view (POV) shot from the second-loop Jess. A short time later, the group enter the interior of the ship, stepping into a labyrinth of dimly lit identical corridors, reminiscent of *The Shining* (1980).[3] Victor (Liam

---

[2] Said by Rose to Christabella.
[3] *Triangle* frequently references *The Shining*, from the overall aesthetic to references to room 237. *Silent Hill* also utilizes references to horror texts to help create meaning from shared genre language, such as Midwich Elementary School (a reference to *The Midwich Cuckoos* [John Wyndham, 1957]).

Hemsworth) calls out, his voice echoing around the eerily empty space as the camera tracks toward him from close to the floor, implying a predatory or voyeuristic point of view. The group turn right, exiting the screen as the camera continues to push forward straight down the main corridor. Their voices can be heard from different directions before the camera abruptly turns left and they walk across the screen from left to right—a path that should logically have been impossible.

When the group enter the ballroom, the time on Jess's watch matches that of the clock, despite Greg and Victor having a different time. Jess is on *Aeolus* time, where a luscious banquet can go rotten in minutes. Barriers become permeable; the camera pushes over Jess's shoulder and through a mirror to follow her retreating reflection, while in Silent Hill, the camera is able to move up and over a wall in a single shot. After Triangle's original Jess knocks the masked killer overboard, she finds a gramophone playing music; it is later revealed that this same song was playing during the fatal car accident. Looking down at the ocean below, Jess sees copies of herself and the group on the upturned yacht shouting for help, revealing that she (or a copy of her, at least) was the unknown person the original group saw as they approached the ship. The shock causes her to bump into the gramophone, causing the music to skip and loop. As it does so, the image on screen hitches and repeats a frame, creating a disorientating jolt that underlines the artificiality of the world.

Symbolism and Repetition

Virtually everything found and experienced in these otherworlds is intrinsically and deeply symbolic. Similar to dreamworlds, they draw from and incorporate details from the real world or the catalyzing traumatic event that created them. On a second viewing, many small, virtually unnoticeable things move to the foreground and become imbued with significance. This is not limited to visual components; often it is the repetition of spoken phrases or music in the film's score that unifies significant moments of memory or discovery. This can highlight the dramatic irony of the text; for instance, the audience may pick up changes in the music, but the character cannot hear them. On occasion, whole characters exist in order to act as symbols, either as an amalgamation of different people and experiences or as a literal personification of a character's emotions (fear, anger, and so on). An argument can be made, for example, that Jess's journey(s) through the loop are a way of her making sense of her grief, with the insinuation that she is unable to move on to the afterlife until she can come to terms with Tommy's death and her treatment of him. In this context, her companions are in fact representations of Elisabeth Kübler-Ross's model for grief recovery: denial (Greg); anger (Victor); bargaining (Sally); depression (Downey); and acceptance (Heather).[4]

In the case of purgatorial landscapes, the threat of being forced to repeat the event—of being forced to re-live the event by remembering it—forever hovers in the atmosphere. In her book *Unclaimed Trauma: Narrative and History*, Cathy Caruth builds on Freud's theory of the repetition of trauma, writing that "Freud wonders at the peculiar and sometimes uncanny way in which catastrophic events seem to repeat themselves for those who have passed through them" (1996: 1). She also notes that sometimes, "these repetitions are particularly striking because they seem not to be initiated by the individual's own acts but rather appear as the possession of some people by a sort of fate, a series of painful events to which they are subjected, and which seem to be entirely outside their wish or control" (1996: 2). Partly due to the nature of the looping narrative, *Triangle* is filled with repeating patterns, objects, musical stings, and dialogue. While the loops are not exactly the same (there are minor changes in dialogue and Jess's path around the ship, for example), they are a constant reminder of trauma—and of mystery. The distress call over the yacht radio is revealed to be from Sally, the music on the gramophone, and symbol on the drum in the *Aeolus* ballroom was drawn from the marching band playing during the car crash. Some of the most disturbing moments of the film occur when the longevity of the loop is underlined—this may be the first time *this* Jess has been through the loop, but it has actually been happening for a very long time. Scenes such as Jess coming across hundreds of her broken lockets reiterate that, despite Jess's best efforts to change the pattern, she is destined to perpetually repeat the loop. It initially appears that by killing and replacing her abusive doppelgänger, Jess has been able to break the cycle (as well as punishing her malevolent urges). However, when Jess accidentally hits a bird and must dispose of it, she comes across a huge pile of dead birds wrapped in newspaper, reminiscent of the huge pile of Sally corpses covered by Jess's cardigans seen earlier in the film. This moment confirms to both Jess and the spectator that she is still trapped and that her fate is inevitable.

---

[4] Heather is completely comfortable with who she is and what she wants, despite the machinations of Sally. She disappears from the ship during the storm, never making it to the *Aeolus*, because Jess cannot countenance the possibility of acceptance at this point (in a deleted scene, it is shown that she is unintentionally responsible for Heather's fate).

Alters and Doppelgängers

The notion of a double or alter is a key feature of the Gothic, leading to a focus on an "aesthetic of interior disorientation and divided selves" (Davenport-Hines 1998: 304). Davenport-Hines writes, "Individuals' strange, violent behaviour and disturbed psyches have always dominated gothic manners; gothic has had a constant histrionic appeal to the jejune orders of humanity who are always looking forward to the next emotional crisis" (1998: 303). Gothic alters can be simultaneously grotesque and terrifying as well as beautiful and passionate despite being shadows, reflections, or corpses.[5] These more graceful examples of alters underline the melancholic and romantic atmospheres of the Gothic text, even in twenty-first-century examples such as *Silent Hill* (2006), *Black Swan* (2010), or *The Others* (2001).

Mothers and children are doubled in *Silent Hill* and *Triangle*, all caught perilously between life and death. *Silent Hill*'s Alessa has several alters and agents that roam the ghost-town: the original (Alessa) who was burned until near death and now resides in a hospital underneath Silent Hill; her "evil" counterpart, Dark Alessa, who manifested from Alessa's pain and "told her it was their turn. I promised, they would all fall under her darkest dream"; and finally, Sharon, who is "what's left of [Alessa's] goodness" and was adopted by Rose and Chris. To parallel this, there are three mothers present in *Silent Hill*: Rose (Sharon's mother), Dahlia (Alessa's mother), and Christabella (the town matriarch, called Mother by its citizens). Jess is also split into multiple selves, including a merciless and cold killer whose head-wound matches the one inflicted on the "real world" Jess after the car accident. Jess dissociates herself from her violent actions throughout the film, telling Greg that she does not want him to see her face as she kills him "because this is not me. I'm somewhere out there on the upturned yacht and you're with me." She tells Tommy that she will not shout at or hit him anymore "[b]ecause the woman that did those things to you is not Mommy." Even when Jess directly confronts her doppelgänger in the ballroom, she can only say "You're not me." Ostensibly, however, Jess is split into two: the multiple Good Mothers of the supernatural world who constantly try to return to their son and the Bad Mother of the real world who abuses him. However, in Jess's quest to get back to Tommy, she ultimately—and unintentionally—becomes the Bad Mother. As Arnold writes:

---

[5] See Arata (1990) and Stevenson (1988) for examples of this phenomenon in *Dracula* (Bram Stoker 1897).

> In contrast to the self-sacrificing films in which the mother volunteers her absence in order to enable the child to fulfil his/her proper socialisation, the Bad Mother continues to "haunt" from afar. She refuses to let go even in death or insists on holding the child back through her overwhelming dominance of the child.
>
> (2013: 93)

While Jess's actions initially appear to fulfill the requirement of the self-sacrificing Good Mother, she in fact "continues to 'haunt' from afar ... refusing to let go even in death" (2013: 93). Jess justifies her decision to re-enter the loop by trying to save Tommy, but in doing so she continually resurrects and kills both of them. As such, she not only becomes a Bad Mother, but Creed's archaic mother, the "parthenogenic mother, the mother as primordial abyss, the point of origin and of end" (1993: 17), who overwhelms and entombs the child. She traps herself in the loop, unable to ever become the true Good Mother.

Maternal Space

Alongside Silent Hill and Triangle, other horror films such as The Others, The Dark (2005), and television series Stranger Things (2016–present) feature mothers searching for their children in ghostly otherworlds where discourses of "good mothering" are questioned. Jackson argues:

> the mother-child bond is often portrayed as redemptive, but only if and when it can be released from the grip of bourgeois patriarchy ... suggest[ing] that the bourgeois family has become, if it has not always been, a violent and oppressive institution, and the identity positions it demands are ultimately unsustainable.
>
> (2016: 185)

Rose is only able to be reunited with Sharon after her husband has been ejected from Silent Hill and forced to stop investigating; Jess can only be reunited with Tommy once the other members of her group, including a love interest (and potential father figure to her son), have been killed.

However, Arnold suggests that liminal maternal spaces such as these "reveal the impossibility of re-articulating motherhood within the Symbolic patriarchal universe" (2013: 105–6). She goes on to explain:

> In order for the mother to find a new language, to operate from her own position, to speak of her own desire, she must be excluded from the patriarchal universe. She must speak from the space of Otherness, which in the films is

often a supernatural place, an alternative, parallel universe. Therefore, even as these films offer a maternal perspective, a maternal space, they still function in opposition to the dominant patriarchal paradigm which in the films is represented as the "normal", Symbolic world of the father figure. The oscillation between the normal male universe and the supernatural female universe maintains the hierarchy which validates the masculine world and is suspicious of the female world.

(2013)

In *Silent Hill*, for example, the real world is brightly lit, rational, patriarchal and follows institutional law and order, the opposite of the dark, foggy, decrepit, obscure, and supernatural maternal space that Rose finds herself in. Here, the paternal story is in control; Chris is never able to find out the truth of what really happened in *Silent Hill* or to his daughter because patriarchal power blocks him both literally (the police who escort him out of *Silent Hill* and arrest him at the orphanage) and figuratively (Chris is unable to access the supernatural maternal space and therefore cannot bear witness to the story). Nevertheless, as Arnold notes, it is the paternal narrative that is set in the real world and is therefore portrayed as "normal," with the film ultimately privileging this perspective in its final moments:

> [T]he final shot of the film belongs to the father, who looks around longingly for the family he senses but cannot see … By comparing the mother's space, which is filled with grey and dark tones, with the father's bright, sunny space, the film renders the latter more appealing. Thus, even though the mother's narrative has dominated most of the film (in contrast to the father's, which is almost irrelevant), the father's narrative concludes the film.
>
> (2013: 110)

"Not Even the Darkness Wants Her"

The purgatorial worlds of *Silent Hill* and *Triangle* are liminal, transgressive nonspaces where patriarchal law gives way to the obsessive, archaic matriarch. Designed to induce helplessness, these spaces challenge the concept of the Good Mother, constantly demanding sacrifice and selflessness before returning their children, now Othered, doubled, and undead. Once inside the otherworld's boundaries, the inhabitants are trapped in a stasis filled with suffering—a dissociative and dream-like holding-pattern that can only end with the sacrifice of the Good Mother or the obliteration of the Bad. The otherworlds cultivate perpetual anguish, but to achieve "satisfaction" ("revenge") as Dark Alessa puts it, the punishment must fit the crime. For Jess, who takes out her frustrations that "every day is the same" on her son, she is imprisoned in an indefinite series of loops where she is forced to confront her various failings as a mother. The townspeople of Silent Hill, however, are subjected to a much more visceral and tangible punishment under Alessa's wrath; kept awake in a nightmare that tortures them physically and psychologically in an echo of the misery they inflicted on Alessa. They have succumbed to Alessa's "darkest dream," where only Good Mothers (Rose and Dahlia) can survive; as Dark Alessa coldly tells Rose, "the dream of this life must end and so too must the dreamers within it."

Works Cited

Arata, S. D. (1990), "The Occidental Tourist: *Dracula* and the Anxiety of Reverse Colonization," *Victorian Studies*, 33(4): 621–45.

Arnold, S. (2013), *Maternal Horror Film: Melodrama and Motherhood*, Basingstoke/New York: Palgrave Macmillan.

Buckland, W. (ed.) (2009), *Puzzle Films: Complex Storytelling in Contemporary Cinema*, Chichester: Blackwell Publishing Limited.

Caruth, C. (1996), *Unclaimed Experience: Trauma, Narrative, and History*, Baltimore: Johns Hopkins University Press.

Creed, B. (1993), *The Monstrous-Feminine: Film, Feminism Psychoanalysis*, London: Routledge.

Davenport-Hines, R. (1998), *Gothic: Four Hundred Years of Excess, Horror, Evil, and Ruin*, London: Fourth Estate.

DiQuinzio, P. (1999), *The Impossibility of Motherhood: Feminism, Individualism, and the Problem of Mothering*, New York and London: Routledge, 1999.

Foucault, M. (1986), "Of Other Spaces: Utopias and Heterotopias," *Diacritics*, 16: 22–31.

Frank, A. W. (1995; 2013), *The Wounded Storyteller: Body, Illness and Ethics*, 2nd ed., Chicago: University of Chicago Press.

Hirch, Foster, *The Dark Side of the Screen: Film Noir*, Cambridge, MA: Da Capo Press, 1981.

Jackson, K. (2016), *Gender and the Nuclear Family in Twenty-First Century Horror*, Basingstoke/New York: Palgrave Macmillan.

Kalmus, N. M. (2006), "Colour Consciousness," in A. Dalle Vacche and B. Price (eds), *Color: The Film Reader*, New York: Routledge.

Kristeva, J. (1982), *Powers of Horror: An Essay on Abjection*, Leon S. Roudiez (trans.), New York: Columbia University Press.

Kübler-Ross, E. and M. D. Ira Byock (2011), "On Death and Dying: What the Dying Have to Teach Doctors, Nurses, Clergy & Their Own Families" Reissue ed. edition. New York: Scribner.

Powell, A. (2005), *Deleuze and Horror Film*, Edinburgh: Edinburgh University Press.

Richardson, N. (2010), *Transgressive Bodies: Representations in Film and Popular Culture*, Surrey: Ashgate Publishing Limited.

Silent Hill (2006), directed by C. Gans, Canada and France: Alliance Atlantis.

Stevenson, J. A. (March 1988), "A Vampire in the Mirror: The Sexuality of Dracula," *PMLA*, 103(2): 139–49.

The Others (2001), directed by A. Amenábar, Spain: StudioCanal.

Tidwell, C. (2013), "'Everything Is Always Changing': Autism, Normalcy, and Progress in Elizabeth Moon's *The Speed of Dark* and Nancy Fulda's 'Movement,'" in K. Allan (ed.), *Disability in Science Fiction: Representations of Technology as Cure*, 153–68, Basingstoke: Palgrave Macmillan.

Triangle (2009), directed by C. Smith, United Kingdom and Australia: Icon Films Distribution.

6

Pray and Obey: The Horror (and Purgatory) of Religious Fundamentalism

Nicola Young

In the twenty-first century, religious fundamentalism, characterized by the application of strict literalism to scripture and strong separation between believers and outsiders (Hunsberger 1995), grows in popularity and influence, suggesting the beginning of a shift away from the increasing secularism of the previous century (Emerson and Hartman 2006). The fundamentalist movements depicted in this chapter's films, *Silent Hill* (Gans 2006) and *We Are What We Are* (Mickle 2013), are "world rejecting" (Wallis 1984: 10) in that adherents perceive the prevailing social order as deviant. This chapter will consider the role of world rejecting religious fundamentalism as a source of gendered horror in contemporary US horror film, using a framework inspired by possible worlds theory to draw out the aesthetically mediated and real-world conversant construction of these film worlds. I will demonstrate the function of religious fundamentalism in horror as a creator of worlds in which women can question and subvert the structures that oppress them, troubling and re-appropriating concepts of necessity and possibility, through case studies of *Silent Hill* (with reference to its sequel *Silent Hill: Revelation* [Bassett 2012]) and *We Are What We Are*. While it will be seen that the possible worlds of both films are quite different, the effect of religion as world-creator is strikingly similar.

It is important to state that this chapter is not concerned with religious fundamentalism in the natural world, but how filmic fundamentalism functions as a source of horror. However, these films draw from real-world sources in their world creation—primarily from millenarian movements (featuring unconventional behavior, prophesy, and withdrawal from general society). Most importantly, these groups "do not accept the culturally transmitted conception of reality" (Barkun 1974: 142), creating and inhabiting a perceptual and moral reality that is militant in its opposition to modernity (Marsden 1980). However, I will attempt to avoid the tendency to elide these filmic representations into our perception of the religions they are inspired by (Cutrara 2014: 31), aided by the ability of possible worlds theory to provide a focus on the metaphysical function of religion in film. Deleuze (1989: 68) reminds us that film "does not just present images, it surrounds them with a world" and the focus here will be on that world, its structures, and possibilities.

This chapter is also indebted to Irena Makarushka (2009), who considers how the idea of woman is "reflected in the different modes and modalities of expression particular to religion and film," changing over time to reflect shifting cultural values (113). I share this view of religion and film as a meaning-making process, which aims to create order through symbols and signifiers and the articulation of societal roles. Furthermore, in this specific configuration of religion and film, "woman is neither outside the margins nor at the margins of the political; instead, she constitutes and unsettles those margins," moving past simpler constructions of women as either comforting or dangerous to find space for complexity (Zerilli 2005: 2).

In taking an artwork seriously as a world, we may begin with the concept that "World" is both a philosophical concept and an example of that concept (Heidegger 2008: 174–5)—a world is both the totality created by art and the natural world, in a relationship both connected and separate. The significance of a work in this regard appears in how the "world is conversant with itself" (Hayot 2012: 54), in which its worldedness underlies the narrative and delineates the rules that constitute the world as a totality. These rules may be unspoken, as much in the foreground as the background, and in the balance between the diegesis and the "knowableness" of the unspoken (for example, the viewer may not be told that pens exist in this world but may safely assume an answer from other signifiers).

Possible worlds theory arose in opposition to "logical positivism," which posits that nonactual objects or states are meaningless (Hempel 1950), through the study of modal logic, which introduced the concepts of necessity and possibility to analytical philosophy (Lewis 1986). Modal logic considers the range of possibilities emerging from actual states and objects. Possible worlds arise from the natural world but are ontologically separate even while within, corresponding to possibilities that are "ways things could have been" (Lewis 1979: 182) and these counterfactuals demonstrate how different conceptual structures give rise to different possibilities (Gyllensten 1988: 274). This concept has been used in literary studies (Eco 1984; Doležel 1998) to define how the audience conceives possibilities within the fictional world. Doležel (1998: 115) outlined a framework to interrogate the plausibility of fictional worlds, a full description of which is outside the scope of this chapter, but which convincingly demonstrates that supernatural worlds have no less plausibility as they contain normative principles which permit or even require implausible things to exist, as is the case with *Silent Hill*. Buckland (1999) demonstrated that the special effects used in *Jurassic Park* (Spielberg 1993) generate a possible world that draws out extreme propositions from an actual state without losing possibility. Possible worlds take plausibility and follow the thread, sometimes to the very limit of rationality. For this chapter, however, the methodology used is inspired by, but not truly possible worlds theory. Following Zerilli (2005), the primary focus is not on testing the modality of the work but celebrating the ambiguities that arise when the film's (female) characters test the world's modalities themselves.

The selection of possible worlds theory also pertains to nostalgia, which arises through a loss of ontological stability resulting from clashes with modernism (Pavel 1988: 255). In their nostalgia, these filmic religious communities generate their own possible worlds within the narrative (complete worlds in opposition to the "actual world" of the narrative), with each interrogating modal claims of necessity and inevitability, and each community explores the possibilities available to "find out a suitable model for realia" (Eco 1988: 346). Furthermore, I will argue that reading the films in this manner will illuminate the tendency to conceptualize natural-world religious communities as parallel worlds, both in and separate from the world. Before considering the specifics of the respective film worlds, it should be noted that the possible worlds on display in these films are each "dyadic, or modally heterogeneous" (Doležel 1998:187), featuring two (or more) realms within the same diegesis with different modalities. Each film contains a "first world," which bears some degree of deliberate similarity to the natural world, and each world contains at least one other world, which may be characterized as purgatorial (in both senses, that of an intermediate state, and that of a state of suffering), particularly for female inhabitants, who have limited ability to traverse between worlds.

Silent Hill (2006) and its sequel *Silent Hill: Revelation* (2012) follow the story of Rose, Christopher, and their adopted daughter Sharon as they travel to an abandoned town named Silent Hill in search of answers on Sharon's origins and sleepwalking. They piece together Sharon's links to the town and its religious fundamentalist community, The Brethren (known as The Order in *Revelation* but referred to throughout this chapter as The Brethren), and particularly to their tortured antagonist Alessa, with whom Sharon shares a soul. The plot is strikingly similar to that of the "survival horror"[1] games from which they are adapted, in which the objective is to kill to survive, justified by the presentation of a "binary opposition of Good and Evil" (Perron 2018: 203). This is in line with the tendency identified by Keller (1996: 11) of religion itself to encourage believers to construct binaries in which they are victimized by, but unified against an evil outsider, who must be purged. Keller's work demonstrates the gendering of these binaries (innocence and vice are feminine, whereas the agency of good and evil is masculine) as well as the importance of ambiguity as a radically subversive medium (1996: 127).

Silent Hill has three realms: the first world (not dissimilar to the natural world) and a gray world, both of which appear to exist outside and inside of the town's boundaries; and a dark world, which is specific to the town. The gray world is the most explicitly purgatorial, although the gray and dark worlds share many similarities. The interplay between these worlds is central to these films, and their construction is aesthetically mediated. Visually, the worlds are separated by weather and by color: we see a variety of colors in the first world and many of the scenes are lit with yellow light reminiscent of sunlight. *Silent Hill* exists in the first world but is abandoned, with access prohibited as a result of the fire that still burns under the town. When Rose (Radha Mitchell) enters the gray world, what appears to be snow falls, although it is soon determined to be ash. The light is gray, and compared to the first world, any other colors are muted. The foggy landscape also appears emptier than in the first world, and the roads are buckled, causing a distorted and blurred effect. Long shots of Rose demonstrate her relative size and frailty in comparison to the town and increase the sense of emptiness. The transition between the gray and dark worlds is spectacular, with a transition from day to night that happens in seconds (and we may determine, therefore, that time does not flow in line with the first world) and the walls and other surroundings melting and cracking from gray to black and red. A particular feature of this landscape is fire at the bottom of stairs and openings, calling to mind traditional representations of hell sitting beneath the natural world such as in John Martin's painting *Le Pandemonium* (1841). Despite the fire, it is no longer snowing ash, but raining torrentially.

Another key world construction device is the aural landscape. Again, the first world is characterized by dialogue, extra-diegetic music, and "naturalistic" sound effects (traffic noises are present by the road, for example) that reinforce

---

[1] Specifically, *Silent Hill* (Konami, 1999) and *Silent Hill 2* (Konami, 2001), although elements from other games in the series appear in the films.

the impression that this world is one with the natural world, validating the possibility of each of the other realms by their relation to this one. The gray world is almost silent: there do not appear to be any birds in the town and there is certainly no traffic. Like the attention paid to the visual transition between the purgatorial and hell worlds, the transition is given an aural signifier in the form of air-raid sirens which punctuate the quiet. The dark world is as loud as the purgatorial world is quiet, using the quiet-loud sound design to great effect.

The worlds also construct and delineate themselves through their inhabitants. The first world represents human society regardless of whether humans are physically on screen: aside from one pastoral scene, the landscape is full of human infrastructure in good working order. Through this (and through the shocked reactions of the human characters on entering the gray and dark worlds) we perceive that the first world allows for the fantastic only in limited ways (Sharon [Jodelle Ferland] is part of Silent Hill but can exist in the first world). The gray and dark worlds are occupied by inhuman and grotesque beings. Although human characters pass between these worlds, it does not appear that the monsters do, at least while alive—"Colin the Janitor" appears in the gray world as a corpse and is reanimated in the dark world. The monsters in each world are different in form and representation. The danger of the gray world beings appears somewhat incidental (they may spit or drip acid) in comparison to the deliberate and often weapon-wielding violence of the dark world's denizens. The gray world monsters are ghostly representations of what haunts The Brethren (Colin's corpse, for example, which symbolizes the town's shame and spurs Rose on her quest). The dark world monsters represent the evil visited on Alessa (also Jodelle Ferland) reflected on the town, for example, the threat of penetration (Pyramid Head) and the torturous medical procedures required to save her life (the Nurses). The framing of the monsters assists with world construction: creatures appear as we follow the point of view of a human character, or in the frame behind human characters. This framing of the fantastical elements is key to the films' merging of the special effects into the diegesis, giving existential weight to the monsters who interact with the same environment as the humans.

With The Brethren, we see the same blending of fantastic and naturalistic elements where they are visually constructed to resemble religious communities, such as the Plymouth Brethren, with men in high necked gray and black suits and women in long dresses with their hair and shoulders covered (although they are also covered in ash and somewhat ghoulish in appearance). In *Revelation*, the group has moved on to ceremonial robes more reminiscent of Catholicism. The Brethren founded Silent Hill, and their crucifix-like symbol adorns many of its buildings, as do their fire and brimstone religious paintings. While they resemble in many ways a Christian fundamentalist sect, they appear to worship a female deity (as shown in their paintings, although these may also be read as prophetic of the coming of Rose).

The Brethren make sin central to their conceptual framework, with strict punishments for sinners, including women who have sinned by being sinned against. Led by their charismatic and cruel leader Christabella (Alice Krige), they tortured Alessa for the sins of being fatherless and abused and burned her alive as a witch, causing the fire that destroyed the town. Even when in the dark world, which as noted is most aligned with Alessa, The Brethren refuse responsibility and acceptance of their own deaths in the fire. They believe that they are holding back the dark world through strict adherence to their faith, although this is shown to be fallacious toward the end of the first film when the dark world arises despite their piety and even their church cannot save them. Both films make clear that The Brethren created all of the worlds they have inhabited—the first world (prior to the fire) was created by their strict literalism and punishment of "sin," and the other two worlds were created by their abuse of Alessa. The Brethren were able to carry out such acts due to their adherence to the if-then proposition that if they did not violently cast out sinners the world would be lost, highlighting a common conceptualization of fundamentalist groups as capable of extreme violence, an idea propagated by stories about groups like the Army of God,[2] whose membership has included several active terrorists (Henderson 2015).

The three worlds of Silent Hill are constructed through the relativity between worlds, positioned so that the reality of the first supports the reality of the next. Each world has internal consistency; however, there is no space here to list every rule on which they rely. However, there are several primary rules, the first of which is the rule of traversability. We are shown that the gray and dark worlds sit in the same physical space as the first world on several occasions. In one key scene, Christopher (Sean Bean) and Rose are in the same area but in different worlds; he can feel something of her presence, and it appears that the distance between these worlds is not insurmountable. Indeed, in *Revelation*, Rose has found a way to send Sharon back, whereas Rose (potentially because she has died and Sharon has not) may not physically return to the first world once she has entered the gray for the first time. In this regard, we see a dichotomy

---

[2] The Army of God is a Christian terrorist organization operating in the United States, particularly known for using violence to oppose abortion services.

between the land of the living (the first world) and the land of the dead (the gray world as purgatorial between first and dark worlds) (Deacy 2012), in which either is excluded from the other. The barrier between the gray world appears porous and yet not—the first world is physically (the bridge to it has collapsed) and metaphysically (they are "out of phase" with each other) detached from the others and most who enter the gray/dark worlds can never really leave. The difficulties of traversability underline the sense that these are complete (albeit porous) realms.

The second rule is that sin has true power, although not necessarily the power The Brethren expected. The pain they visited upon Alessa grew into her creative power and she exclaims "Now is the end of days and I am the reaper" as she returns that pain in apocalyptic fashion. While as noted, The Brethren are not a specifically Christian group, the language used throughout is overwhelmingly representative of Christianity. In considering such a world, we appreciate that it is not the natural world, but it has meaning in the way it engages in modalities that account for the way things are and the way things could/should be (Laure-Ryan 1991: 48), so our engagement with these films has relevance to our conceptual engagement with natural world religious institutions. As discussed below, the primary mechanism here for this exploration is the actions of the primary female characters. *Silent Hill* ultimately suggests that to avoid the darkness, it may be necessary to radically alter the natural world to reduce or prevent the popularity of potentially dangerous forms of fundamentalism.

We Are What We Are centers on the Parkers, whose mother, Emma (Kassie Wesley DePaiva), dies suddenly in the opening scene. Father Frank (Bill Sage) and his three children have no time to mourn, as they need to prepare for their traditional religious ritual, which can only be performed by the women, and which involves cannibalism. The small town in which they live is unaware of their unusual religious practices or their "bible," the diary of an ancestor recounting her religious conceptualization of her own community's starvation-induced cannibalism (itself a reference to natural world events such as the stories of the Donner Party in 1846 [McGlashan 1918]). An ongoing torrential rainstorm washes up the evidence of the Parker's crimes, recalling the biblical forty days and forty nights of rain, foreshadowing the Parker's upcoming reckoning with their God. The world of *We Are What We Are* is, at first glance, much more similar to the natural world than those explored in *Silent Hill*. However, this is also a dyadic world, in which the Parkers live in a realm that sits physically within the first world but is markedly apart. One very clear narrative and aesthetic choice in the landscape that constructs the Parker world is that it is an ossuary, literally a place of worship full of bones. The town may itself be doing rather poorly, particularly in light of the damage being caused by the ongoing torrential rain, but the surprise and horror caused by the washing downstream of human bones signifies that the first world here is built on natural-world foundations and moral codes.

Unlike *Silent Hill*, however, the primary manner of aesthetic mediation between the two worlds lies in the points of difference between the Parkers and their neighbors. The film features an interesting use of expository hairstyles; the Parker girls begin the film with tightly plaited hair, which becomes looser as they begin to question their religion, although they retain their demure clothing throughout, visually similar to female members of the Fundamentalist Church of Jesus Christ of Latter-Day Saints (Adams 2007). The local townspeople, on the other hand, dress in contemporary clothes suitable for the rural environment. In this respect, the Parkers recall the aforementioned nostalgic tendencies of fundamentalism, in which "modern ways of life ... were pernicious and must be resisted" (Brasher 2014: 14). Male Parkers also wear somewhat anachronistic clothing, but the Parker doctrine does have a particular focus on women's roles and behavior based on the extremity of their difference.

The Parker religion is heavily focused on tradition ("we'll do it the way we've always done it") and strongly teleological (focused on the end times) and their world is partially constructed by their linear understanding of time, making their nostalgia even more striking. Frank appears to be a clockmaker, with the walls of his shed lined with clocks. Frank believes he is tasked with ensuring that the Parkers continue, event after event, toward culmination, telling Rose (Julia Garner) and Iris (Amber Childers) that "we go on, we must." In this view, the Parkers are divinely called to continue their practices until God signals the end is arrived, meaning that the sisters are not permitted to traverse to the first world for fear they may not return. This again places the sisters in a purgatorial state not shared by their father, as he may traverse between worlds, and takes some control over the marching of events, where they may only wait. The diary supports Frank's view of their religion as it guides his family through its gristly practices with an abundance of religious justification, similar to that employed by The Brethren in *Silent Hill*.

The boundaries between the first and Parker worlds are also delineated by the gaze of other characters, who see the Parkers without knowing, as though they are obscured. Their nearest neighbor spends a significant amount of time watching the Parkers; however, in a darkly comical moment following Emma's death, she brings them a vegetarian lasagna, demonstrating that those who know the Parkers best do not know them at all. Similarly, deputy Anders (Wyatt Russell), who is in love with Iris, is incapable of perceiving the danger, unable to understand Iris when she states that he would not like her if he knew what she was. As in *Silent Hill*, there is some degree of traversability for the Parkers, who can enter the first world, although the other characters are not able to enter the Parker world at all, rendering them apart and unknowable. Therefore, despite the relative lack of explicit visual and aural separation between the worlds, the separation is no less effective here.

The first world here is also similar to the natural world in a manner that enhances the sense of realism in both worlds. The first world has businesses, traffic, people, and objects that would be expected in the twenty-first-century natural world as well as naturalistic sound effects matching the visual scene and dialogue. The Parker world shares some of these features, but the color palette (other than the red of blood) is muted and gray/beige, shown to great effect when the girls gather, surrounded by gray curtains, to watch the outside from the window, the background obscured by a reflected haze of rain. Perhaps unsurprisingly, their world is centered around the dinner table, a ritual altar of immense significance. Gathering at the table/altar to eat and pray decreases the possibilities of the world on each occasion as it further aligns the children with Frank and emphasizes their apartness from the first world. The Parker world is separated less by physical borders than it is by the doctrine and practicalities of their religious practice.

It should be no surprise that a key rule of the Parker world is "we are what we are"—a deterministic view of the world in which people can only be what God wishes them to be, and all that matters is carrying out God's will. Boethius (523AD) theorized that God exists in eternity, which is a place outside of time. Therefore, God can see the past, present, and future simultaneously, and is guiding us toward his eventual aim. The Parkers believe in this form of determinism, which enables the externalization of moral concepts and reduces individual culpability. Again, in a manner that recalls *Silent Hill*, this is a world in which women do have a particular religious significance and even leadership, but in a manner that upholds the institution and requires them to do terrible things. The Parker girls carry out their family's ritual murders and partake in cannibalism. However, the girls trouble their world to the point of its destruction, opening their own anti-deterministic (if not necessarily cannibalism-free) future. In this regard, the film positions the natural world (by its closer relationship with the first world) as inherently anti-determinist. In *We Are What We Are* as in *Silent Hill*, whatever the role of women, the worlds turn on a gulf between the religious and secular. In constructing these parallel and purgatorial worlds, they highlight a tendency to imagine fundamentalist religious communities as existing in other realms with a dyadic relationship to the natural world.

In all three films—the two *Silent Hill* movies and *We Are What We Are*—"the wages of sin is death" (Romans 6:23) or sin is the source of all suffering. Sin in natural world Christianity should be understood as an act that offends God (such as Eve's eating the apple in Genesis 3) and all three films feature religious characters who fail the most basic of God's commandments, "thou shalt do no murder" (Matthew 19:16-19). They do so in a twisted attempt at piety, unaccepting of doctrine that describes their acts as sinful. Belief in tangible evil is also featured, with religious leaders exerting control through personal experience of the divine. In *We Are What We Are*, God told the Parker ancestors to eat, and they thrived. In *Silent Hill*, they have proven the existence of the afterlife. Faith has been replaced by knowledge for the believers, presenting a more complex than may be expected picture of their belief structures.

As noted above, these worlds restrict women by not allowing them to participate in the first world. The construction of women is reciprocal—the worlds cannot function without the participation of their female inhabitants, but they require women to be held to particular roles. Having constructed possible worlds, these religious communities are ultimately undone by the introduction of female agency, where women act in solidarity with other female characters rather than upholding patriarchal norms. Just as the religious communities are willing to do violence for God, these women do violence for love and the possibility of self-determination. Where these female characters truly trouble the world, though, is in their rejection of the gendered binaries outlined earlier— they feminize the action of doing good and evil, refusing their place as paragons of virtue or scapegoats. Rose (*Silent Hill*) in particular is an adoptive mother who acts as a divine surrogate for God (as noted in the first film "mother is God in the eyes of the child"), with all the creative and destructive power that such a role entails. *Silent Hill* explicitly considers the role of the mother, testing Rose's capacity to sacrifice herself to its limits ("be careful what you choose"), and positioning Rose in opposition to Alessa's biological mother Dahlia (Deborah Kara Unger), who failed the same test. Unlike some mother archetypes,[3] however, Rose's love for Sharon is expressed through action and violence. With

---

[3] For example, the "Good Mother," characterized by self-abnegation, or the "Bad Mother," characterized by selfishness (Kaplan 1990)—these archetypes are presented as binary and relational, from the position of the child or husband.

Sybil (Laurie Holden), the police officer who followed them to Silent Hill, Rose admonishes The Brethren boldly, telling them the truth they have ignored for many years, "you burned in the fire that you started, and nothing can save you, because you're already damned." Rose refuses their counterfactual ("if we don't burn the witch, we ourselves will be damned") as she allows Alessa to enter their sanctuary to slaughter the gathered Brethren. Rose gives a different counterfactual: "You should be careful how you fight evil, your weapons can turn back on you," or if we burn the witch, we ourselves will burn, as the film culminates entirely as a result of her action.

These particular female protagonists trouble the very structure of the worlds when they accept ambiguity in their relationship to the worlds they inhabit. As noted above, Rose surrenders to Alessa's revenge to accomplish her goals, marking her victory with blood. In *We Are What We Are*, The Parker sisters spend much of the film quietly questioning the dominant doctrine while outwardly complying. However, it is not until they are called upon to carry out the sacrificial ritual that they find that the counterfactual on which their lives are built ("[i]f God told our ancestors to eat human flesh, it must be righteous") does not carry the same status of necessity for them. They do carry out the ritual, but Rose immediately states she will not do it again. Iris's relationship with Deputy Anders, and his horrific death at the hands of her father, adds further fuel to their quiet discussions, particularly as Frank rages outside screaming scripture and slashing plants in his fury at Iris. Having decided that they are not required to live this way the sisters plan to escape, but when their father attempts to feed them poison, the girls turn their religious tradition against him. We also see in the final scene that the girls and their brother are safe and driving away to their future, although Rose's hand on the Parker bible suggests that they may carry on with their ways even as they determine their own futures.

In conclusion, the use of possible worlds theory in the analysis of religion and film has enabled readings of these films which outline the ability of religious fundamentalism horror to open fantastic and radical spaces. By accepting the concept that films contain self-contained worlds and by working through how and why those worlds are constructed, we can begin to see how audiences conceptualize fundamentalist religion. As was the case with *Silent Hill*, we find that these worlds are haunted by the meaning we give them as much as by the meaning they create. We find that fundamentalism functions not purely as a source of horror but also as a creator of dyadic or hybrid worlds, in which believers (and particularly women) are restricted in their ability to traverse from one to the other. As has been seen, the extremity of the presentation of these worlds (and the extremity of the fundamentalism within them) stretches the limits of the possible, giving these films a specific capacity to consider gendered possibilities and to consider new ways of being.

Works Cited

Adams, B. (2007), "FLDS Women and Their Dresses," *Salt Lake Tribune*, August 14. https://web.archive.org/web/20120321142305/http:/blogs.sltrib.com/plurallife/2007/08/flds-women-and-their-dresses.html.

Barkun, M. (1974), *Disaster and the Millennium*, New Haven: Yale University Press.

Blizek, W. (2009), "Using Movies to Critique Religion," in W. Blizek (ed.), *The Bloomsbury Companion to Religion and Film*, 39–48, London: Continuum.

Boethius (1999), *The Consolation of Philosophy* [523 A.D.], Victor Watts (trans.), London: Penguin Classics.

Brasher, B. (2014), "The Apocalyptic, Gender and American Christian Fundamentalism," in B. Brasher and L. Quinby (eds), *Gender and Apocalyptic Desire*, 14–21, New York: Routledge.

Buckland, W. (1999), "Between Science Fiction and Science Fact: Spielberg's Digital Dinosaurs, Possible Worlds and the New Aesthetic Realism," in S. Redmond (ed.), *Liquid Metal: The Science Fiction Reader*, 24–36, London: Wallflower Press.

Cutrara, D. (2014), *Wicked Cinema: Sex and Religion on Screen*, Austin: University of Texas Press.

Deacy, C. (2012), *Mapping the Afterlife: Theology, Eschatology and Film*, Abingdon: Routledge.

Deleuze, G. (1989), *Cinema 2: The Time Image*, H. Tomlinson and R. Galeta (trans.), Minneapolis: University of Minnesota Press.

Doležel, L. (1998), *Heterocosmica: Fiction and Possible Worlds*, Baltimore: Johns Hopkins University Press.

Eco, U. (1984), *The Role of the Reader: Explorations in the Semiotics of Texts*, Bloomington: Indiana University Press.

Eco, U. (1988), "Report on Session 3: Literature and Arts," in A. Sture (ed.), *Possible Worlds in Humanities, Arts and Sciences: Proceedings of Nobel Symposium*, 65, 343–56, Berlin: de Gruyter.

Emerson, M. and D. Hartman (2006), "The Rise of Religious Fundamentalism," *Annual Review of Sociology*, 32: 127–14.

Gyllensten, L. (1988), "Possible Worlds—A Chorus of a Multitude of Souls," in A. Sture (ed.), *Possible Worlds in Humanities, Arts and* Sciences: *Proceedings of Nobel Symposium*, 65, 272–92, Berlin: de Gruyter.

Haunton, C. (2009), "Filming the Afterlife," in W. Blizek (ed.), *The Bloomsbury Companion to Religion and Film*, 260–9, London: Continuum.

Hayot, E. (2012), *Literary Worlds*, Oxford: Oxford University Press.
Heidegger, M. (2008), *The Basic Writings [1937]*, D. Krell (trans.), New York: HarperCollins.
Hempel, C. (1950), "Problems and Changes in the Empiricist Criterion of Meaning," *Revue Internationale de Philosophie*, 41: 41–63.
Henderson, A. (2015), "6 modern-day Christian Terrorist Groups Our Media Conveniently Ignores," *Salon*, 7, April 7, 2015. https://www.salon.com/2015/04/07/6_modern_day_christian_terrorist_groups_our_media_conveniently_ignores_partner/.
Hunsberger, B. (1995), "Religion and Prejudice: The Role of Religious Fundamentalism, Quest, and Right-Wing Authoritarianism," *Journal of Social Issues*, 51(2): 113–29.
Jurassic Park (1993), directed by S. Spielberg, Universal City: Universal Pictures.
Kaplan, A. (1990), "The Case of the Missing Mother," in P. Erens (ed.), *Issues in Feminist Film Criticism*, 126–36, Bloomington: Indiana University Press.
Keller, C. (1996), *Apocalypse Now and Then*, Minneapolis: Fortress Press.
Laure-Ryan, M. (1991), *Possible Worlds, Artificial Intelligence and Narrative Theory*, Bloomington: Indiana University Press.
Lewis, D. (1979), "Possible Worlds," in M. Loux (ed.), *The Possible and the Actual*, Ithaca, N.Y.: Cornell University Press.
Lewis, D. (1986), *On the Plurality of Worlds*, Oxford: Blackwell.
Makarushka, I. (2009), "Women, Religion and Film," in W. Blizek (ed.), *The Bloomsbury Companion to Religion and Film*, 113–22, London: Continuum.
Marsden, G. (1980), *Fundamentalism and American Culture*, Oxford: Oxford University Press.
McGlashan, C. (1918), *History of the Donner Party: A Tragedy of the Sierra Nevada [1880]*, San Francisco: A Carlisle & Company.
Pavel, T. (1988), "Fictional Worlds and the Economy of the Imaginary," in A. Sture (ed.), *Possible Worlds in Humanities, Arts and Sciences: Proceedings of Nobel Symposium 65*, 250–9, Berlin: de Gruyter.
Perron, B. (2018), *The World of Scary Video Games: A Study in Videoludic Horror*, New York: Bloomsbury.
Silent Hill (2006), directed by C. Gans, Paris: Davis Films.
Silent Hill: Revelation (2012), directed by M. J. Bassett, Paris: Davis Films.
Wallis, R. (1984), *The Elementary Forms of the New Religious Life*. London: Routledge.
We Are What We Are (2013), directed by J. Mickle, Toronto: Entertainment One.
Zerilli, L. (2005), *Signifying Woman*, Ithaca, N.Y.: Cornell University Press.

Part Three

Female Development in Purgatorial Spaces

7

The New Eden? The Female-Centered Purgatorial Space of *Dollhouse*

Erin Giannini

The concept of purgatory—a place between heaven and hell in which imperfectly "purified" souls, whether through doctrine or timing (i.e., before Christ)—is held to expiate their sins and eventually advance to heaven, has only existed in Catholic doctrine for approximately a millennium. Its parameters continue to be debated and revised in contemporary times, with Joseph Ratzinger (Pope Benedict XVI) writing in 2007, "Purgatory is not ... some kind of supra-worldly concentration camp where man is forced to undergo punishment in a more or less arbitrary fashion. Rather it is the inwardly necessary process of transformation in which a person becomes capable of Christ, capable of God, and thus capable of unity with the whole communion of saints" (2007: 230). It is similar in scope to the idea of Gehenna in Judaism and Barzakh in Islam but was not generally adopted by the Protestant denominations that split from the Catholic church in the mid-1500s.

In Dante's *Divine Comedy*, written fewer than 200 years after the concept of Purgatory was accepted into Catholic doctrine, the Garden of Eden sits atop Mount Purgatory, an allegory for Adam and Eve's—and humanity's more generally—state of innocence before the fall, i.e., the consumption of the apple from the tree of knowledge. This placement is unique to Dante. Yet, by placing it at the summit of his Purgatory, whose residents suffer only to expiate their sins and thus ascend, Dante seems to suggest that this expiation allows them to return to that original state of innocence. This too is a promise made to potential Actives in the series *Dollhouse*—that they will be returned to a state of innocence without the complications of the modern world—for the duration of the time they spend there. This time, however, is in the service of a corporation that simultaneously exploits them, essentially creating a high-end sweatshop in which individuals are "rented" to the moneyed class for "engagements" ranging from romantic/sexual to spy or negotiator, all of which occurs outside of the public eye.

This unseen labor has real-world analogues. Despite a law passed nearly twenty years ago intended to crack down on abuses, Los Angeles, California nevertheless has a sweatshop problem, with retailers such as Forever 21, TJ Maxx, and Marshall's finding creative ways to skirt regulations and continue to offer discount prices to consumers (Kitroeff and Kim 2017). These sweatshops operate on LA's outskirts, employing vulnerable, and thus easily exploitable, individuals. These people, a majority of whom are women, work outside the view of the average shopper doing piecework for pennies in frequently dangerous and/or toxic conditions, with few recourses to legal or governmental assistance. In essence, sweatshops operate as an open secret to maximize profits by essentially erasing the identities of its workers in favor of the logos of the brands (see Klein 2000).

Setting *Dollhouse* in the same city—Los Angeles—is one element that allows the series to serve as a metaphor for these workers (frequently women) exploited by powerful corporate entities: a series about a biomedical corporation—called Rossum, in a nod to Karel Capek's play *RUR* (Noone 2010: 21–34)—that uses its technological prowess to erase the memories and personalities of select individuals and reprogram them for the "needs" of wealthy clients. *Dollhouse* makes it abundantly clear from its first episode that these "workers" (known as "dolls" or "Actives") were chosen precisely because they were both vulnerable and socially isolated. As a global concern, Rossum operates Dollhouses around the world in defiance of the law, positioning these Dollhouses, and their workers, literally and figuratively underground. These workers, both Actives and employees, are overwhelmingly women, serving as both the exploited workers (Actives) and the gatekeepers for the corporate order (e.g., LA Dollhouse head Adelle DeWitt [Olivia Williams], programmer Bennett Halverson [Summer Glau]). For the Actives, like the garment workers in Los Angeles and around the world, the "solution" to their difficult circumstances consigns them to a kind of corporate purgatory. Yet gatekeepers such as Adelle DeWitt are also subject to a loss of identity (employees cannot discuss their job with anyone outside the corporation) and exploitation, despite their seemingly more powerful roles. The presence of women in leadership roles within this corporate purgatory makes no appreciable difference in how those within it are treated.

Thus, in this chapter I will examine the ways in which *Dollhouse* offers a critique of these corporate practices by positioning the corporate-run Dollhouses as purgatory, in contrast to both the "real" world and the "hell" of the "Attic," a form of punishment for employees and Actives in which they live out their worst fears in an endless loop. If within Catholic doctrine, Purgatory serves as a place of purification for souls neither damned nor entirely saved, these corporate purgatories offer neither expiation nor release for those whose labor is exploited, and identities erased.

"What We Do Here Helps People": Cleaning the Slate

The series *Dollhouse*, about a medical corporation named Rossum whose more legitimate enterprises are funded by the use of beautiful, programmable people (known as "Actives" or "Dolls") rented to the highest bidder to fulfill their fantasies, offers a particular exchange to those to whom they make an offer. In exchange for "allowing" their personalities to be erased and their bodies to be used, Rossum not only pays them extravagant sums, but promises to take care of the problems, such as grief, mental illness, or illegal activities, that made them vulnerable in the first place. When not in use, these Actives exist in a state of childlike innocence, with no desires, will, or independent thought. The environment in which they remain resembles a high-end spa, with extras such as massage facilities and pools that cater to their physical needs. Quotidian issues such as rent or the need for a job are dispensed with, as is literacy, complex thought, and privacy (even shower facilities are under video surveillance ["Man on the Street," S01.E06]). These Dollhouses are thus positioned as both Eden[1] and Purgatory, and the one in which the viewer spends the most time is led by Adelle DeWitt, who views its residents as children "in my care" ("Belonging," S02.E04). Yet, despite her claims, her actions frequently undermine this assertion and position her as yet another exploitative force.

The first episode of the series opens with Adelle DeWitt making Caroline Farrell (Eliza Dushku) an offer: a "clean slate." Subsequent episodes reveal that Caroline, in a plan to take down the Rossum Corporation after she discovers their

---

[1] This is mentioned directly in the series. Paul Ballard, who has been seeking the Dollhouse, and Caroline Farrell in particular, locates a man he thinks is the original architect of the LA Dollhouse: Steven Kepler (Alan Tudyk). Kepler designed it to be self-sustaining, including recycling air and water, and nearly completely off the grid. While this is obviously to keep it secret, Kepler is nonetheless proud of his work on an environmental level: "They told me this place was the new Eden" ("Briar Rose," S01.E11). From an environmental perspective, Kepler is correct; even after being abandoned for years, the space is able to sustain its residents and shield them from the rogue technology.

experiments on both animals and people ("Echoes," S01.E07), has committed numerous felonies and is likely to be charged with performing terroristic acts ("Getting Closer," S02.E11). Adelle offers to make this all disappear, in exchange for five years of Caroline's life, in which her original "personality" would be removed and replaced by new ones at clients' behest. Once the original version of themselves is removed, they are renamed; for the Los Angeles Dollhouse (where the series is primarily set), they are given designations based on the NATO alphabet. While Caroline—and it is revealed later, Carl William Craft (Alan Tudyk)—is approached and offered a place in the Dollhouse because of illegal or violent acts, for others, the erasure process is sold as a form of treatment for post-traumatic stress disorder (Victor/Anthony Ceccoli [Enver Gjokaj]), paranoia (Mike [Teddy Sears]), or prolonged grief (November/Madeleine Costly [Miracle Laurie]). Removed from the context of "sin," the personality erasure suggests a kind of expiation of troubling external or internal circumstances by returning them to a child-like state, after which they will "ascend" into physical, mental, and financial health with their original personality intact.

Yet the journey to get there is itself fraught with both physical and mental minefields. Because of their reduced state, they cannot provide informed consent for neither the personalities with which they are imprinted, nor the actions said personalities undertake while in their bodies. For the former, the initial consent when they enter the Dollhouse, despite their legal or psychological vulnerabilities, is taken as consent for everything from the initial "wiping" procedure to whatever use to which their bodies are put. With regard to the latter, not only do "romantic" engagements abound—themselves problematic in terms of consent—but even limiting examples to the first season, imprinted Actives are kidnapped and psychologically abused ("Stage Fright," S01.E03), knowingly blinded and placed in a religious cult ("True Believer," S01.E05), or subjected to interrogation and police misconduct ("Ghost," S01.E01). This is justified, by Adelle and the other Dollhouse staff, by the fact that the memories of these events are immediately removed when the engagement is complete. Yet, when it is revealed that Echo is capable—even after numerous "wipes"—to retain both memories and personalities, Adelle's response does not express concern over the psychological toll this might take, but rather concludes: "Echo might be useful to us in ways we haven't yet realized" ("A Spy in the House of Love," S01.E09), explicitly putting the needs to the Dollhouse and the Rossum corporation over her professed desire to "protect" the Actives in her care. As Samira Nadkarni suggests, Adelle is positioned a "transgressive mother," defined as a "gender neutral portrayal of maternal work that, while outwardly displayed as socially acceptable, often transgresses these boundaries in ways that could connote an abuse of the authority granted by the act of mothering itself" (2014: 84). The idea that Adelle—or Rossum—cares for the Actives is thus "another fantasy" (2014). Indeed, when Adelle is demoted midway through season 2, she goes to great lengths to regain her old position, including providing Rossum with a dangerous technology with potentially devastating global consequences ("Meet Jane Doe," S02.E07). While she asserts that she does this to protect "her" Actives from the new management, the loss of respect and status she undergoes by the now exclusively male leadership, including comments on her appearance, likely played a strong role (Giannini 2017: 172).

Further, both the initial removal process and the regular "wiping" procedure are shown to cause physical pain to the Actives ("Ghost," S01.E01), pain that they are not allowed, by virtue of the technology, to remember. That this is a form of torture is made explicit in the second season, when Echo is reunited with Rossum employee Bennett Halverson (Summer Glau), whom she'd befriended as Caroline Farrell in her attempt to bring down the corporation ("Getting Closer," S02.E11). When their plans went awry, Caroline sacrifices herself to prevent Bennett from being blamed; however, Bennett reads her actions as abandonment and, when they are reunited, takes her revenge ("The Left Hand," S02.E06). Bennett's prowess with the Rossum technology allows her to recreate the pain of the imprinting process (without imprinting her) to a conscious Echo over and over with no recourse, despite the fact that Echo does not contain Caroline's memories. "You can't even call out for God; we take that from you too" (S02.E06). Bennett's connection to both Caroline and the Actives more generally is suggested more than once, including Caroline—pre-incarceration—echoing Dollhouse programmer's words "are you ready for a treatment?" to Bennett (she's coloring Bennett's hair), and the way Bennett herself is presented as lost and empty before essentially "imprinting" on Caroline's more dominant personality (S02.E11). Indeed, when LA programmer Topher (Fran Kranz) meets her for the first time, his initial assumption is that she is an Active ("The Public Eye," S02.E05). That neither the pain nor the engagements are recalled by most of the Actives thus makes the Dollhouse a purgatory without transcendence, and the neurosurgical changes wrought to the Actives to make them receptive to the imprinting and wiping process are irreversible, meaning that they never quite escape from Rossum's grasp.

Adelle's promise to exchange their negative circumstances for better ones once they have served their time is also revealed to be hollow. Madeleine Costly (Miracle Laurie)—formerly November—entered the Dollhouse due to the debilitating grief she felt when her daughter died of cancer. The "new" version of Madeleine has this grief removed, as well as significant financial resources. Yet what is seen of her post-Dollhouse life is not one of happiness; rather, her social interactions seem shallow and her life empty of meaning. When asked if she's happy, she simply replies: "I'm not sad" ("Instinct," S02.E02). She's later horrified to discover that Rossum installed a "sleeper" protocol in her that turned her into an assassin ("The Public Eye," S02.E05), and is subsequently used as a scapegoat to give Rossum more political and financial power ("The Left Hand," S02.E06). A more egregious case is that of Priya Tsetsang (Dichen Lachmann), who becomes the Active Sierra in the first episode of the series. It is revealed that Priya was taken from a mental hospital, with the promise that the Dollhouse technology would alleviate her paranoid schizophrenia. Topher, who recommended her for the treatment, considers his work with her as a significant achievement. It is revealed, however, that Priya's diagnosis was induced by a prominent Rossum neuroscientist, Nolan Kinnard (Vincent Vintresca), after she rejected his sexual advances, allowing them to "rewrite" her as a Priya who loves him ("Belonging," S02.E04). This was made easier by Priya's status as an undocumented individual, and thus separated from family and friends and, despite the episode airing in 2010, resonates with the contemporary treatment of undocumented immigrants and asylum seekers in the United States (Campos and Cantor 2017: 1–27). That is, it:

> demonstrates ... that the "real-life" institutions permit it to happen. Behind Nolan Kinnard's power is also the support of the medical institution and an incredibly rich and powerful corporation, not to mention the inequities inherent in Nolan's status as a wealthy, educated American ... and Priya's status as a poor, struggling artist and undocumented worker from Australia.
>
> (Zhang 2012: 405)

Priya, therefore, was not even given the nominal choice like the others; she is trapped in Dollhouse's purgatory neither as an escape nor as a form of treatment, and at the whim of another, making it even more of a hell.

"Even the Apples Were Monitored": Work and the Outside World

While the Dollhouse is a purgatorial space for the empty Actives, in which they are unable to learn and grow from their numerous bodily experiences, it can also be viewed as such for the non-Actives employed there. The first season establishes that, due to its illegal activities, the LA Dollhouse is literally underground, designed to be a self-sustaining ecosystem ("Briar Rose," S01.E11; see St Louis and Riggs, 2010: n.p. for an analysis of how the Briar Rose fairy tale accords with the series' thematic concerns). While the imprinted Actives and their Handlers interact with the outside world, the other staff, including programmers Topher and Ivy (Liza Lapira) and Adelle and physician Claire Saunders (Amy Acker), are rarely seen outside the Dollhouse—Topher and Claire claim they are agoraphobic. Former Actives and employees also suffer severe penalties if they even suggest that the Dollhouses exist: "A former Active once made a passing reference to us in his blog ....it was his *last* entry" ("The Public Eye," S02.E05). It is thus seemingly difficult to maintain relationships outside of their work with Rossum because of the secrecy involved.

This may be why many of the employees, the series suggests, have their own problematic pasts or issues prior to their work with Rossum. It is implied, if not outright stated, that part of why some of the staff are willing to work at a place they rarely leave and cannot discuss with anyone outside is their own past actions. In her attempt to convince Topher to do something he feels is against his moral code, Adelle tells him: "The cold reality is that everyone here was chosen because their morals had been compromised in some way" ("Belonging," S02.E04). While the details of such compromises are untold, it suggests that more conventional—and legal—employment is out of reach. Yet, like the highly problematic consent of the Actives, whether or not Rossum's employees realize precisely what they are signing up is questionable. And so when Adelle tells Boyd: "[Y]ou work for Rossum. That means your options tend to slim to three: carry out Rossum's work without question, the attic or death. The moment you stepped into this house, you, in effect, gave us your life" ("The Attic," S02.E10), it seems unlikely such a statement was part of any employee's initial interview. While the treatment of the Actives by these employees ranges from caring (Dr. Saunders) to abusive (handler Joe Hearn [Kevin Kilner] who repeatedly rapes Sierra while she's in Doll state ["Man on the Street," S01.E06])—with dismissiveness being the dominant element—there is actually little that separates them; both employees and Actives are equally trapped within this corporate purgatory.

These employees have the single advantage over the Actives in that they retain their own personalities and memories, yet all are subject to the whims of the corporation. As per example, a Rossum employee from Japan is placed in the Attic—in a nightmare scenario during which he literally consumes himself—simply because he identified a security weakness, and that knowledge made him a security risk ("The Attic," S02.E10). If purgatory is a place that allows its residents expiation of their sins in order to ascend,

Dollhouse only allows this for a select few of its employees. Adelle, who turns over technology that Topher invented—and was horrified by—to Rossum in order to regain her position as head of the LA Dollhouse, becomes the leader of the small group dedicated to taking down the corporation rather than supporting it. Yet this redemption is, at best, problematic; while she claims her actions were necessary in order to more effectively work as a double agent against Rossum's machinations (which included selling off Active's bodies permanently to the highest bidder, rather than returning them to their original personalities ["Epitaph One," S01.E13]), they nonetheless were instrumental in causing a technological global apocalypse ("Epitaph One"; "Epitaph 2: The Return", S02.E13). It thus became a case of sacrificing millions to save a few. Adelle does, however, become the parental figure to both the group and others affected by the events that she initially claimed to be at the start of the series and, when the technology is defeated, leads the group of survivors in order to rebuild a world devastated by that technology ("Epitaph 2: The Return," S02.E13).

In comparison, Topher's arc is far more straightforward. He is initially presented as gleefully amoral,[2] considering the Actives "toys" he can "play" with ("Haunted," S01.E10; "Belonging," S02.E04)—trying out new technologies, such as turning Echo's eyes into a camera ("True Believer," S01.E05), or tweaking hormone levels to create lactation without birth ("Instinct," S02.E02)—with little concern for the consequences. He is quick to dismiss Actives's behavior as instinctual (he assumes the clear bonds formed between Echo, Victor, and Sierra are merely "grouping" ["Gray Hour," S01.E04]) or nonsensical (Echo volunteering to be imprinted to help solve an internal crisis within the Dollhouse ["A Spy in the House of Love," S01.E09]). It is only when one of the Dollhouse's past mistakes returns—the accidental uploading of multiple imprints and the subsequent murderous rampage of early Active Alpha (Alan Tudyk)—that Topher begins to feel the consequences of his actions ("Omega," S01.E12). When he is directly confronted with his view that he treats the Actives as playthings, he takes decisive action to help Sierra/Priya confront Nolan Kinnard, who forced

---

[2] Despite this, the series underscores that Topher is not in fact a sociopath. In the episode "Belle Chose," in which Adelle, Boyd, and Topher are deciding whether to treat Terry Karrens's brain injuries, whose uncle is an influential Rossum shareholder, Topher compares Karrens's brain scan to his own. "See these dark areas?" he tells Adelle. "That's because Terry Karrens doesn't use that part of his brain. And that's where you'd find stored such things as empathy, compassion, an aversion to disemboweling puppies" (S02.E03). That Topher's scan does not show these dark areas is the show's way of telling us that sociopathy is not a factor in Topher's amorality.

her into the Dollhouse to be rewritten to his specifications; when it goes horribly wrong, he accedes to Priya's request to remove the memory of it, so he alone will be the one who carries the knowledge ("Belonging," S02.E04).

Even as he is developing more of a conscience, his interest in the technology and desire to figure things out nonetheless lead him to perhaps his biggest "sin": making the wiping and imprinting technology wireless and thus bringing about what he terms the "thought-pocalypse" ("The Hollow Men," S02.E12); that is, the ability to erase and imprint everyone, which reduces the global population to either empty vessels or mindless killers. By naming this episode—in which Topher comes to the realization that everything he understood about himself and those around him was wrong—after T. S. Eliot's post-First World War poem of regarding loss of identity and morality, the series underlines its connection to nearly all of the characters within the series, but Topher in particular. Eliot's *The Hollow Men* is characterized by despair, "candidly suggesting that the web of spiritual and moral degeneration will go on and no human efforts can bring about any change" (Khanna and Patel 2022: 10). The reveal that Boyd was not the fatherly moral center of the group but rather the mastermind behind Rossum's worst actions leads to his defeat at Echo's hands and the destruction of Rossum's headquarters, but as the final moments of the episode reveal, it changed nothing. The world still became a wasteland. Topher is thus broken, becoming one of the "hollow men" himself, and spends the next decade in physical and psychological pain before he is able to work out how to fix what happened. In what could be viewed as a form of substitutionary atonement,[3] he sacrifices himself as part of the effort to return everyone else to their original selves. By expiating his sin of pride and willful blindness to the consequences of his inventions, he becomes the one capable of emptying the Dollhouse's purgatory. He enacts the "clean slate" Adelle initially promises the Actives by reversing Rossum's actions and returning humanity—though not the broken world around them—but to a state of, if not innocence, then at least a form of freedom.

---

[3] In *The Cabin in the Woods* (2012), written by Whedon, Kranz plays the character of Marty, who is given a similar choice. In the film, a meta-narrative take on horror films, Marty is told that if he does not die to appease the "Old Ones"—ancient gods who require a yearly sacrifice in order to not destroy humanity—it will mean the literal end of the world. In this instance, Marty makes a different choice than Topher, determining that a world that requires such sacrifices is not worth saving and "maybe it's time to give someone else a chance."

Conclusion: "We're Not Anybody, We're Everybody"

The recently concluded series *The Good Place* (2016–20) is a rare example of a show that takes place entirely in the afterlife. While the four human characters are—due to their actions on Earth—consigned to the Bad Place, their version of it is absent of the mindless torture inflicted on others (e.g., being twisted or burnt). The torture they endure is psychological; they think they are in "paradise" but it's actually "a filthy dumpster of our worst anxieties" ("Michael's Gambit," S01.E13). Despite this, each character improves ethically and psychologically, forming a supportive community with one another. However, like in *Dollhouse*, once they discover the truth, their memories are wiped, eliminating the progress they have made. This continuous resetting—and the humans' progress despite it—makes their particular hell more of a purgatorial space from which they eventually ascend once the rebooting has stopped, and they are free to become their best selves ("Patty," S04.E12).

Dollhouse's purgatory remains earthbound and not entirely transcend-able. Throughout most of the series, the Actives continued to be wiped and reset, with only Echo, due to a biological quirk, able to resist the process and retain her knowledge. While Rossum is destroyed ("The Hollow Men," S02.E12), the technology is not, and thus both the former Actives and humanity as a whole are vulnerable to having their minds erased. Further, those the viewer comes to know throughout the series (Sierra/Priya, Victor/Anthony, and Echo/Caroline) are at risk of being "wiped" a final time by Topher's final reset, erasing a decade's progress and—in the case of Priya and Anthony—the memory of their son ("Epitaph 2: The Return," S02.E13). In an earlier episode, in which the Actives went through a planned exercise to address pressing issues and therefore prevent them from "glitching" ("Needs," S01.E08), Echo's "need" was to set everyone free from their bondage within the Dollhouse, leading them out into the light. Yet in the end, it is Adelle who does that, acknowledging to Echo: "Funny that the last fantasy the Dollhouse should fulfill would be yours" ("Epitaph 2: The Return," S02.E13). Instead, Echo, Priya, and Anthony elect to remain in this particular purgatory as the only way to retain their humanity. For them, to ascend is to lose themselves. It underscores the essential ironies at play within the series: that the place that for the Actives was a hellish purgatory ends up being their salvation.

Works Cited

Alighieri, D. (2005), *The Divine Comedy: The Vision of Paradise, Purgatory, and Hell [1308–20]*, Rev. H. F. Cary (trans.). https://www.gutenberg.org/files/8800/8800-h/8800-h.htm.

Cabin in the Woods, The (2011), directed by D. Goddard, Vancouver: Lionsgate.

Campos, S. and G. Cantor (2017), "Deportations in the Dark: Lack of Process and Information in the Removal of Mexican Migrants," *American Immigration Council*, September 17, 1–27. https://www.americanimmigrationcouncil.org/sites/default/files/research/deportations_in_the_dark.pdf.

Dollhouse (2009), "Ghosts," season 1, episode 1, directed by J. Whedon, New York: Fox.

Dollhouse (2009), "Stage Fright," season 1, episode 3, directed by D. Solomon, Fox.

Dollhouse (2009), "Gray Hour," season 1, episode 4, directed by R. Hardy, Fox.

Dollhouse (2009), "True Believer," season 1, episode 5, directed by A. Kroeker, Fox.

Dollhouse (2009), "Man on the Street," season 1, episode 6, directed by D. Straiton, Fox.

Dollhouse (2009), "Echoes," season 1, episode 7, directed by J. Contner, Fox.

Dollhouse (2009), "A Spy in the House of Love," season 1, episode 9, directed by D. Solomon, Fox.

Dollhouse (2009), "Haunted," season 1, episode 10, directed by E. Keene, Fox.

Dollhouse (2009), "Briar Rose," season 1, episode 11, directed by D. Little, Fox.

Dollhouse (2009), "Omega," season 1, episode 12, directed by T. Minear, Fox.

Dollhouse (2009), "Epitaph One," season 1, episode 13, directed by D. Solomon, Fox.

Dollhouse (2009), "Vows," season 2, episode 1, directed by J. Whedon, Fox.

Dollhouse (2009), "Instinct," season 2, episode 2, directed by M. Grabiak, Fox.

Dollhouse (2009), "Belle Chose," season 2, episode 3, directed by D. Solomon, Fox.

Dollhouse (2009), "Belonging," season 2, episode 4, directed by J. Frakes, Fox.

Dollhouse (2009), "The Public Eye," season 2, episode 5, directed by D. Solomon, Fox.

Dollhouse (2009), "The Left Hand," season 2, episode 6, directed by W. Stanzler, Fox.

Dollhouse (2009), "Meet Jane Doe," season 2, episode 7, directed by D. Little, Fox.

Dollhouse (2009), "The Attic," season 2, episode 10, directed by J. Cassaday, Fox.

Dollhouse (2010), "Getting Closer," season 2, episode 11, directed by T. Minear, Fox.

Dollhouse (2010), "The Hollow Men," season 2, episode 12, directed by T. O'Hara, Fox.

Dollhouse (2010), "Epitaph 2: The Return," season 2, episode 13, directed by D. Solomon, Fox.

Giannini, E. (2017), *Joss Whedon versus the Corporation: Big Business Critiqued in the Films and Television Programs*, Jefferson: McFarland & Co., Inc.

Good Place, The (2017), "Michael's Gambit," season 1, episode 13, directed by M. Schur, New York: NBC.

Good Place, The (2020), "Patty," season 4, episode 12, directed by M. Sackett, NBC.

Khanna, M. and R. C. Patel (2022), "Moral Predicament in T. S. Eliot's 'The Hollow Men' and 'The Waste Land,'" *Research Journal of English*, 7(1): 7–15.

Kitroeff, N. and V. Kim (2017), "Behind a $13 Shirt, a $6 an Hour Worker: How Forever 21 and Other Retailers Avoid Liability for Factories that Underpay Workers to Sew Their Clothes," *Los Angeles Times*, August 31. https://www.latimes.com/projects/la-fi-forever-21-factory-workers/.

Klein, Naomi (2000), *No Logo: Taking on the Brand Bullies*, New York: Picador.

Nadkarni, S. (2014), "'In My House and Therefore in My Care': Transgressive Mothering, Abuse, and Embodiment," in S. Ginn, A. Buckman and H. Porter (eds), *Joss Whedon's Dollhouse: Confounding Purpose, Confusing Identity*, 81–95, Lanham: Rowman & Littlefield.

Noone, K. (2010), "Rossum's Universal Robots," in J. Espenson (ed.), *Inside Joss' Dollhouse: From Alpha to Rossum*, 21–34, Dallas: Ben Bella Books.

Ratzinger, J. (2007), *Eschatology: Death and Eternal Life*, Washington DC: Catholic University of America Press.

St. Louis, R. and M. Riggs (2010), "'A Painful, Bleeding Sleep': Sleeping Beauty in the Dollhouse," *Slayage: The International Journal of Buffy+* (Special Issue: Fantasy Is Not Their Purpose: Joss Whedon's *Dollhouse*) 8.2-3, no. 30–31, n.p. https://www.whedonstudies.tv/uploads/2/6/2/8/26288593/stlouis_riggs_slayage_8.2-3.pdf.

Zhang, A. (2012), "'Buffy' and 'Dollhouse': Visions of Female Empowerment and Disempowerment," in M. A. Money (ed.), *Joss Whedon: The Complete Collection, the TV Series, the Movies, the Comic Books, and More*, 401–6, London: Titan Books.

8

The Vampire in the Attic: Constructing Monstrous Female Identities in Liminal, Purgatorial Spaces

Taryn Tavener-Smith

Introduction

This chapter is concerned with the liminality associated with the purgatorial elements evident in *Slade House* in relation to Norah Grayer's monstrous-feminine identity. Although the term "liminality" originated with the French folklorist Arnold Van Gennep (2013), the anthropologist, Victor Turner, reformulated this theory as a framework to evaluate the practices of rites of passage carried out by tribes in Central Africa (1992: 48). As Turner points out, Van Gennep's theory outlined three stages in this transition: "separation; margin (or limen); and reaggregation" (1992). While the first and last stages are easily understood as the separation of initiates from society and later their reintegration into the social group during the process of transition, Turner argues that the "more interesting problem is provided by the middle (marginal) or liminal phase" (1992: 49). Turner's special interest is in the limen as a "threshold," or space of "midtransition," a condition of being "be-twixt and between established states" (1992: 48). Those who find themselves in this in-between space are known as luminaries who "evade ordinary cognitive classification [...] for they are not this or that, here or there, one thing or the other" (1992: 48). Turner observes the "invisibility" characteristic of liminality, arguing that it is a paradoxical condition: "being *both* this *and* that" (1992: 48, original emphasis). In *The Spectralities Reader: Ghosts and Haunting in Contemporary Cultural Theory* (2013), Maria del Pilar Blanco and Esther Peeren argue that Turner's theory of liminality, despite its original anthropological focus, is strongly relevant in its application to literature. As I argue in this chapter, Turner's theory of liminality informs the vampiric, monstrous-feminine identity in Mitchell's novel. This identity, then, is associated with the "margin" (Turner 1992: 48) as it may be likened to a state that establishes itself as being both "be-twixt and between" (1992: 49): vampires are *both* human *and* monster.

Slade House Summary

The novel is set in the grand Slade House on Slade Alley in downtown London and spans across thirty-six years. Mitchell's narrative is clearly separated into chronotopes: 1979, 1988, 1997, 2006, 2015. Every nine years the twins, Norah and Jonah Grayer, entice a new visitor into the attic to extract and devour the souls of "potential psychics" (Mitchell 2015: 175). They do this to absorb the powers of their victims, thereby preserving their own lives as vampiric beings. The twins' victims include mother and son, Nathan and Rita Bishop; police investigator Gordon Edmonds; psychic sisters Sally and Freya Timms; and Horologist, Dr. Iris Marinus-Fenby. Mitchell's vampires are called "Atemporals," which are immortals who "attempt to force consciousness into successive bodies, [by] consuming the souls of those humans [...] to whom they are especially attracted by virtue of their paranormal capacities" (Mitchell 2015: 223; O'Donnell 2015: 161). Because of their fragility, the Grayers are bound to the house and rely on its prison-like qualities to halt time and aging. In the novel, Slade House acts as a time capsule that keeps the twins locked within its confines while ensuring they remain preserved within the bodies of the hosts, whose souls they have devoured. If the house's attic is a purgatorial space, then the house itself is the life preservation system that keeps the twins "in thrall to these [...] birth-bodies to anchor our souls to the world of the day" (Mitchell 2015: 137). The Grayers entice victims into the house's purgatorial attic by establishing a "kind of reality bubble" (2015: 172) that lures those with life-preserving psychic powers inside.

While exploring Slade House's perimeter before entering, characters acknowledge the possibility of the house's entrance as a "membrane between worlds" (2015: 99). Indeed, once any visitor crosses the threshold of that hidden "small black door" (2015: 23), there is no escape from the horrifying in-between condition that ensues. For example, Nathan and Rita Bishop are coerced into the house under the guise that its owners (the Grayers posing as mother and son) are hosting a soirée, where aspiring musician, Rita, will play the piano alongside renowned violinist, Sir Yehudi Menuhin. Nathan's interest is piqued by the house's expansive grounds and by the prospect of making a friend (Jonah posing as a young child) his own age. However, Slade House's utopic disguise soon wears off as Nathan's worst nightmare of being mauled by a bull mastiff is replayed on a loop while he and Jonah play foxes and hounds around the estate's perimeter. Similarly, ParaSoc (Paranormal Society) members (Axel Hardwick, Todd Cosgrove, Angelica Gibbons, Lance Arnott, and Sally Timms) are coerced into the house through the staging of an elaborate Halloween party, which gives the investigative teens an opportunity to snoop around the property to solve the mystery of their missing predecessors, Nathan and Rita. By the time the cracks in the prison begin to show, it is already too late, and the group find themselves trapped within the house's confines. It is in this way that the Grayer twins are able to coerce victims inside with the intention of confining them to the purgatorial attic, where their soul-imbibing ceremonies take place.

Once victims are trapped, the Grayers host their ritualistic soul-imbibing ceremonies, preserving their lives upon consumption. During these rituals, victims are placed in front of a mirror in the attic alongside the twins, allowing them to watch in horror as their souls are sucked from their bodies through their foreheads. In the novel, the mirror functions as a purgatorial threshold where two worlds meet with "death as a door to the afterlife" (Mitchell 2015: 114). Sally provides a telling account:

> The Grayer twins' hands then begin to weave through the air like Todd Cosgrove's did earlier, leaving short-lived scratch marks on the air. Their lips move and a murmur grows louder and louder as something solidifies above the candle, cell by cell; a kind of fleshy jellyfish, pulsing with reds and purples. [...] Tendrils grow out of it, tendrils with sub-tendrils.
>
> (Mitchell 2015: 137–8)

As Sally's soul is removed, she sees its reflection, which she describes as "shimmering," which makes her realize that "souls are real" (2015: 138). She describes her soul as "the most beautiful thing I've ever seen" (2015: 138). Like Sally, each chapter's protagonist reflects on the uniqueness of their souls alongside the realization that what they see in the mirror represents who they *really* are. This revelation, however, comes too late and is coupled with the unveiling of the Grayers's true vampiric identities, which, in turn, incite terror while unveiling the truth about those who pose a moral, and in this case mortal, threat. It also unveils a "truth" about each victim that each has formerly been unable to see while characterizing the Grayers as the novel's villains. These realizations arguably emphasize Mitchell's comment on the emptiness and demand of modern existence, embodied here in the voracious, soul-destroying appetites of the vampiric Grayer twins. Ultimately, this imbibing of souls maintains their immortality, classifying the Grayers as "soul vampires" (2015: 174) while emphasizing the attic as the space where one life ends, to offer renewal to a further two lives: those belonging to the twins. After each ceremony, the twins occupy victims' host bodies for nine years before returning to their birth bodies in the attic and imbibing new souls.

Slade House's Monstrous-Feminine Identities

In Barbara Creed's seminal book, *The Monstrous-feminine: Film, Feminism, Psychoanalysis,* she examines the marginalized role of female villains in fiction, revealing how their monstrosity is related to society's "conception [...] of what it is about women that is shocking, terrifying, horrific, abject" (1986: 67). Creed's theory responds to patriarchal attempts to represent women as "abject" and "monstrous" by celebrating "woman's potential to disrupt the patriarchal symbolic order" (Creed 1993: 3). This approach allows feminine narratives to write against the grain by opening a "place" for women, thereby elevating them from passive "others" into roles of "active, terrifying fury, a powerfully abject figure, and a castrating monster" (1993: 16). The "monstrous-feminine" thus emphasizes the role of "gender in the construction of [the female villain's] monstrosity" (1993: 3), by foregrounding gender itself—rather than the notions of the "monster" or "evil," for example—as potentially monstrous within society's patriarchal conception. Creed's (1993) concept relates to Norah's enactment of the monstrous-feminine, which occurs in her characterization as a contemporary form of vampire who sexually dominates and thus terrifies men. Creed's monstrous-feminine argues that this common, yet variable, trope of female abjection

> wears many faces: the amoral primeval mother (*Aliens*, 1986); the vampire (*The Hunger*, 1983); the witch (*Carrie*, 1976); the woman as monstrous womb (*The Brood*, 1979); woman as bleeding wound (*Dressed to Kill*, 1980); the woman as possessed body (*The Exorcist*, 1973); the castrating mother (*Psycho*, 1960); and the woman as beautiful but deadly killer (*Basic Instinct*, 1992).
>
> (1993: 1–2)

Other such examples of novels focusing on vampires while emphasizing sexual possession as a function of gender inequality in society include Joseph Sheridan Le Fanu's *Carmilla* (1872), Bram Stoker's *Dracula* (1897), and, more recently,

Anne Rice's *Interview with the Vampire* (1976). *Carmilla* addresses the strict sexual mores of the time in which it was written while representing a "sexual possession" (Signorotti 1996: 607) which is similar to Dracula's motivation and in many ways is Stoker's response to Le Fanu's earlier work. These similarities are comparable with *Slade House*: each novel depicts vampires or vampiric figures exerting their power over their victims, partly through sexual possession. Gothic representations of this kind of control, Bubke argues, serve to illustrate societal fears about "sexuality, religion and morality by transferring the knowledge gained from [society's] own reactions to the presented narratives" (2018: 2). Patriarchal social anxieties about sexuality can be related in particular to women's sexual possession exerted over men (Creed 1986), a theme also evident in *Slade House*.

Similar arguments are presented by Creed's contemporaries, including Natalie Wilson, who maintains that the "monstrous-feminine serves as a powerfully political metaphor for our times" (2020: 181) while acknowledging women's frequent association with monstrosity based on the possession of their "mere female bodies" (2020: 182). In the novel, Norah encounters similar monstrous representations in relation to her female form, as it is her female role that is frequently used to lure victims into the house while capitalizing on her feminine identity. This is seen in the novel when Gordon enters the house and meets Chloe Albertina Chetwynd (Norah, in fact, occupying another body), a wealthy widow living alone in what appears to be the decaying Slade House. Norah's enactment of the monstrous-feminine occurs in her characterization as a vampire who sexually dominates men. As time passes, Chloe and Gordon begin an intimate romantic relationship. Before long, time becomes distorted when Gordon realizes he has spent more time inside Slade House than he initially anticipated. It appears that time is alterable within the confines of the house. While on one of his many visits, Chloe beckons Gordon up the staircase. As he follows her enticing calls, he encounters a display of portraits. The most startling is the portrait of "Nathan Bishop, as seen by Fred Pink in Slade Alley in 1979" (Mitchell 2015: 69). Gordon hears vague warnings about Chloe's motives whispered to him from an invisible source and it is at this moment that he realizes that the remnants of Nathan's soul haunt Slade House, as the unidentified voice explains: "I'm not a lot […] I'm my own leftovers" (2015: 69). As Gordon retreats, he suddenly notices his own "more-real-than-real" (2015: 70) portrait staring back at him. Seeing his portrait prefigures his consumption by the twins and he ends up as "just the residue" (2015: 82) of his former self. As the description above suggests, Norah is characterized as a version of the monstrous-feminine through her terrifying sexual domination.

In this way, the monstrous-feminine disrupts the conventional view of "woman as victim of the (mainly male) monster" (Creed 1993: 1). Instead of viewing femininity as a pale opposition to monstrosity, Creed and her contemporaries take a feminist approach to show that the "monstrous-feminine emphasizes the importance of gender in the construction of her monstrosity" (1993: 1). Femininity itself, according to Creed's (1993) study, is viewed as monstrous and terrifying within a patriarchal context. More stereotypes in fiction exist, then, than that of the woman as helpless victim.

Similar perspectives are observed in the works of Cristina Santos (2014), who explores representations of feminine monstrosity in fairy tales such as *Little Red Riding Hood* and *Snow White and the Seven Dwarves*. Santos problematizes those oversimplified representations of female characters as "monster" while recognizing the underlying complexities present within each construction. Santos goes on to emphasize the "moral ambiguity" (2014: 128) present in such portrayals while underscoring the limitations of representing female characters in this way. She highlights the Evil Queen's status as prisoner of a patriarchal system, which confines her to a world to which she remains bound: "I'm the Queen but practically a prisoner" (2014: 128). Similarly in *Slade House*, Norah experiences this sense of imprisonment, as she embodies the role of the monstrous-feminine through her consumption of others, while also relying on the confines of the attic for self-preservation. In this way, Norah arguably embodies a liminal state that supersedes her position as vampiric parasite—she is also stuck in limbo oscillating between the roles of jailer of her victims and prisoner herself within a purgatorial space within the house. Such complexities of the monstrous-feminine are evidenced in the realization that Norah's role problematizes the adherence to those "monstrous demands" imposed on female characters by patriarchal society, while simultaneously subverting them, which is considered monstrous (Bacon 2011: 22).

Slade House as a Liminal and Purgatorial Space: The Vampire in the Attic

While vampires are not considered central to Gothic fiction, they certainly form part of the genre's cast of monsters. Notably, "like the mythical creature itself, the fictional vampire has undergone several transformations throughout these years, and still in the 2000s it has seen a resurgence in different media" (Rinne 2013: 1). In *Slade House*, the Grayer twins' consumption of their victims' souls, linked to their immortality, positions them as vampiric figures. Yet the Grayers are not vampires in the traditional sense; rather than sucking blood for immortality, they devour souls. This consumption of souls, rather than blood, serves as an exchange of sorts, which still occurs when they drain the life force of others in order to gain eternal life. These energy exchanges are observed in earlier vampire fiction and lore dating back as early as the restless dead in Ancient Greek times where vampires drained people before leaving them for dead (Johnston 2013). Similar instances of energy vampires are observed later, in the nineteenth century in works such as Sabine Baring-Gould's "Margery of Quether" (1891) and Florence Marryat's *The Blood of the Vampire* (1897). Similarly in *Slade House*, the twins take from others everything they possibly can. Because of their urgent desire for blood (or souls, in the case of the Grayer twins)—indeed, for extracting the very life force from others—vampires are notoriously menacing figures. In terms of the vampire, Rinne observes that their "acquisitiveness is seen as one facet of their monstrous nature" (2013: 31). This is observable not only in the desire to acquire blood, but also wealth, with blood perhaps becoming a metaphor for economic power, thereby reflecting the values of contemporary society beyond the pages of Mitchell's novel.

Equating blood to economic power "recasts capitalism as a form of economic vampirism" (Morrisette 2013: 637). For example, in Anne Rice's *The Queen of the Damned* (1988), Maharet summons the supernatural to ensure her family's accrual of wealth. While retaining several characteristics of the earlier representations of vampires, contemporary depictions (such as those observed in *Slade House*) thus tend to rewrite certain elements, including the ways in which the vampire feeds parasitically on its victim. Whereas popularized representations of the vampire, such as Bram Stoker's *Dracula* (1897), sucked the blood of their victims as a means of sustenance, contemporary reimaginings of vampires, like Mitchell's Grayer twins, feed off the living less literally. Other such examples of vampires, which feed off qualities such as youth, souls, or creativity, include George Sylvester Viereck's *House of the Vampire* (1907) and Algernon Blackwoods's *The Transfer* (1912). Kris Hirschmann argues that the "scare factor" of vampire accounts for contemporary society's preoccupation with them: "[T]hey stalk, feed, and kill without mercy, using their otherworldly powers to subdue and seduce their human prey" (2011: 6). As such, the vampire is positioned as a liminal figure straddling the constructed border between the "human" and "monster" and thus troubling this dichotomy. Yet, alongside this, and more so since the 1970s, the vampire's popular image is now more often that of a misunderstood troubled soul in light of Anne Rice's groundbreaking work on the subject (Williamson 2003).

In *Gothic*, David Punter and Glynnis Byron provide the following evaluation of the vampire's changing role:

> In nineteenth century vampire fiction, the representation of the vampire as monstrous, evil and other serves to guarantee the existence of good, reinforcing the formally dichotomized structures of belief. Vampire fiction of the latter twentieth century becomes increasingly skeptical about such categories [and] the oppositions between good and evil are increasingly problematized.
>
> (2004: 248)

This treatment of the vampire figure is evident in *Slade House* and in Norah's character as, even though she is clearly established as a villain in *Slade House*, we observe a rare complexity in her. Her multifaceted nature is strongly evident in the last chapter of *Slade House*, which she narrates herself, thereby allowing the reader insight into her experiences from her own perspective. Norah's embodiment of "human," observed in her form and desperate attempts at self-preservation, and her role as "monster," evident in her ability to cheat death, reinforce her liminality. This complexity emphasizes the human side of Norah, which is relevant to my argument that vampires are liminal figures caught between, and thus dismantling, the apparent oppositions of "human" and "monster."

David Punter goes on to describe the vampire as possessing a "grotesque exaggeration of character and location" while characterizing the vampire as a parasite, an organism that lives off others (2012: 1). Notably, the vampire concerns him/herself with "absorbing other lives [to] indefinitely prolong his own" (Pedlar 2006: 138). The Grayers', and in particular Norah's, inherent necessity to consume to remain alive emphasizes her feminine monstrosity and the centrality of consumption within the novel. Consumption though has its price, and the attic, and indeed the house fills with the detritus, or "leftovers" of what the vampires have consumed. This simultaneously reinforces the notion of the domestic space as a purgatorial one, where the residue of the "no longer alive" actively seeks to release themselves from the liminality they find themselves trapped in.

For example, Nathan warns Gordon about Chloe's intentions to devour his soul: "She'll take your life, and more," and cautions him to find and use the "*weapon in the cracks*" (Mitchell 2015: 69, original emphasis), thus referring to the fox head hairpin that Rita left behind (an example of the way in which the narrative sections of the novel are linked through attention to recurring supernatural and liminal objects). Notably, "things 'fall down the cracks', arguably even between the narratives (thus emphasizing liminality), but when the ghost of the policeman [Gordon] hands his successor [Sally] a real knife, something starts to change" (Craig 2015). With the passing years and the growing instability of the house, Norah realizes the inevitability of her and Jonah's downfall when she argues that their feeding ritual, which she terms their "operandi" (Mitchell 2015: 78), is far too reliant on external factors. While Jonah smugly denies that they are at risk, Norah is aware of the fragility of their immortality and warns him:

> The operandi works provided our birth-bodies remain here in the lacuna, freeze-dried against world-time, anchoring our souls to life. The operandi works provided we recharge the lacuna every nine years by luring a gullible Engifted into a suitable orison. The operandi works provided our guests can be duped, banjaxed and drawn into the lacuna.
>
> (Mitchell 2015: 78, original emphasis)

Unlike Jonah, Norah fears especially the remnants of previous victims that haunt the house (by this point, Nathan, Rita, and Gordon). She points out, for example, that Gordon's "residue was substantial enough to *speak* with the guest" (Mitchell 2015: 136, original emphasis), suggesting that the ghosts can undermine the process necessary for the twins' immortality. Indeed, Gordon warns Sally of the house's dangers proclaiming "They … don't … e … ven … let … you … die … pro … per … ly" (Mitchell 2015: 115). This statement emphasizes the role of purgatorial liminality in not just trapping Norah, but as a state she confers on all those she "feeds" upon as well. Of note is how the feeding occurs in the attic, a space within oneiric thinking, that is often connected to the mind or imagination which then sees Norah's vampirism as one that devours her victims' hopes and dreams of the future to extend her own, yet her own future is only to remain within the purgatory she can never leave. Slade House's hauntings lend to the liminality in the novel as characters find themselves occupying the margin between the realms of the living and the dead, and between their own narrative and the next.

The house as the novel's purgatorial setting, with its cellars, attics, and mysterious passages, "exacerbates unease about boundaries generally" (Helyer 2000: 725), and as importantly the idea of thresholds, both between worlds and of ways of being within them. Norah in particular exhibits this not just in her feminine monstrosity and its purposeful containment from the patriarchal world beyond the house, but in her essence as a vampire that, like the space she inhabits, is caught on the thresholds "between visibility and invisibility, life and death, materiality and immateriality, and their association with powerful affects like fear and obsession" (Blanco and Peeren 2013: 1). Historically, borderlines in vampire fiction have played a significant role and are often figured as "obstacles [that] protect humans from vampires" (Buzwell 2014: 5). Such imaginary thresholds between the human and the monster are evident, for example, when vampires are unable to pass through the doorway of humans' homes without invitation. In popular representations, "vampires had to live in hiding from the human world, existing in a liminal, supernatural realm, as is the case in *Dracula*, [and] *Interview with the Vampire*" (Bubke 2018: 8). In this way, the "threshold-myth" in vampire fiction served to "prevent unwanted guests from entering [and] signifies an insurmountable protection" (2018: 26). However, *Slade House* inverts both these "conventions" by preventing the vampires from crossing the threshold of their own house and leaving it—signifying their inherent separation from the world of humans and the living—and in having to live alongside humans to cement their permanence in the world they wish to remain bound to.

Yet, this self-made purgatory is not as permanent as they had hoped. As such, the rising sense of unease felt by Norah is proven to be prescient when an explosion in the house causes a crack, which destabilizes the structure allowing time to creep in. The focus of Norah's purgatorial space then shifts from the confines of the house to that of her own skin that begins to age rapidly and horrifyingly, reflecting her own internal decay. She narrates the last chapter of the novel and describes how her skin begins "sagging like a grotesque, ill-fitting sleeve" while a "white-haired witch stares back, aghast" (Mitchell 2015: 231). The reflection Norah sees is of her own aged, decaying figure reduced to her mortal, now decrepit shell. In this way, Norah is reduced to an evil force, a crone. This imagery not only invokes the supernatural imagery of the witch—Creed maintains that the role of the witch is one of the few roles considered "exclusively female" (1993: 15)—but also manifests her inner-corruption and what Creed describes as the "woman-as-monster" (1993: 12). Finally, when Norah's body disintegrates and the mirror is destroyed, her soul is left to wander the earth until a new host can be inhabited, seeing her embody Mitchell's thesis of the dangers of consumerism and exploitation, but also the indefatigability of female resistance.

Ultimately, Norah outlives her brother, Jonah, thereby triumphing as a female villain, a victorious *female* monster. However, the stability she craved—the purgatory of the house and the corporeality of the bodies she inhabited—was lost, forcing her to roam the earth in search of a new host. Although she achieves her aim and occupies the body of an unborn fetus, her days of a certain future are gone revealing the instability of the contemporary moment and the new kind of purgatory, she finds herself in, that of never-ending precarity.

Conclusion

David Mitchell's *Slade House* re-evaluates conventional representations of the female vampire figure, casting the role of the female villain as monstrous in relation to patriarchal society's conception of conventional female characters. Here, the monstrous female, Norah, subverts one-dimensional stereotypes of women as victims revealing them as patriarchal, purgatorial structures (Creed 1993; Santos 2016; Wilson 2020). As such, the novel comments critically on the state of contemporary society by addressing themes pertaining to moral choice, speculation about the origins of evil, feminist views, sexual possession, power imbalances, and the fear of moral and physical decay in relation to identity creation. *Slade House* also comments on the purgatorial nature of "traditional" patriarchal identity, which positions the reinforcement of boundaries and thresholds of these spaces of our own volition. However, as seen in the figure of Norah, she more than Jonah—who literally remains trapped within the belly of the purgatorial beast (house)—is capable, from her position of monstrosity and outsidership, to forge herself a liminal future beyond her former domestic purgatory. Yet, this too is problematic in Mitchell's narrative as while being seen as monstrous within patriarchal society, she simultaneously embodies the inevitable exploitation of late consumerist society so that her continued existence can never be a new beginning, but only a continual questioning of how the past continually feeds on the present.

Works Cited

Bacon, S. (2011), "Binging: Excess, Aging, and Identity in the Female Vampire," *MP: An Online Feminist Journal*, 3(3): 21–37.

Blanco, M. del P. and E. Peeren (eds.) (2013), *The Spectralities Reader: Ghosts and Haunting in Contemporary Cultural Theory*, London: Bloomsbury Academic.

Bubke, C. (2018), "Being Human: Monstrous Humans and Human Vampires in *Dracula*, *True Blood* and the *Sookie Stackhouse* Novels," *The Dark Arts Journal*, 3(1): 1–17.

Buzwell, G. (2014), "*Man Is Not Truly One, but Truly Two: Duality in Robert Louis Stevenson's* 'Strange Case of Dr Jekyll and Mr Hyde,'" *British Library.* https://www.bl.uk/romantics-and-victorians/articles/duality-in-robert-louis-stevensons-strange-case-of-dr-jekyll-and-mr-hyde.

Byron, G. and D. Punter (2004), *Gothic*, Oxford: Blackwell Publishing.

Craig, S. F. (2015), *Ghosts of the Mind: The Supernatural and Madness in Victorian Gothic Literature.* Thesis. Mississippi: The University of Southern Mississippi.

Creed, B. (1986), "Horror and the Monstrous-Feminine: An Imaginary Abjection," *Screen,* 27(1): 44–71.

Creed, B. (1993), *The Monstrous-Feminine: Film, Feminism, Psychoanalysis*, London: Psychology Press.

Gennep, A. V. (2013), *Rites of Passage [1909]*, M. B. Vizedom and G. L. Caffee (trans.), New York: Routledge.

Helyer, R. (2000), "Parodied to Death: The Postmodern Gothic of *American Psycho*," *Modern Fiction Studies,* 46(3): 725–46.

Johnston, S. I. (2013), *Restless Dead: Encounters between the Living and the Dead in Ancient Greece,* California: University of California Press.

Kahane, C. (1980), "Gothic Mirrors and Feminine Identity," *Centennial Review,* 24(1): 43–64.

Kelly, S. (2014), "Book Review: *Slade House* by David Mitchell," The Scotsman: Scotland's National Newspaper.

Machinal, H. (ed.) (2011), "*Cloud Atlas:* From Postmodernity to the Posthuman," in *David Mitchell: Critical Essays,* Canterbury: Gylphi Limited.

Mitchell, D. (2015), *Slade House,* London: Routledge.

Morrisette, J. J. (2013), "Marxferatu: 'The Vampire Metaphor as a Tool for Teaching Marx's Critique of Capitalism,'" *The Teacher,* 637–42.

O'Donnell, P. (2015), *A Temporary Future: The Fiction of David Mitchell,* London: Bloomsbury Academic.

Pedlar, V. (2006), *The Most Dreadful Visitation: Male Madness in Victorian Fiction,* Liverpool: Liverpool University Press.

Punter, D. (2012), *A New Companion to the Gothic,* Oxford: Blackwell Publishers.

Rice, A. (1988), *The Queen of the Damned,* London: Sphere.

Rinne, A. (2013), "'I Am the Vampire for These Times': Representations of Postmodernity in Anne Rice's *The Vampire Chronicles*," Thesis. Tampere: University of Tampere.

Santos, C. (2014), "It's Not All about Snow White: The Evil Queen Isn't that Monstrous After All," in A. S. Dauber (ed.), *Monsters in Society: An Interdisciplinary Perspective,* 41–51, Leiden: Brill.

Santos, C. (2016), *Unbecoming Female Monsters: Witches, Vampires, and Virgins,* Washington DC: Lexington Books.

Signorotti, E. (1996), "Repossessing the Body: Transgressive Desire in 'Carmilla' and 'Dracula,'" *Criticism,* 38(4): 607–32.

Turner, V. (1992), *Blazing the Trail: Way Marks in the Exploration of Symbols,* Tucson: University of Arizona Press.

Williamson, M. (2003), "Vampire Transformations: From Gothic Demon to Domestication," *Vampires. Myths and Metaphors of Enduring Evil,* 101–7.

Wilson, N. (2005), "Excessive Performances of the Same: Beauty as the Beast of Reality TV," *Women & Performance: A Journal of Feminist Theory,* 15(2): 207–29.

Wilson, N. (2020), *Willful Monstrosity: Gender and Race in 21st Century Horror,* Jefferson: McFarland & Co., Inc.

9

"Into the Further We Go": Exploring Gender, World-Building, and the Return of the Fantastic in the *Insidious* Franchise

Mark Richard Adams

The *Insidious* franchise has been developed across a decade which has seen a large number of social, cultural, and political changes, including a reinvigoration of far-right ideology in opposition to an expansion of progressive thinking and awareness of social issues. Horror films have often reflected the times in which they were made, and the changes and different interests of the four *Insidious* films suggest they are adapting and evolving in relation to contemporary society. This chapter will begin by looking at a horror history, looking at times when the genre seems predominantly, albeit not exclusively, nihilistic in tone and how this reflected their contemporary cultures. I will be contrasting this often very grounded and "real world" set horror, with periods where the genre more widely embraces the fantastic, where it creates its own mythologies, and builds its own fictional worlds, which exist with their own rules and characters. The fiction world of *Insidious* is increasingly centered around the character of Elise, an older female lead who is at odds with both the traditional Final Girl, and the elements of the nuclear family in the first two films of the series. Thus, I will explore the Blumhouse *Insidious* franchise, and the strange, somewhat agnostic, mythology it constructs over four films in order to tell its stories of demonic entities and ghosts, and a psychic, superhero woman.

This chapter will begin with exploring how horror has a history of responding to changes in culture and society, looking at notable periods in the 1970s and early twenty-first century when the genre predominantly featured films offering a distinctly nihilistic tone. This section will serve to explore what we mean by nihilistic horror, identify particular cultural moments that give rise to it, and then lead into the contemporary rise of fantastical horror through current horror auteur figures such as James Wan and Jason Blum. I will be exploring how they construct fantastical narratives with a strong focus on world-building and lore, which is then utilized to examine contemporary societal issues. While the world remains in a state of turmoil, horror seems to have moved away from nihilism toward a more progressive exploration of the issues that exist through such franchises as *The Purge* (2013), *The Conjuring* (2013), *Paranormal Activity* (2009), and, of course, *Insidious* (2010). Part of this involves the refocusing of the genre upon strong female lead characters, albeit ones that do not abide by the more conventional action woman trope. Elise, as the leading figure of the *Insidious* franchise, reflects the growing representation in mainstream media, the expansion of gender roles, and the fight against more contemporary oppressive structures within culture.

"There Is No Magic": A Brief History of Nihilistic Horror

In George Romero's *Martin* (1977) as Martin Madahas (John Amplas) prepares to break into the suburban home of a housewife and murder her for her blood, he envisages a very different scenario where she entices him through the darkened corridors of a gothic mansion. This sequence, one of several similar scenes, highlights a prominent stylistic shift in the aesthetic of horror from the 1940s to the 1970s. Horror has often been a genre that reflects the nature of the society it was a product of and films such as *Martin*, *The Last House on the Left* (1972), *The Texas Chain Saw Massacre* (1974), and *It's Alive* (1974) are among those that demonstrate the influence of cultural change within 1970s America.

In earlier films the narrative threat has more often come from without, but Robin Wood has argued that across the decades, it has made a "steady geographical progress towards America" (2003: 77). He suggests horror "is always external to Americans, who may be attacked by it physically but remain (superficially, that is) uncontaminated by it morally" (Wood 2003: 77). America felt it was not ultimately responsible for the horrors it faced and could still stand as the moral force standing to fight against outside oppression. However, during America's involvement in the Vietnam war over fifty thousand troops lost their lives and the government spent over a hundred-billion dollars on the war effort, both of which had a heavy impact culturally and economically. Through extensive news coverage, the American public was made aware of atrocities committed not by the enemy but by their own troops, destroying any sense of moral superiority in the war and literally bringing real-life horrors into the very heart of American culture. By 1972 films were already beginning to reflect an increasingly negative outlook and Waller emphasizes that "the horror film has engaged in a sort of extended dramatization of and response to the major public events and newsworthy topics in American history since 1968" (1987: 12). Suddenly horror was not something distant, a foreign supernatural force that came to destroy the morally superior United States, but a very close, very real threat from within America itself. Crane describes these films as "relentlessly and antagonistically grim" featuring "sustained, unavoidable anguish with no promise of catharsis" and that "when forced to suffer, the audience is not allowed to do so in realms far removed from ordinary life … horror is visited upon the audience in familiar harbours" (2002: 166–7). This nihilist sentiment saw corruption and decay stem from the very heart of the country, rising up to destroy the modern youth, children of the flower power generation, and attack the very fabric of society.

Whereas the previous decades had presented the monstrous as demonic creatures, vampiric stalkers, and alien mutants, now the horror stemmed from "ordinary" men and women, driven to extremes not only by their own circumstances but by the very decay inherent in society itself. The villains of *Martin*, *The Hills Have Eyes*, *Chain Saw Massacre*, *It's Alive*, *The Last House on the Left*, *Blue Sunshine*, and many others are all products of economic failure, scientific experimentation, governmental conspiracy, and, most importantly, a sense of inherent corruption within society. Within these films there is a realization "not only that the monster is the product of normality, but that it is no longer possible to view normality itself as other than monstrous" (Wood 2003: 85). Just as America's faith in its own righteousness had been permanently damaged following Vietnam and Watergate, so was its willingness to believe in the fantastic, the extraordinary becoming suddenly terrifyingly ordinary. *Martin* rejects the conventional interpretations of the vampire, consistently subverting the iconography associated with them as the titular character rips down garlic cloves and, most tellingly, removes a pair of fake fangs, exclaiming "You see? There is no magic." This is perhaps as good a summary of nihilistic horror as you could find, an admittance to the removal of the fantastic.

The threat of the contemporary world extended beyond societies' own corruption to incorporate other signifiers of the modern, that is, science, technology, and rationality. These notions are tied in to not only the loss of the fantastic in these films, but also the loss of faith, patriarchal power, and the institution of religion; what would have once been demonic is now explained through science. Even the films of the period that do appear to overtly deal with the demonic, notably *The Omen* (1976) and *The Exorcist* (1973), are not entirely comfortable with the issue and not only address it directly but offer up the possibility of rational explanations for events. They constantly question the spiritual nature of the threats by offering up explanation of psychiatry and paranoia, as the priest in *Martin* suggests, the nature of evil and the demonic is "a difficult subject, something that has to be dealt with." Charles Derry suggests these films expressed the audiences concern that, "if we could not find God reflected in the modern world, perhaps we could at least find the devil" (1987: 169) but it seems even the devil comes from within society.

Flower power and the 1960s had encouraged liberal thinking toward alternative religions which perhaps led to American cinema being "dominated by the pessimistic, mystic mode of horror" (Waller 1987: 169) but it is clear that any form of religious connotation to the horrors should either be entirely rejected and at the very least called into question. Religion, authority, and morality are all questioned and shown to be lacking in these films and the contemporary alternative of technology and science is shown to be equally destructive. There is no room for faith or hope within 1970s horror, only for rationality, as "the modern world has substituted science for religious faith" (Blake 2002: 159), a rationality that ultimately only serves to reveal the self-destructive course that American society appeared to be heading on.

It is worth noting now that we should not seek to imply that the filmmakers were making deliberate political statements in these films but more so that, as Laura Mee states, "they are products of their time rather than explicit comments on it" and that "it is important to understand such factors as having been predominantly applied retrospectively" (2020: 119). The early noughties would see another era of more nihilistic horror, exemplified by the "torture porn" cycle popularized with the *Saw* franchise. Following the postmodern and more humorous approaches to horror of the late 1990s, these films were notably more violent, graphic, and sadistic in their approach, often emphasizing the deconstruction of the human body (*Saw, Captive, Hostel, Paradise Lost, The Hills Have Eyes*, and more). While many have attempted to make connections between these films and the events of 9/11, Mee has put forward the case that these films, like those from the seventies, are not deliberate in their political discourse and while "horror remakes clearly feature images and themes relevant to cultural concerns in the 2000s, these often manifest in ambiguous ways" (2020). Mee thus suggests that many of the "allegories" in post-9/11 films are rather inconsequential, reflecting more the generic conventions of horror and that the images and themes that are present are actually more part of the overall cultural zeitgeist than a deliberate intention to engage with 9/11 politics. The 1970s nihilistic cycle was followed by a slasher genre that became increasingly supernatural in its narratives, and the nihilistic noughties also gave way to an era that moved away from overt splatter to a greater exploration of the fantastic in horror. While there may be an element responding to events in society, it can be equally argued that in both eras the interests of audience simply shifted. Audiences who have watched several years of prominent torture porn films, often grounded in a nihilistic view of the contemporary real world, might find narratives featuring more subtle and fantastical elements a clear contrast to what they are used to. I would argue that the truth lies somewhere between the two, and audiences tired of both nihilistic horror movies, and a sense of continuing frustration in global politics, might turn to the fantastic aspects of the genre as a way to explore and address with the collective cultural trauma.

Building Imaginary (Horror) Worlds

The global box office success of the *Paranormal Activity* franchise was an important moment, not only for popularizing an era of found footage, but also for putting Blumhouse onto the horror map, with the company going on to launch numerous horror franchises. The series' increasingly complicated plotline would set a template for world-building that the company would continue in their various franchises. The first *Paranormal Activity* starts off simply as a paranormal haunting, though the film soon reveals that a demon is responsible. The demon was sent to these characters after being exorcised by the lead character Katie's sister in the films sequel/prequel, which ends with the now-possessed Katie taking her nephew prisoner and killing her relatives. *Paranormal Activity 3* goes back to the sisters' childhoods and establishes that a coven of witches has been responsible for the series events. These witches place the abducted baby in an adoptive family and monitor him during the events of *Paranormal Activity 4*. Meanwhile the fifth film looks at other cursed children and ends with a time-traveling door which takes the protagonist back to events of the first film. The 3D *Ghost Dimension* features rupture in reality, time travel, other dimensions, and a plot by the coven of witches to give the demonic Toby a human form. The franchise continues on in another sequel, which will no doubt continue to develop the already-complicated narrative. These elements build up across the films of the franchise, often in the background of the film's narrative, but nether-the-less providing a unifying context and narrative drive to the found footage franchise. Mark Wolf, in his study on world-building, sees the creation of fictional mythology as being about "giving them a history and context for events ... they often reveal how characters and ongoing problems came to be, so that story events seem more meaningful" (2012: 23). The *Paranormal Activity* narrative is built up slowly, and often in background details, but it does construct something arguably more fantastical and complicated than a standard vengeful spirit or haunting narrative more traditionally seen in the genre. It builds a mythology and this more expansive world-building and engagement with fantastical elements would become a staple of Blumhouse Pictures.

Blumhouse Pictures has thrived following the success of *Paranormal Activity*, and expanded into other horror films, as a contemporary house of horrors, producing a variety of films that have increasingly explored the fantastic in the genre, not only originating a menagerie of monsters, but also constructing unnatural worlds which they inhabit. Blumhouse's productions generally do not try to place a singular threat into a real-world scenario, but rather construct worlds which feature a *Twilight Zone*-esque "what if?" question at the heart of them. Audiences are often expected to simply accept the proposition of the Tethered's existence (*Us*), the rise of *The Purge*, or that a girl might be caught in a time loop, dying again and again (*Happy Death Day*) rather than building in clear explanations that fit our normative reality. These narratives take time to introduce a world similar but at the same time different to our own. Wolf suggests that "once an imaginary world's initial differences from the actual world are established, they will often act as constraints on further invention, suggesting or even requiring other laws or limitations that will define a world further as an author figures out all the consequences of the laws as they are put into effect" (2012: 23). Of the Blumhouse franchises, the *Purge* series perhaps embodies this the most, with the television spin-off especially, exploring the ramifications of the central conceit. I suggest the success of so many Blumhouse franchises in part stems from the high concept ideas they utilize at their core. *Insidious* begins with a central twist on the haunted house concept, with its tagline proclaiming, "It's not the house that's haunted," expanded in the film itself to clarify that the young son Dalton is the target of the supernatural forces. As with the others, this relatively simple starting concept is expanded to build an imaginary horror world which constructs its own form of purgatorial realm. It is more interested in the development of this world as the core feature of the horror than any singular horror icon, setting it apart from the traditional trajectory of horror franchises.

In building a fictional world, Wolf identifies how "unless we are told otherwise, we expect the laws of physics in a secondary world to be the same as those of the Primary World," the latter a term used for our own reality in relation to the fictional one (2012: 54–5). Newly created elements will have a basis in the Primary World, even if this is an existing myth as is usually the case in the horror genre, such as the recurrence of specific rules for vampires in fiction. Of course, these do vary, and fantasy horror narratives may build their first act around establishing the parameters of the supernatural threat. Horror franchises are predominantly built around their villains and the worlds they inhabit are, by and large, indistinguishable from the Primary World, aside from the presence of the monster itself. There are some exceptions, such as the character of Kristen (Patricia Arquette) in *A Nightmare of Elm Street 3: Dream Warriors* (1987) who has the narratively useful ability to mentally pull other sleeping characters into her dreams, and thus interact with them. Freddy Krueger (Robert Englund) is the supernatural entity in a world of ordinary teenagers, but Kristen is given this ability which allows the titular Dream Warriors to unite against Freddy. Notably this third film is arguably the one that most embraces the fantasy elements of the franchise, also drawing in religious mythology and featuring the spirit of Freddy's deceased mother. Wolf suggests that "for works in which world-building occurs, there may be a wealth of details or events (or mere mentions of them) which do not advance the story, but which provide background richness and verisimilitude to the imaginary world" (2012: 2). This is perhaps part of the reason many horror franchises tend not to be too expansive in their world-building. The nature of the threat is often the singular icon, a commercial figure who is vital to marketing, and thus any story that is developed must remain centralized around that individual. In cases when the franchise attempts to move away from this, such as *Halloween III: Season of the Witch* (1983) or *Friday the 13th Part V: A New Beginning* (1985), there has been a backlash from audiences and the series has rapidly returned to foregrounding their icons. Wickham Clayton attributes *A Nightmare on Elm Street* (1984) for the revival and evolution of the slasher films in the mid-1980s, with a "increased tendency toward supernatural storylines" within the genre (2020: 32–3). However, the franchises rarely moved beyond their focus on a central icon, and entries that did would often be negatively received, such as 1990's *Jason Goes to Hell: The Final Friday*. In some cases, where the initial film of a franchise features multiple antagonists, the franchises branding imperatives might reduce and remove other elements to solely focus on the primary icon, arguably the case with both Leatherface (*The Texas Chain Saw Massacre*) and Pinhead (*Hellraiser*), among others.

Unlike the majority of ongoing horror series, the *Insidious* franchise is not built around a solitary villain figure or antagonist. Rather it is unified by an ever-expanding internal mythology that incorporates elements of different theological canons, but is, unlike the other prominent contemporary world-building horror franchise, *The Conjuring* series, not directly connected to Biblical lore. Wolf notes how makers of worlds "often reference or acknowledge their predecessors and the worlds that have gone before them" (2012: 226). This is the case with *Insidious*'s use of demonic and spiritual entities, even though it avoids ever specifying the series as being connected to any specific religious belief, possibly derived from Box Office imperatives to be accessible to a global audience. Simon Marsden has explored the notion of the "death of God" as a historical moment where horror fiction tries to deal with the reduced importance of Christianity within culture. Marsden states that "the experience of the death of God is part of the context in which their narratives take place: implicitly or overtly, their fictions depict the struggle of individuals to come to terms with divine absence" (2019: 121). More contemporary fantastic films seem to continue this exploration, with *The Conjuring* reaffirming Christian metaphysics, while the *Insidious* franchise opens its world up to individual interpretation, creating a space uniquely suited to audiences projecting their own belief system or values onto it. *Insidious* deals with familiar themes and theologies; it is consistently careful to avoid positioning them as evidence of religious truth for any single denomination, instead constructing its own fictional purgatorial world out of familiar iconography and terminology familiar from our Primary World but not bound to it.

"A Place Not Meant for the Living"

The "Further" is the key purgatorial world of the *Insidious* franchise, from which the varied antagonists across the series originate. Rather than entities existing as spirits trapped somehow in the mortal world, unable to pass on, the hauntings are instead a manifestation of their desire to cross back into the real world from the "Further" where they have become stuck. Central to the world-building in the *Insidious* franchise, the Further is named by Lin Shaye's character, Elise Rainier. In the first film we get a brief explanation, although Elise specifies this is her own belief, and that she named it the Further. She states that "[t]he Further is a world far beyond our own, yet it is all around us. A place without time as we know. It is a dark realm filled with the tortured souls of the dead. A place not meant for the living." The sequels expand on this, suggesting the Further is a place everyone passes through after death. Where the deceased go afterwards is left deliberately vague although some form of afterlife is implied. The Further is thus a place in between life and the afterlife, the realm of lost spirits of deceased humans, and the more insidious demonic entities who were never alive to begin with. Its closest religious concept would be a form of purgatory, although the franchise is clear that while many human spirits reside there, the demonic entities are somehow native to the Further. Audience knowledge of Primary World mythology, and wider genre knowledge, helps position these entities as either ghosts or demons within the minds of the audience, but the film does not delve into any deeper metaphysical explanation as to their nature than this.

The films adopt a format akin to the "monster of the week" formula of television fantasy series, whereby each installment features a new entity with a different motive and nature, albeit equally as dangerous. The first *Insidious* film focuses on Josh (Patrick Wilson) and Renai Lambert (Rose Byrne), whose son Dalton (Ty Simpkins) slips into a coma and appears to be subject to hauntings. Josh's mum reveals that Josh, like Dalton, could astral project as a child, and this drew the attention of entities. Josh's memory was suppressed by the psychic Elise (Lin Shaye), who arrives with her assistants Specs (Leigh Whannell) and Tucker (Angus Sampson), to aid the family. Dalton has become trapped in the Further by the Lipstick Faced Demon, and as his mortal body weakens, different spirits vie to enter it and return to life. The Demon, however, is not something that was once a normal man, but is an otherworldly entity itself, and thus a much larger threat. Josh enters the Further to rescue Dalton with Elise's help and succeeds. However, there he encounters the Bride in Black, the spirit that haunted Josh as a child. Josh is possessed and, unknown to the others, murders Elise. In *Insidious: Chapter 2* Josh remains possessed by The Bride in Black, revealed to be Parker Crane, a serial killer who was tormented by his overbearing mother. Josh's body deteriorates and the spirit of Crane's mother urges Crane to kill again as a way to survive. The real Josh, meanwhile, is trapped in the Further where he eventually encounters the spirit of Elise who has returned from an afterlife; she explicitly cannot talk about to help them defeat Crane. Eventually the spirits are overcome, Josh reclaims his body, and Elise, as an unseen spirit, follows Specs and Tucker to aid on their next paranormal investigation. The *Insidious: Chapter 3* antagonist is The Man Who Can't Breath, a displaced spirit, trapped in the apartment building. Unlike the other entities, he does not seek to possess people to enter the world of the living. Rather, he drives his victims to despair through their pain and suffering, drawing them into the Further. The very Clive Barker-esque climax sees the Man Who Can't Breathe seemingly tenderly stroking, almost comforting, his victim, as she slowly slips into death, and thus to join him in his suffering. Elise is able to call on the departed spirit of his victim's mother to offer her closure to her personal issues and defeat the Man Who Can't Breath. *Insidious: The Last Key* features another Demon as its main antagonist, one that is linked to Elise's own past with her abusive and murderous father. Key-Face has been utilizing human men to kidnap and imprison young women, feeding off their fear and despair. His victim's souls appear in a prison-like space within the Further, where Key-Face continues to feed off and torment them. Elise refuses to feed the cycle of violence Key-Face needs and is able to summon her own Mothers spirit before the three generations of their family destroy the demon and free the trapped souls. In the real world, Elise is reunited with her estranged brother and her two nieces, including the equally psychically gifted Imogen (Caitlin Gerard). The film ends with Elise being summoned to the house from the first film, which will lead to her eventual demise.

Gender and the Final Girl

While each *Insidious* film features its own victims of the denizens of the Further, as the series progresses, the character of Elise steps forward as the central icon of the franchise. This is where we see the central exploration of gender and family emerging within the *Insidious* franchise, that begins with a more conventional focused on the nuclear family, before exploring and deconstructing familial relationships in the latter half of the series. The importance of a major horror franchise being led by an older woman should not be overlooked, especially in light of historical examinations of the role of gender in the genre.

The notion of the Final Girl has reached mainstream cultural consciousness but began in one of the seminal studies of gender in the horror film. Carol J. Clover suggested "the image of the distressed female most likely to linger in memory is the image of the one who did not die: the survivor, or Final Girl" (1992: 35) and the power of this idea has continued to influence the horror genre, whether in deliberate subversion, postmodern referencing, or embracing the slasher format as established by Clover's work. There were many other theorists studying the role of gender in horror (Barbara Creed, Brigid Cherry, Barry Keith Grant, and others) and what becomes noticeable across the works is that while there is a plethora of different positions women can take with the genre, there is very little for older actresses. Creed's work looks at the roles often associated with women; the archaic mother, the possessed mother, the monstrous womb, the vampire, or the witch and it becomes increasingly clear that while there is more variety of roles for younger women, older women are inherently unknowable, sexless, or monstrous (1993). While horror has diversified, and made attempts to strengthen the Final Girl role, *Insidious* more interestingly and directly breaks the mold by making older actor Lin Shaye the primary star and central icon of the franchise.

The first film initially positions Josh as the main character to explore the Further, and the sequel features Carl, an old friend of Elise who takes up her role following her death. The trajectory at this stage feels familiar, with a younger male lead, and an older, wiser figure with vital occult knowledge that can help the hero. However, by the end of Chapter 2 Elise herself has returned as an unseen "Guardian Angel" to protect the characters from demons and spirits. The following films are prequels, focused entirely on Elise before her death, and firmly establishing her as the franchises recurring hero, with neither Josh nor Carl returning in any prominent capacity. *The Last Key* explores her personal backstory and reunites her with the spirit of her deceased mother, allowing them to overcome Key-Face together. Writer Leigh Whannell, responsible for all four movies as well as starring in them as Specs, has stated in an interview "We've kind of established Lin in this particular film as kind of this superhero, so that would be kind of interesting to explore in the other films" (John Squires 2016). The use of the word "superhero" is particularly interesting, as it is trans-generic, and not something usually associated with horror films. That *Insidious* embraces the fantastic is partly why it is able to blend genres, and as contemporary culture features many television series, books, and film narratives featuring monster slayers, audiences are more willing to engage with it. A scene in *Chapter 3* exemplifies the formalist elements that go into constructing Elise as a form of horror superhero. Attacked by Parker Crane, Elise is able to break free of their grip and flings the spirit across the room in a clear feat of strength. The camera pushes in, and we get a slightly low angle, creating a heroic image of Elise who delivers a one-liner, "come on, bitch" as she beckons her enemy. It is a moment not out of place in the action genre and uses cinematic language to demonstrate the strength of Elise, cementing her as a hero able to fight back.

Insidious 5 has been announced and sees the return of Josh (Patrick Wilson also directing this time) and Dalton and will follow up from where Chapter 2 ended. With Elise deceased at this stage, the question remains whether or not the franchise will continue to center on her. The fourth film, set just before the original, introduces Elise's niece, Imogen, who takes after her psychic aunt. Chapter 2 last depicted Elise as a "Guardian Angel," invisible to those around her, but following Specs and Tucker as they investigate the paranormal. It remains to be seen what will happen, but there seems to be many possible avenues for Elise to continue to play a central role from beyond the grave. We might argue that, despite the issues facing the world today, there is a growing sense of optimism in younger generations through their engagement with social issues, their criticisms of conservative ideologies, or the rise of prominent left-leaning political thinking. Is it a coincidence then that Lin Shaye's Elise in the *Insidious* films, like Donald Pleasance's Dr. Loomis or Peter Cushing's Van Helsing, sees the return of a recurring protagonist who can defeat the monsters? Might we be seeing the return of the fantastic, and of hope, to the horror genre, albeit still balanced with oppressive, patriarchal forces of evil?

Conclusions

The grounding of the fantastic in real-world stories allows these films to engage their more elaborate ideas without losing the audiences belief. The greater mythologizing of the supernatural horror as magical, demonic, and supernatural is often grounded in itself by aligning it with very real human evil. Whereas the more nihilistic movies focus on the destructive and violent bodily destruction, often lacking any hope of escape, the films of Blumhouse Pictures and others have shifted away from this cinematic despair. The current films align the supernatural and human, often misogynistic, evil together as forces equally to be faced by the protagonists of these films.

I would suggest horror films have moved on from a nihilistic acceptance of the world as it is and are now engaging more with themes of dealing with trauma and fighting back. It is increasingly clear to everyone, with the rise of Trump, the rise of the alt-right, the attacks of basic human freedoms by the United States' own Supreme Court, just how bad things have become. Audiences, culture, and films seem less likely to go silently into the night. Horror is not going to necessarily wallow in a nihilistic acceptance of a brutal world. Horror fiction is now embracing the fight back, through increased representation and diversity within and without the film's various worlds, but also with messages of the possibility of hope. In each *Insidious* film, the evil force is ultimately defeated, at least temporarily, and characters survive, learn, grow, and often overcome their own trauma. The agnostic approach to the Further might speak to a more secular society, but we should also not forget capitalist imperatives to sell a product globally. The worlds Blumhouse builds are not exactly our own, and they feature threats that are both fantastical and personal, but it is often the case in confronting the former, the characters can resolve the latter. The imaginative engagement with world-building and fantasy perhaps speaks of a more optimistic era of horror, where the young and the old, and more importantly, the female, are actively and intelligently engaging with the very real horrors that exist, suggesting that we can not only fight them, but that we should fight them, and that perhaps we might win, in the end.

Works Cited

Blake, L. (2002), "Another One for the Fire: George A. Romero's American Theology of the Flesh," in X. Mendik (ed.), *Shocking Cinema of the Seventies*, 151–65, Hereford: Noir Publishing.

Clayton, W. (2020), *See! Hear! Cut! Kill! Experiencing Friday the 13th*, Mississippi: University Press of Mississippi.

Clover, C. J. (1992), *Men, Women and Chain Saws: Gender in the Modern Horror Film*, New Jersey: Princeton University Press.

Crane, J. L. (2002), "Come On-A My House: The Inescapable Legacy of Wes Craven's The Last House on the Left," in X. Mendik (ed.), Shocking Cinema of the Seventies, 169–77, Hereford: Noir Publishing.

Creed, B. (1993), *The Monstrous-Feminine: Film, Feminism, Psychoanalysis*, London: Routledge.

Derry, C. (1987), "More Dark Dreams: Some Notes on the Recent Horror Film," in G. A. Waller (ed.), *American Horrors: Essays on the Modern American Horror Film*, 162–74, Illinois: University of Illinois Press.

Marsden, S. (2019), "Horror and the Death of God," in E. Beal and J. Greenaway (eds), *Horror and Religion: New Literary Approaches to Theology, Race, and Sexuality*, 119–35, Melksham: University of Wales Press.

Mee, L. (2020), *Reanimated: The Contemporary American Horror Film Remake*, Edinburgh: Edinburgh University Press.

Squires, J. (2016), *Insidious: The Next Chapter Now in Development*. https://www.dreadcentral.com/news/161672/insidious-next-chapter-in-development/ (Accessed June 1, 2022).

Waller, G. A. (1987), "Introduction," in G. A. Waller (ed.), *American Horrors: Essays on the Modern American Horror Film*, 1–13, Illinois: University of Illinois Press.

Wolf, M. J. P. (2012), *Building Imaginary Worlds: The Theory and History of Subcreation*, London: Routledge.

Wood, R. (2003), *Hollywood from Vietnam to Reagan... and Beyond*, New York: Columbia University Press.

10

Coded Outcry: Margaret Atwood's *The Handmaid's Tale* (1985 and 2017–Present) and *The Testaments* (2019)

Gina Wisker

Introduction

The Handmaid's Tale (1985) is hellish, unforgettable, inescapable as history, the present, and the likely future. Once written, read, and repeatedly discussed and written about, replayed in film and TV versions (and also a comic book), its expressed engagement with the all-encompassing destructive powers, the refusal, denials, and the torturous punishments of oppressive regimes and individual meanness are a bleak testament to our times past, present, and a terrifying warning of our future. Revisited, it is always too much, too worrying, too grim, and sometimes just a little too minimally hopeful as it tells us of our ways and times. I am going to argue that *The Testaments* (2019), on the other hand, offers insight and active hope and does so partly because in form and tone it resembles a comedy first in the sense of Dante's *Divine Comedy* (1308–20) and then Shakespeare's comedies and late romances. More so, I will argue for the power of testimony and witnessing, not just from those we can sympathize with, like the sisters Agnes/Jemima and Nicole/Daisy, but also from those that are more problematic, such as Aunt Lydia, who, while seemingly being part of, and enforcing, the Purgatory known as Gilead, offers the chance of dissent and a reckoning, and maybe even a future beyond it.

Dante's *Divine Comedy* is not comic as we would define it today but is a "'comedy' in the medieval-Aristotelian sense that it leads from misery to a state of happiness" (Thomson 2018: n.p.), and so the three books *Inferno, Purgatorio*, and *Paradiso* trace Italian poet Dante Alighieri's own journey through hell and torment to joy, led by the Roman poet Virgil. It is in the vernacular (Italian) as would be a discussion or a diary entry (such as Aunt Lydia's). In terms of the world of Gilead, *The Handmaid's Tale* is Atwood's *Inferno*; *The Testaments* her *Purgatorio*. One wonders if Atwood intends a *Paradiso* but I would think a tone of joyful celebration would be unusual for her throughout an entire book (rather than appearing minimally in an uplifting, but wryly tempered piece of closure), so I doubt it.

If we explore the meaning of purgatory when considering Atwood's novel, we appreciate that it is a time of torment and expiation of guilt, leading to resolution, as the *Merriam-Webster Dictionary* indicates:

> Purgatory answers the human need to believe in a just and merciful cosmos, one in which ordinary people, neither hardened sinners nor perfect saints, may undergo correction, balance life's accounts, satisfy old debts, cleanse accumulated defilements, and heal troubled memories.
>
> (*Merriam-Webster*)

The Testaments, for which Margaret Atwood co-won the Booker Prize with Bernadine Evaristo in 2019, is a novel based on a comic rather than a tragic form, so redemption of a sort and resolution are at its core. Diversity, rather than a single reductive vision and version, is one strategy of its comic and redemptive energies. The focus on three main women characters with different perspectives offers the opportunity to move beyond the individual testimony of Offred, the possible survivor of Gilead, and instead offer corroboration and their three different perspectives on the experience and the meaning of events. Although still in Gilead, the harsh world of *The Handmaid's Tale* some years later, the action of this novel and its women characters take from the rich possibilities and diversity offered in comedy where the view of one will be counteracted and undermined by another, where there are disguises, escapes and irony, satire, and occasional near slapstick. The single worldview of *The Handmaid's Tale* and patriarchal fundamentalism gives way in *The Testaments* to a richer, more diverse set of expressed worldviews. In the earlier novel, other than the secret records of Offred, there is no guiding human voice, only that of the repressive state parroted back from people turned into obedient functionaries because all are controlled by internalized regulations, valuations, and devaluations, and where there is therefore very little opportunity to speak except in coded or vacuous phrases, such as "Praise be." Repression, secrecy, and then the honesty of testimony reappear in *The Testaments* with Aunt Lydia's self-confessed manipulation of language and worldview, her acts of subversion through keeping her critical revelatory diary log in the page of Newman's tracts (1864: 1833–4). Variation and honesty also emerge through the differently conditioned, expressed perception and interpretations of Daisy/baby Nicole, "Jade" (brought up in free Canada by adoptive revolutionary parents) and her sister Agnes/Jemima (brought up in Gilead and escaping from a potentially abusive arranged marriage by learning to become an Aunt). The three-part diversity offers room to question, reimagine, undermine, challenge, and to poke fun—even if it is dangerous unlicensed fun—at the monomaniac minded, and enforced behavior aligned with the dominant, coded worldview of *The Handmaid's Tale*, where sneaking personal testimony out could bring death and where religious mouthings cover over any alternative ways of seeing the world.

This essay explores beyond *The Handmaid's Tale* (1985), briefly mentioning the television adaption, and focusing on Atwood's *The Testaments* (2019), a novel with a darkly comic set of three voices, variously escapees from the purgatory of Gilead (which is itself destabilized). It argues about the importance of articulacy and of women's empowered agency as expressed in the testimony of the three women, and through the darkly comic forms, the confusions, varied mishaps and cruelties, and eventual resolutions. While the moment and trajectory of *The Testaments* resembles that of being in purgatory, the tone is reminiscent of that of satire from Alexander Pope to Monty Python's cruel zany fun debunking social and religious hypocrisy. It is also reminiscent of some Shakespearean comedy and late romance with twinning, disguises, threats, and a carnivalesque undermining of an often forcibly maintained status quo, dangers avoided, and a new order established or restored. The novel situates its characters and readers in a purgatorial world but does not leave us there. Through the witnessing of both testimony and testaments comes a way of dealing with past and present trauma, without overlooking its problematic tendency to return and recur, while through the comic emerges new energy so there should eventually be a glimmer of some hope and change.

As *The Testaments* begins, the world is already post-apocalyptic, dystopian, misogynistic. Women, segmented according to their functions as infertile domestics ("Marthas"), infertile trophy wives for commanders, insider bullying "Aunts" and fertile "Handmaids," are set against each other, in a powerful mechanism to enable the dominant patriarchal regime to control economic and political power, human life, as well as women's bodies and their reproduction.

There is an element in the television version (2017–present) of *The Handmaid's Tale* ("Night," season 1, episode 10) where the Busby Berkeley synchronized red-cloaked and white-wimpled Handmaids circle Janine (Madeline Brewer), the deviant one who did not understand that speaking out of ignorance and wanting to retain and love your own child was a crime. The "girls" are meant to stone her in a "particicution," but unlike Shirley Jackson's "The Lottery" (1949), they drop their stones and refuse. This incident is visually, psychologically, and politically powerful and empowering. It does not occur in *The Testaments*, which Atwood took in a different direction from the series—on which she was an advisor—although other forms of refusal and prevarication, disingenuity, lying, and subversion are rife. In the original book and television series this act expresses a form of female agency seen only under threat, threat of punishment for both speaking out and attempting escape, as it affected Offred (Elisabeth Moss). In the third season of the series the different ranks of women form an underground railway following the example of Harriet Tubman (1820–1913), who led African Americans to freedom in the North of the United States during slavery. Through this the Handmaids, working with the Marthas and one sole wife, enable the children to escape to Canada, represented as a country of peace and individuality up in the snowy North. Offred does not escape to the North, but her model is the positive agentic one they all emulate. Nor is Offred present in *The Testaments* except as a memory and example, in this horrendous purgatorial world. The freedoms expressed by women emerge from the three voices of those whose stories, whose testimonies we read: Offred's first daughter, Agnes/Jemima, by her husband Luke, the legendary baby Nicole/Daisy/"Jade," her daughter with Nick the chauffeur, a member of the underground, and, maybe most surprisingly, the iconic Aunt Lydia—played by Anne Dowd in the series—the violently and psychologically manipulative Aunt, of whose statue the toe (like that of Churchill's in the Houses of Parliament in the UK), is kissed by acolytes. Aunt Lydia's statue is her memorial (Stanley 2020) and, unlike her testament, a public representation of her power. Lydia herself is one of Atwood's "spotty-handed villainesses" from the eponymously named book (Atwood 2005), a bully, and a radical proto-feminist who tells her tale to indict her enemies but also to pass on other versions of events, and truths forbidden by the regime. In Gilead, women and girls are denied anything but domesticating education, reading is frowned upon and writing of any creative or critical kind forbidden. The oppression and silencing of women is rife, the norm in Gilead, which has all the characteristics of the denial of difference, the genocidal disappearance of those considered socially without value (Murphy 2006) or victims of an oppressive fascist state including Hitler's Nazi Germany which resembles Gilead with its "enthusiastic book-burnings that have been going on across our land" (Atwood 2019: 4). In Gilead it is considered that women were also incapable of responding to education, which was not "important for females to meddle with because they had smaller brains that were incapable of thinking" (2019: 15). Without reading and education there is little room for the imagination or a counterculture. Of the imaginative freedoms enabled by reading, by education beyond the domestic crafts, we are told that "boys could taste that freedom; only they could swoop and soar; only they could be" (2019: 16). The girls are curtailed. Without a counter-voice, resistance is difficult to imagine, construct, and enact and so they believe "Our minds were too weak for reading. We would crumble, we would fall apart under the contradictions" (2019: 304). They are silenced and unable to offer any form of witness or testimony as a result, as Aunt Lydia notes, which she secretly disobeys, and writes her own testimony, "[F]irst-hand narratives from Gilead are vanishingly rare—especially any concerning the lives of girls and women. It is hard for those deprived of literacy to leave such records" (2019: 412). Aunt Lydia, however, while maintaining an iron grasp on the girls' education and expression, exercises her own deviant and carnivalesque freedom of speech.

Aunt Lydia's secret journal is hidden in the leaves of a Cardinal Newman tract (appropriately, *Apologia Pro vita Sua* [1864], a defense of one's own life), in the library, from which women are banned, except for some of the Aunts, and some who aspire to be Aunts. Through her own abusive power and collusion and through her insider insights and occasional revelations and use of loopholes, Lydia speaks out and though she could well be found out and will certainly die (as punishment or naturally, of age), her strong female voice emerges as one of resistance, resilience, agency.

Purgatory and Trauma Testimony

In her work on trauma, *"Dear You": Witnessing Trauma in the World of The Handmaid's Tale* (2022), Caroline Wood argues that in her relationships between memory, intimacy, and witnessing trauma, June/Offred is bearing witness to trauma. We can also argue that her own testimonies and those of her daughters go beyond trauma to creative problem solving, embracing life, and a leap for freedom. Wood first traces Gilead's "abuse of memory, both individual and collective" (2022: 5). Next, she sees the television series as resembling a revenge tragedy, a way for June/Offred to manage trauma, which is then inherited by her daughters, Agnes and Nicole. The route of inherited trauma is damaging and dangerous, and bearing witness requires someone to listen and respond, a form of mutuality which only really happens in *The Testaments* when "for the very first time in *The Handmaid's Tale* universe, *The Testaments* also illustrates how witnessing for one another enables Agnes and Nicole to begin processing their trauma" (2022: 5). Offred has only her future listeners to share her trauma and testimony with, and like sending a message in a bottle she has no idea if there will be a respondent let alone one who understands her. Arguably Prof James Darcy Peixoto, going through, interpreting, and lecturing on the tapes many years later, does not witness or understand, and misinterprets with a patriarchal scholarly distance, as he no doubt will when he responds to Aunt Lydia's hidden testament upon its discovery. However, in the world of these books and then of the television show, audiences can access Offred's testimony and witness her trauma and the way she deals with it. Over the years, since the publication of *The Handmaid's Tale*, many of us, even those who saw the novel as far-fetched, can appreciate her predicament. While the fundamentalist religious far right regimes of (parts of) the Middle East might have set Atwood off on her painful, scathing revelations about Gilead, Gilead was also based on the seventeenth-century United States in which fundamentalist religious settlers escaped repression in Europe only to establish and deal out their own extremism in new Puritan and other religious-based settlements and regimes. It is, however, repression, brutality, and hypocrisy that Atwood denounces and so the hypocritical repression of some religious and other fundamentalist or totalitarian regimes rather than religion in itself. As she notes of *The Handmaid's Tale*: "the book is not 'antireligion.' It is against the use of religion as a front for tyranny; which is a different thing altogether" (Atwood 2017: n.p.). It is, however, also anti-repression and anti-sexist. In 2022, it is still the case that in some of the Middle East and some parts of Asia women are veiled, kept indoors under what might well resemble house arrest, ostensibly to preserve their purity and guarantee their domestic and child-bearing role. In 2022 in the United States, meanwhile, the repeal of Roe vs Wade (1973) has in many states flung away women's rights to make decisions about their own bodies and, however painful, about abortion. Gilead is never far away, even today.

Atwood testifies to the historical probity and the unwelcome longevity of some of the most brutal repressive and silencing regimes and specific acts in history when she notes of *The Handmaid's Tale*, and before *The Testaments* was written:

> [I]t's an antiprediction: If this future can be described in detail, maybe it won't happen. But such wishful thinking cannot be depended on either.
>
> So many different strands fed into *The Handmaid's Tale* (1985)—group executions, sumptuary laws, book burnings, the Lebensborn program of the

SS and the child-stealing of the Argentine generals, the history of slavery, the history of American polygamy... the list is long.

(Atwood 2017: n.p.)

The Handmaid's Tale and *The Testaments* each emerge from, and testify to, the damage done by trauma (Luckhurst 2008; Nordini 2016). Much trauma narrative grows from the destruction caused by legacies of war, including the literary legacy of the First World War in poetry and prose, of the genocide of the Holocaust and racist genocide of Transatlantic slavery. There is also trauma that springs from misogyny, the abuse and debasement of women. Recent narratives that testify to this include for example Eimar McBride's *A Girl Is a Half Formed Thing* (2013), in which trauma brought about by abuse from Girl's uncle leads her to abjection, perceived self-worthlessness, and her eventual suicide. Trauma narratives by and for women often focus on bodily abuse, sexual violence, rape, or on the death of infants. Toni Morrison's *Beloved* (1987) gathers together all of these, in a context of the trauma of slavery. Deborah Madsen (2011) builds on the work of Dominick LaCapra (1994) and reports of experience of the Holocaust when she warns of the problems of autobiographical writing about trauma which can normalize or assimilate these personal reports, and where she is concerned that:

> A historical juxtapositioning of the autobiographical with the fictional leads to "normalising" of traumatic experience ... The untranslatability of trauma makes survivor discourse especially reliant upon cultural scripting for its own meaning, even when it may resist these cultural ideologies.
>
> (Madsen 2011: 6)

Commenting on the importance of bearing witness to trauma to make sense of it before re-entering the community, Susan Brison notes:

> Piecing together a shattered self requires a process of remembering and working through in which speech and affect converge in a trauma narrative. Saying something about the trauma does nothing to it, the communicative act of bearing witness to traumatic events not only transforms traumatic memories into narratives that can then be integrated into the survivor's sense of self and view of the world, but it also reintegrates the survivor into community, re-establishing bonds of trust and faith in others.
>
> (Brison 2003: x–xi)

As part of the purgatorial moment and the purgatorial world, Aunt Lydia, Daisy/Nicole, and Agnes/Jemima inhabit, they must bear witness to their own and others' painful (or in Lydia's case pain-giving) experiences through spoken and written testimony, telling their own and sometimes others' stories through the vehicle of the novel, and specifically through Aunt Lydia's secret writings. In some texts, ghosts might embody or re-enact trauma and so enable those they haunt to cope, confront, and move on (Caruth 1995). However, in *The Testaments*, there are no Gothic ghosts, only other more solid traces in memory, monuments, testaments, tales retold, re-shaped, passed on and in notes secreted in religious tracts, in plain sight. Offred is a trace and a memory while Nicole, Agnes, and Aunt Lydia are very much alive, creating different versions of testimony and witnessing, the young women for each other, Aunt Lydia on the entire history of Gilead, those she is protecting, including herself and those who will be brought to some form of punishment once her witness testaments have been found, after her death. It is the stories of those who succeed and survive which last, as Aunt Lydia knows, and she ensures she is a victor in her testament.

Lydia is a legacy from a very dark past as she initially led the re-programming of the handmaids-to-be in *The Handmaid's Tale* (1985) and her modus operandi was in those days physical brutality and controlling mind games. However, she gradually shows she is managing her own testimony, her own testament, in this purgatorial world. The two young women, Nicole and Agnes, born of the new generation, have very different perspectives and upbringings. It is their growing mutual understanding which partly enables the tone of the text to change from the threat and hopelessness of *The Handmaid's Tale* through the dangerous querying and struggle for some form of free speech and alternative ways of living in the television series, into the relative honesty and hope of *The Testaments*, where this purgatorial world, it seems, can be eventually purged and possibly there might be a more honest and positive future. Witnessing to and testifying about their own different histories and values and worldviews enables the two young women to begin to understand each other.

Testaments: A Comic Form and Hopeful Futures

The Testaments, in following the hellish world of *The Handmaid's Tale*, resembles "*The Purgatorio*" the middle part of Dante's *The Divine Comedy*, and Margaret Atwood uses a full range of the broadest understanding of comedy to manage the novel's trajectory through testimony of trauma, an existence in a purgatorial world, to revival and hope. We will look at some of the variety of her comic energies, from satire and irony, to farce and then focus on the contestatory, survival, and celebratory energies of comedy in this Purgatorial world, which in form, action, and trajectory resembles both a Shakespearean comedy, principally *Twelfth Night* (1600–2), and a late romance, *The Tempest* (1611).

Atwood's comic range is both functional and delightful. The Marthas cooking and talking about marriage and the infertility of the wives in the kitchens of Gilead are hilarious. They spring straight from a sit-com:

> "Better them than us," said Zilla. "They can never have husbands," said Rosa. "Not that I'd want one myself, but still. Or babies either. They can't have those." "They're too old anyway," said Vera. "All dried up." "The crust's ready," said Zilla.
> (Atwood 2019: 238)

Discussing Atwood's humor as using satire, parody, and a low form of burlesque "involving a recurrent gap between a lofty subject and the low register of language depicting it" (Dvorak 2021: 124), Marta Dvorak argues that "Atwood favours grotesque realism" (2021: 125) which clarifies how she moves between registers in her comic writing so the serious is undermined by the banal and ridiculous, and in this case the "dried up" infertility of the wives is directly compared to a pie "crust." Further, the confusions, alternative opportunities, and new solidarities embodied in the friendship of the half-sisters in *The Testaments* resemble the dangers, life affirming muddle, truths, and resolutions of *Twelfth Night* (1600–2) and, as I shall argue, also Shakespeare's late romance, *The Tempest* (1611).

As with their mother, June/Offred, the half-sisters Daisy/Nicole/"Jade," and Agnes/Jemima, each have more than one name, don disguises, and play a variety of roles to fit into the societies and scenarios in which they find themselves. This use of name change, disguise, role play resembles such activities in for example *The Merry Wives of Windsor* (1597–1601) and *A Comedy of Errors* (1589–94), with all the confusions and misrecognitions sometimes enabling escapes and resolutions of persona and social difficulties. In *Twelfth Night*, the noble, shipwrecked twins, Viola and Sebastian seem lost at sea, but through disguise, gender swopping, and an ability to fit into whatever positions and interactions present themselves, they deal with this traumatic experience and emerge anew into positive relationships, each falling in love and bringing a vital reason for life to their new noble partners. The comic heart of the play is also part of its purgatorial heart, the spiteful toying with pompous Malvolio, an alarming managed cruelty at the core of that moment of misrule, twelfth night, when he is imprisoned and tormented in what begins as a jest, which undermines his self-esteem and with it his identity. This amused managed cruelty is also very much the tenor of Aunt Lydia's control over the women under her rule in latter day Gilead, her control over approved memory, and over her own revelatory written versions and comments she keeps to control the future. In the purgatorial world of *The Testaments*, mirroring the cruel, critical, dangerous fun seen in *Twelfth Night* is Aunt Lydia's attempt at exposing everything of the regime and her own seemingly obedient, yet totally controlling self-serving and self-preserving actions.

Although revenge lies at its heart, *The Tempest* is near tragedy yet has the healing resolution of comedy. Prospero's loss of power, the enslavement of Caliban and Ariel, fear for the next generation, should Miranda's idealized innocence be threatened, and Ferdinand drowned in the tempest, give way to catharsis and the beginning of calmer order. Prospero forgives his enemies, his brother Antonio who usurped him, and Alonso and Sebastian, and Ariel is freed. Traumatic histories are faced, revenge is curtailed, and the union of Ferdinand and Miranda provides resolution and promise of continuity.

In similar vein to the above two examples, there is an energetic excess and a balance of diverse views in Atwood's novel which embodies/dramatizes the generosity of the comic spirit, but which also suggests the more biblical version of testaments in offering differing versions of events. The energies offered in *The Testaments* by different perspectives from Aunt Lydia, Daisy/Nicole, and Agnes/Jemima suggest opportunities for querying, altering, undermining, and exposing the controlling lies of the past, and for positive change in the present, for being other than single mindedly repressive and or repressed in word and deed. The richness of these revealing testaments can help to settle the trauma of the past and offer a life-affirming variety which derives in part from there being not just one firmly imposed but several versions of events.

This is the energy of comedy, however dark it might be. In her own testament, Aunt Lydia's tone about the ostensible importance and representational nature of her statue – treated as if a religious shrine by some – and her theft of the votive food gifts to the statue, evidence life energies bursting out from the constrained controlled history, repressed present and future. The voices of the three women, and the energies of writing an alternative history, kept secret in a religious sanctified space are the low energies of ridicule of the life-denying and the pompous through use of the burlesque, and the riotous, alternative, energies of a reaction against oppression, the carnivalesque (Bakhtin 1984).

Canada, Gilead, and Atwood

Margaret Atwood deliberately juxtaposes Canada, her home, Toronto and where she both studied and has established her archives (Thomas Fisher Rare Book Library, University of Toronto), with the brutal, misogynistic, fundamentalist state of Gilead, a dystopian version of the United States and particularly of Harvard, Massachusetts where she took her master's degree at Radcliffe College, in 1962. While Harvard is central to *The Handmaid's Tale* since it is over its walls that the hooded figures of those speaking out against the Gilead regime hang and dangle, a warning to maintain the rules and silences imposed by the regime, Canada always features as an alternative place of freedom and safety. It is impossible to reach Canada in *The Handmaid's Tale,* although Offred, climbing into the back of the car at the novel's end, hopes she will get there, to her husband and child. In the television series women of all types and roles show solidarity in uniting to enable escapees across the border, and Canada, home to Offred's child baby Nicole, is both a liberated place of safety and one from which revolutionary energies travel to explore and undermine Gilead from within. Hope and alternative worldviews might come from Canada, but they need to find fertile ground in Gilead itself to be able to encourage and feed counter-revolutionary energies. Fascist states impose a lockdown of the mind and its creative expression. Even thinking otherwise is dangerous should your thoughts be given away by a slip of the tongue, a note of paper or confiding in the wrong person. However, *The Testaments* offers some hope. Those controlled and expressing utter devotion, even wielding the worst violence in the name of fascistic states, can, if Aunt Lydia is to be taken seriously, think and speak in oppositional ways sometimes. Through the energies of an insider, carnivalesque disrespect can subtly take control of the story, creating engagement and suggesting the potential to develop and reward alternative expressions and actions. Alternative perspectives and voices of dissent can lurk in the most committed of a regime. In *The Testaments* it emerges quite early on that Aunt Lydia is one such counter-voice, unlikely though this seems given her sadistic commitment to violent control of mind and body in her training of the handmaids. Collusion leads to survival. However, should the moment of truth arrive, the ultimate intention of some of her testaments which undermine received values and versions of events might only be to save her own skin, by pointing the finger at those in power.

These testaments serve also, though, as a very tangible piece of evidence that the human spirit can overcome the worst oppression and violence that humans impose on humans. From within her history of power, lies, and cruelty, Aunt Lydia can render ridiculous the very acts of the regime which keep her in her position in Gilead, exposing others while expressing a darkly comic energy through ironic comment on her own deified position, and on the craven lauding of her and the world maintained by the laws of the regime. Through the secret content and intent of her testaments, we are exposed by Lydia herself to her insider information about the cruelties she has carried out, the evils she has upheld and because of this she emerges as both a real member of the dark side of a regime and the one who will ensure that dirt will fly and that those in power will be punished.

Testimony is a necessary response to centuries of silencing and a social habit of ignoring, denying experience. But even testimony is not confined to the factual, historical detail of events. Feelings, hopes, desires, fears are a part of lived experience, and the fantastic, imaginative lives of people explored, voiced, are dramatized in the speculative, the mythic, the Gothic. In *The Handmaid's Tale*, The *Maddaddam* trilogy especially *Oryx and Crake* (2003–13) and *The Testaments*, testimony enables some sort of salvaging from the troubled moments of past and future, where, to quote Aunt Lydia, the "corrupt and blood-smeared fingerprints of the past must be wiped away to create a clean space for the morally pure" (Atwood 2019: 4). Lydia's role here is witnessing, writing, testifying. She acknowledges that it is possible that "all my efforts will prove futile, and Gilead will last for a thousand years" (2019: 277). However, "[s]ome days I see myself as the Recording Angel, collecting together all the sins of Gilead, including mine; on other days I shrug off this high moral tone" (2019: 277). But she is writing to reveal, and in doing so hopefully to topple the regime since "[e]veryone at the top of Gilead has lied to us" (2019: 304). Testimony, testaments are invaluable and vulnerable, and need both writer and reader, as well as some form of conservation. The potential is always there for obliteration of the truth and history telling, the reading and the potential to act on what is read. Lydia in a moment of power threatens: "I would destroy these pages I have written so laboriously; and I would destroy you along with them, my future reader. One flare of a match and you'll be gone—wiped away as if you had never been" (2019: 317).

Testaments are powerful.

Conclusion

In talking about *The Handmaid's Tale* and predicting the work that followed it, Margaret Atwood clarifies the roles of testaments, testimony, witnessing to trauma, and so acknowledgment which can hopefully lead to decisions and positive change.

She emphasizes the creative energies of a range of forms of writing including in the main that of comedy, but also fantasy, sci-fi, dystopian fictions, and Gothic fictions. While her use of comedy, in the broadest sense, resembles

Shakespearean comedy, specifically here *Twelfth Night*, leading to resolution, this mixture of darkness and creative light also resembles that in Shakespeare's late romances, specifically *The Tempest,* which through expressing the worst can release the creative energies to plan ahead and prevent the very worst. This is a positive creative energy which has to first engage and witness the darkness and while the darkness of *The Handmaid's Tale* can only be shared years later when picked over as a historical artifact. Witnessing is crucial as Atwood notes:

> But there's a literary form I haven't mentioned yet: the literature of witness. Offred records her story as best she can; then she hides it, trusting that it may be discovered later, by someone who is free to understand it and share it. This is an act of hope: Every recorded story implies a future reader. Robinson Crusoe keeps a journal. So did Samuel Pepys, in which he chronicled the Great Fire of London. So did many who lived during the Black Death, although their accounts often stop abruptly. So did Roméo Dallaire, who chronicled both the Rwandan genocide and the world's indifference to it. So did Anne Frank, hidden in her secret annex.
>
> (Atwood 2017: n.p.)

The positive energies of *The Testaments* lie in the power of witness, and of the comic rather than tragic or spirit of revenge which drive the novel, expressed through the three female perspectives, moving beyond the confines of a single voice sent off on a tape into a possibly blank future. This comic form in itself allows these perspectives for something more generous and diverse, part of the essentially comic energy of the novel which like Atwood's *Maddaddam* trilogy offers some resolution in its diverse perspectives and its energies. The novel can be seen to suggest validation of a variety of histories of the silenced, and of the power of being able to write, express, share, and read a testimony of women's lives. Aunt Lydia understands the power of individual testimony, witnessing, and of writing, though the writing she covertly produces is itself silenced and banned in Gilead. She notes: "The collective memory is notoriously faulty, and much of the past sinks into the ocean of time to be drowned forever; but once in a while the waters part, allowing us to glimpse a flash of hidden treasure" (Atwood 2019: 415).

This is a novel offering some form of hope beyond the, seemingly, purgatorial present. In an interview for *Time* magazine, Margaret Atwood responded to questions about the green cover (she used crayons, green looked preferable to red, and says green suggested hope) and the title of the novel:

> Atwood has a three-pronged answer to this question, drawing on the structure of the novel—which is told by three narrators—and the religious aspects of

Gilead. "It has several different meanings: last will and testament, Old and New Testaments. And what does a witness give? A testimony, but also a testament," she says. "So it's those three: the witness, the will and 'I'm telling you the truth.'"

(Feldman 2019)

Green is for hope. Perhaps that exists through and beyond the comic and purgatorial world of *The Testaments*. Like the endings of Shakespeare's late romances, testimony, comedy, generosity, and forgiveness could be a way forward from the lies, silencing, disappearances, and darkness. If we are complacent that none of this could happen here, we are reminded at the novel's end that it did and it still does: "axioms of the novel: no event is allowed into it that does not have a precedent in human history. Every published book is a group effort" (Acknowledgements 418).

Even in Gilead, not everything should be wiped away. Nicole and Agnes come to terms with this when Nicole asks Agnes:

"You think that festering shitheap can be renewed?" I said. "Burn it all down!" "Why would you want to harm so many people?" she asked gently. "It's my country. It's where I grew up. It's being ruined by the leaders. I want it to be better." "Yeah, okay," I said. "I get it. Sorry. I didn't mean you. You're my sister." "I accept your apology," she said.

(Atwood 2019: 379)

There is then, in addition to Lydia's honesty and dark revelations, also a spirit of generosity which can feed into developing something beyond the constraints of Gilead, especially enriched by the knowledge that there is an alternative lifestyle not far away. Nicole has traveled between the two places to take testimony between them and to witness each. Ultimately, the investment in the potential for telling the story, it being heard, and for mutual understanding, and for rescuing something from the messiness of history, dominates the novel as it moves beyond purgatory and suggests, if not paradise, then at least a more positive balanced future. Aunt Lydia has a last word here, aware of the power of time and the vitality of the comic form when she says, "Time wounds all heels. Patience is a virtue. Vengeance is mine" (Atwood 2019: 251).

Works Cited

Alighieri, D. (1955), "Purgatorio," in D. L. Sayers (trans.), *The Divine Comedy [1308–20]*, London: Penguin Books.

Atwood, M. (1985), *The Handmaid's Tale*, Toronto: Fawcett Crest.
Atwood, M. (2003), *Oryx and Crake*, New York: Nan A. Talese.
Atwood, M. (2005), "Spotty-Handed Villainesses: Problems of Female Bad Behaviour in the Creation of Literature," in *Curious Pursuits: Occasional Writing 1970–2005*, London: Virago.
Atwood, M. (2009), *The Year of the Flood*, London: Bloomsbury.
Atwood, M. (2013), *MaddAddam*, London: Bloomsbury.
Atwood, M. (2017), "Margaret Atwood 'What *The Handmaid's Tale* Means in the Age of Trump,'" *The New York Times*, March 10, 2017. https://www.nytimes.com/2017/03/10/books/review/margaret-atwood-handmaids-tale-age-of-trump.html.
Atwood, M. (2019), *The Testaments*, London: Chatto and Windus.
Bakhtin, M. (1984), *Rabelais and His World*, London: John Wiley & Sons.
Brison, S. J. (2003), *Aftermath: Violence and the Remaking of a Self*, Princeton: Princeton University Press.
Caruth, C. (1995), *Trauma: Explorations in Memory*, Baltimore and London: The Johns Hopkins University Press.
Dvorak, M. (2021), "Margaret Atwood's Humor," in C. A. Howells (ed.), *The Cambridge Companion to Margaret Atwood*, Cambridge: Cambridge University Press.
Feldman, L. (2019), "Let's Break Down the Most Mysterious Parts of *The Testaments*, with a Little Help from Margaret Atwood," *Time*, September 10. https://time.com/5673535/the-testaments-plot-questions-margaret-atwood/.
Handmaid's Tale, The (2017–present), created by B. Miller, Beverley Hills: MGM Television.
LaCapra, D. (1994), *Representing the Holocaust: History, Theory, Trauma*, Ithaca, N.Y.: Cornell University Press.
Luckhurst, R. (2008), *The Trauma Question*, London: Routledge.
Madsen, D. (2011), "Teaching Trauma: (Neo) Slave Narratives and Cultural (Re) memory," in G. Wisker (ed.), *Teaching African American Women's Writing*, 60–74, Basingstoke: Palgrave Macmillan.
McBride, E. (2013), *A Girl Is a Half Formed Thing*, Norwich: Galley Beggar Press.
Merriam-Webster dictionary online. https://www.merriam-webster.com/dictionary/purgatory.
Murphy, F. (2006), *Trauma Trails, Stolen Generations, and The Ethics of an Authenticity of Suffering*, Erasmus Intensive Programme, Vienna, July 22–August 2, Institut für Kultur und Sozialanthropologie, Hs A.
Newman, J. H. (1864), *Apologia Pro Vita Sua*, London: Longman, Green; Longman, Roberts and Green.
Nordini, G. (2016), *Haunted by History: Interpreting Traumatic Memory through Ghosts in Film and Literature*, All Regis University Theses, 798, https://epub-lications.regis.edu/theses/798.
Shakespeare, W. (1623), *Twelfth Night*, First Folio, London: Edward Blount and William and Isaac Jaggard.

Shakespeare, W. (1623), *The Tempest*, First Folio, London: Edward Blount and William and Isaac Jaggard.
Stanley, L. (2020), *Remaking Memory: On Statues and Memorials*, www.whiteswritingwhiteness.ed.ac.uk/Reading-Lists/memory-statues/.
Thomson, I. (2018), *Dante's Divine Comedy: A Journey without End*, London: Head of Zeus.
Wisker, G. (2011), *Margaret Atwood, an Introduction to Critical Views of Her Fiction*, London: Palgrave Macmillan.
Wisker G. (2021), "Margaret Atwood and History," in C. A. Howells (ed.), *A Cambridge Companion to Margaret Atwood*, Cambridge: Cambridge University Press.
Wisker, G. (2022), *Contemporary Women's Ghost Stories: Spectres, Revenants, Ghostly Returns*, Basingstoke: Palgrave Macmillan.
Wood, C. (2022), "'Dear You': Witnessing Trauma in the World of *The Handmaid's Tale*," BA diss., Bates College, Lewiston, Maine.

Part Four

Spaces of Female Resistance

11

Of Monstrous Spaces: Female Identity in *American Horror Story: Murder House* and *American Horror Story: Hotel*

Pembe Gözde Erdogan

Regarded by some scholars and critics as depraved, trivial, and harmful, horror actually carries a critical and subversive potential. In employing the monster as culture's Other, horror's "true subject," as Robin Wood claims, is "the struggle for recognition of all that our civilization represses or oppresses" (1979: 10). For Wood, all the othered identities within the heteronormative patriarchal society are represented in horror: women, children, lower classes, ethnic groups, and different sexualities. Isabel Pinedo maintains that in contemporary postmodern horror, which involves a questioning of reality, a transgression of boundaries, and a disruption of the everyday world, women are very prominent, both as victims and as heroes (1997: 5, 16). Horror's relationship to female identity is multiform. Many feminist film scholars have explored how horror depicts women as characters within the stories (victims, heroes, monsters) and appeals to them as spectators (Clover 1987; Creed 1993; Pinedo 1997; Williams 2002).

As a contemporary televisual horror show, *American Horror Story* (*AHS*) (2011–present) has given extensive space to the exploration of female identity in America throughout its, as of writing, ten seasons. As Amy King suggests, the show "consistently frames its horrors as American cultural norms that terrorize women" (2017: 557). This chapter aims to analyze how *AHS* explores the ideologies that make up female identity in America in two of its seasons, *AHS: Murder House* (S1, 2011) and *AHS: Hotel* (S5, 2015–16). In this analysis, gender identity is seen as expressed not only in the characters and themes of the seasons but also in their settings. Adopting a postmodern conception of "space," the article aims to dissect and analyze the purgatorial spaces of "the family home" and "the hotel" as "power geometries," symbolic structures of power created out of dynamic social relations (Massey 1994: 265). This study will borrow from diverse fields of scholarship in its exploration of space and identity; namely, feminism, post-structuralist psychoanalysis, postmodern geography, and anthropology. Michel Foucault's theorization of "heterotopias," Barbara Creed's concept of "the monstrous feminine," and Victor Turner's ideas on "liminality" will be used particularly.

AHS is one of the shows that reintroduced the anthology format to American television and its form has been appreciated by scholars for its subversive potential. Much has been said about the show's form and play with time and historicity. For Robert Sevenich, *AHS* is both "expansive" and "fleeting" in its nontraditional anthology format and its adoption of "the troupe theatre model," casting a core group of actors in diverse roles throughout its seasons (2015: 4). This allows space for multiple othered identities to be explored by the same actor. Also, the show's format is seen as performing "temporal drag" by Theresa Geller and Anna Marie Banker, queering the serial form through structural belatedness by incorporating horror's death drive (2017: 40). Each season travels to a different historical setting and within the seasons, flashbacks establish associations among timelines, disrupting the forward progression and exploring "the historicity of its diegetic present by enchaining it with the historical ('actual') past" (Geller and Banker 2017: 40).

This historicity, according to Harriet Earle and Jessica Clark, is one of the characteristics that makes the show about truly "American" horrors. *AHS* not only uses common horror tropes and themes but also blends them with figures from American history, creating a dark historiography of America and revealing the "cultural obsession with crime and depravity" (Earle and Clark 2019: 7). If we shift the focus from history/time to place/space, we see that the settings of *AHS* carry the same heritage of Americanness; they are both actual and symbolic spaces that are inscribed by the weight of this dark historicity. After all, most of the seasons in *AHS* also employ iconic and archetypal spaces, dwellings, and communities: the house, the asylum, the coven, the circus, the hotel, the village, the cult, the summer camp. Some of these settings—the asylum, the circus, and the summer camp—are chosen because they are "heterotopias," "counter-sites ... in which all the other real sites that can be found within the culture, are simultaneously represented, contested and inverted" (Foucault 1986: 24). The others, like the house or the village, are invested with layers of symbolic and archaic meanings through *AHS*'s horrific historicity.

Within the *AHS* multiverse, the two settings/spaces chosen for this study are both located in present-day Los Angeles (LA), the city of dreams; of possibilities;

of the self-made (wo)man. In this vein, LA can be seen as the quintessential American city. Located only a few miles apart, the house and the hotel are both haunted dwellings which have a strong hold on all the people who died within their confines. They are both symbolic power structures that problematize the tenets of American female identity, questioning woman's place between the private and public spheres. Furthermore, both dwellings are liminal, purgatorial spaces in which ghosts of the past are doomed to exist forever. Victor Turner, in his analysis of liminality in rituals, claims that liminal states have liberating powers since the individuals are pushed out of social structures and are free to play (1987 and 2011). For him, people in liminal stages are "in a close connection with asocial powers of life and death" and they are frequently compared to ghosts (1987: 27). *AHS*'s ghosts are forever stuck in a liminal state. As such, this chapter explores how the spaces of the house and the hotel within *AHS* might offer any potential for change or development for their liminal beings and for the understanding of female identity in America.

House as Necrotopia in *AHS: Murder House*

The first season of *AHS* has been a long-time fan favorite and one of the seasons that has been analyzed the most by scholars. *AHS: Murder House* (2011) appropriates many tropes and themes of the traditional haunted house narrative within horror, which foregrounds the house not just as the setting but as almost a separate character. The Harmon family is ideal site for the house's hauntings. The family members are dealing with the crisis of adultery, the scares of pregnancy, and a teenage daughter. Hence, they become perfect candidates to repeat or fall victim to the sins that have been plaguing the house ever since it was built in the LA suburbs in the 1920s. Spectators later learn that the house has "a hold" on everyone who dies within its boundaries and the ghosts in the house are stuck there forever. However, the spectral inhabitants of the house also have a power to make themselves known to the living since they continue to exist in their corporeality within the house. As the season starts a new family enters the house, and two of the three characters of this family can be seen as "liminal" beings full of potential for the future. Vivien (Connie Britton) gets pregnant soon after entering the house and her daughter Violet (Taissa Farmiga) is a teenager. Both are "threshold people," "betwixt and between" two stages in their lives, thus full of potentiality (Turner 1969: 95). In archaic and tribal societies, pregnancy was seen as the transitional period and pregnant women were excluded from the rest of the society during their pregnancy (van Gennep 1960: 41). Equally, in Western culture, the figure of the girl has been seen as "a harbinger of change and transformation" as she is a liminal being "both as a subject moving from juvenility to maturity, and as a hinge between old and new, present and future" (Munford and Waters 2014: 106–7). In *AHS*, however, instead of questioning and changing the ideologies that make up their white American middle-class female identity, both end up as victims to the lethal embrace of the nightmare of domesticity.

Throughout the season's twelve episodes, flashbacks reveal how each of the ghosts died in the house. The flashbacks display, as Dawn Keetley suggests, the dark "repetition" that lies at the heart of the house as "the past rewrites the present, exerting an inexorable shaping force" and lives "accumulate," "layered upon" by the families that lived there before them (2013: 90). What appears is a story of murder, rape, suicide, adulterous men, ineffective fathers, and dead and monstrous children. More importantly, what emerges is the story of women: teenagers, young women, wives, mothers, maids. It is a story of violence and horror at the heart of domesticity reflected in the unhappy and cruel lives of these women and in the dark and evil domestic space of the house. In many ways *AHS: Murder House* can be seen as the televisual representation of Barbara Creed's concept of "the monstrous-feminine." Although this connection has been suggested by other scholars (Komsta 2014), it will be developed further here in order to grasp the ideological importance of the house as purgatorial space.

Using Julia Kristeva's theory of "the abject," Creed outlines how, in horror, female monsters are created by patriarchal ideology as a result of their sexual difference and in relation to their "mothering and reproductive functions" (1993: 7). The abject is "the place where meaning collapses" and it must be "radically excluded" (Kristeva 1982: 2). Creed emphasizes that the concept of border is crucial in horror as monsters represent the abject by crossing fundamental borders between self/other, life/death, human/nonhuman, and so on. Kristeva ties the abject to the female body and to the mother. For her, "[t]he clean and proper body" of the patriarchal symbolic order must not show any of its "debt to nature," to bodily fluids or anatomical functions. As the female body, through its maternal functions, cannot hide this debt, it signifies the abject (1982: 102). Furthermore, for Kristeva, the psyche also marks the mother as abject during our attempts to break away from her as her body becomes "a site of conflicting desires" (Creed 1993: 11). Thus, Creed sees notions of "the material female body" and its maternal functions as central to the concept of the monstrous in horror.

AHS: Murder House is a story of monstrous motherhood, played out in the lives of its characters and epitomized in the house as the locus of stasis and death. The two living mothers of the house represent different sides of the monstrous-feminine mother. Vivien Harmon is the disgruntled wife who is oppressed within the confines of her marriage and within the patriarchal medical profession that seeks to imprison her. While one of her twins is stillborn, representing her stilted life, the other is the ultimate evil-in-human-form, the Anti-Christ. Constance Langdon (Jessica Lange) is the perfect pre-oedipal, sadistic mother. Narcissistic and over-bearing, she refuses to let go of her hold on her children. As the mother of physically and psychologically deformed and diseased children, she can be seen as the Norma Bates of the murder house.[1] The ghosts of Nora Montgomery (Lily Rabe) and Hayden McClaine (Kate Mara) are mothers stuck in perpetual search and yearning for their dead children. We also briefly meet Lorraine Harvey (Rebecca Wisocky), who kills her daughters and herself after her husband's infidelity.

The abject experiences of these mothers and women bind them to the most abject being in the show, the House. As Marta Komsta suggests, the House is the perfect representation of the archaic mother (2014), described by Creed as "the generative …, pre-phallic mother," "the parthenogenetic mother," the "shadowy" figure, the primordial abyss that "threatens to reabsorb what it once birthed" (1993: 20, 25, 27). Kristeva claims that "fear of the archaic mother turns out to be essentially fear of her generative power" (1982: 77). As Creed analyzes the ancient connection made between woman, womb, and the monstrous, she draws on Freud's concept the uncanny to show how the haunted houses in horror are representations of the archaic mother, invoking our connection to our former home, the womb. She suggests that "the symbolization of the womb as house/room/cellar or any other enclosed space is central to the iconography of the horror film" (1993: 55).

AHS: Murder House establishes a link between the house and the female body from its first episode. Vivien's gynecologist compares her aging female body to a house: "Your body is like a house. You can fix the tiles and the bathroom and the kitchen but if the foundation is decaying, you're wasting your time" (E1). He urges her to take hormones in order to preserve the reproductive capabilities of her body. However, Vivien is more concerned with taking back "the control" over

---

[1] Norma is Norman Bates's overbearing mother in Alfred Hitchcock's horror classic *Psycho* (1960). The now-dead mother appears as the cause of her son's fragmented psyche, the true psycho behind her son's murders. Creed also analyzes this famous figure in her book as "the castrating mother" (1993: 139).

her body again after her miscarriage. Women, the female body, and the house itself are then primarily defined by their maternal, familial, and reproductive function. This superimposition of woman and the house is not peculiar to horror, however. Rebecca Munford and Melanie Waters note how the compound noun of "housewife" "weds woman to home, conjoining place and status in a way that implies an uncanny, reciprocal bleed between that which is alive (namely the 'wife') and that which is demonstrably inanimate (the 'house')" (2014: 85). It seems like in Western patriarchal ideology, the idealized domesticated female identity has been written onto the idealized enclosed domestic space of the house. These women are intentionally limited to the private space of the house like the ghosts that are doomed to inhabit its purgatorial space.

Moreover, as Komsta suggests, the basement of the house can be seen as "the symbolic womb," the setting where the house's original owner and creator did his Frankenstein-like experiments and stitched together his own dismembered son to create the house's first "unnatural progeny" (2014: 253–4). The basement is the place where the deformed children of the house (Beau [Sam Kinsey] and Infantata [Ben Woolf]) hide. It is also the place where the Infantata tortures others during scenes obscured from the audience's eyes by flashing lights and darkness. Creed claims that in horror, the womb is highlighted as "a place that is familiar and unfamiliar … through the presentation of monstrous acts which are only half glimpsed" (1993: 55). As such, the basement-as-womb, through its mystery, darkness, and its status as the vessel for the house's dead children, strengthens the metaphor of the house as the mother.

The association between house/woman/womb reaches its culmination point in the season's penultimate episode "Birth." As Vivien gives birth in the house's living room with the help of the ghosts of the house, the implication becomes clear that it is both Vivien and the house that are giving birth. As Vivien's child with her husband dies and she herself dies, her other child, created as a result of her rape by one of the house's ghosts, lives. This monstrous birth by the house cements its status as the archaic mother, who, in its archaic fertility, gives birth to the ultimate agent of evil. It is in the same episode that the medium Billie Dean Howell (Sarah Paulson) describes the house as containing "the evil." She makes associations between the house and heterotopias of prisons and asylums, where "negative energy feeds on trauma and pain" (E11). The birth of the Anti-Christ can be seen as the result of the house's need to "break through" and "move in our world" (E11).

In its association with evil, the house is ultimately associated with death. Keetley calls this "entropic Gothic," a relentless trajectory toward "exhaustion, stasis, dissipation and death" (2013: 89). For her, through its repetitions of events and themes, the show signals toward "sameness, undifferentiation and extinction" (2013: 92). Creed claims that the omnipresence of death in horror harkens us back to the archaic mother as all-encompassing. Death signifies, according to Creed, "a desire to return to the state of original oneness with the mother," a return to the womb (1993: 28). Thus, since it constantly drives its inhabitants toward sameness and death, the house here is the ultimate archaic mother.

House is an archaic space as seen in its inherent equivalences in the series of house=woman=death. However, it is also an actual brick-and-mortar place, a prime real-estate located in the wealthy suburbs of LA. As such, it also represents the middle-class American dream and what people are willing to sacrifice in order to play a part in that dream. It is important to note that most of the women in the show are white and upper-middle-class (with the exception of Moira [Frances Conroy], the maid, who is also white). Susanna Rosenbaum suggests that "in the United States, ideas about good and desired mothers follow ethnic and racial stratifications," where white women are supposed to be have children while reproductivity in other ethnicities is seen as something that needs to be controlled (2017: 13). In *AHS*, this obsession with white upper-class motherhood seems to be criticized as something decaying.

The Murder House is also a simulacrum, as Keetley suggests, an attraction in the "Murder Tour," showing America's obsession with crime and depravity (2013: 92). This was the only season of *AHS* which was given its name by its fans. "Murder House" is the name of the season's third episode where Vivien sees the tour bus in front of her house and decides to explore the bloody history of the house. Thus, the name of the house comes from its name in the "L.A. Murder Tour" and the "Murder House" is an archaic and cultural space that imprisons its characters to an existence in the border between reality and simulation; to a purgatorial plane between life and death; to an existence of stasis, sameness, and need.

In his seminal work, "Of Other Spaces," Michel Foucault claims that "the anxiety of our era has to do fundamentally with space" (1986: 23). He says:

> The space in which we live, which draws us out of ourselves, in which the erosion of our lives, our time and our history occurs, the space that claws and gnaws at us, is also, in itself, a heterogeneous space. In other words, we do not live in a kind of void, inside of which we could place individuals and things ... we live inside a set of relations that delineates sites which are irreducible to one another.
> (1986: 23)

The Murder House, as the space that "claws and gnaws at" its inhabitants, as the space in which their lives literally erode, is also made out of the "set of relations" that define the American nuclear family. Rejecting the idealized connotations of "the home" as safe, permanent, and nurturing, the Murder House reveals the family home as a space of confinement, conformity, violence, and death—maybe not a heterotopia but a *necrotopia*. By laying similar stories on top of one another, *AHS* achieves the concept of what Doreen Massey calls "space-time," stretching out the social relations over time onto a spatial plane. She suggests that "since social relations are inevitably and everywhere imbued with power and meaning and symbolism, ... the spatial is ... an ever-shifting social geometry of power and signification" (1994: 2, 3). The "architectural palimpsest" of the house in *AHS*, this "site of compressed temporality," thus shows how social relations within the American middle-class nuclear family eliminate any potential for change and growth for women within this institution (Munford and Waters 2014: 102). The Murder House is an embodiment of Henri Lefebvre's dictum that "space is political and ideological"—"a product literally filled with ideologies" (1976: 31). As such, the dead zone of the house becomes a purgatorial cage for all the female identities trapped within the confines of American white middle-class ideologies of ideal womanhood and motherhood.

Heterotopia of Potential in *AHS: Hotel*

Watching *AHS: Hotel* (2015–16) four years after *Murder House*, audiences revisit present-day LA at a totally different ideological locale that leads to both spaces acquiring a new social dimension in comparison to each other. The fifth season of *AHS* takes place in Hotel Cortez in downtown LA, an art-deco-style remnant of the old days of Hollywood now overrun with addicts and criminals. Compared to the show's first season, this season has been criticized for having loose and superficial plotlines and for being style over substance (Hale 2015). No doubt the casting of pop icon Lady Gaga as the vampire character "the Countess" has played a part in these critiques. For this study, however, *AHS: Hotel* will be seen as more than its stylized aesthetics. Through its casting of Lady Gaga, its character of Liz Taylor (Denis O'Hare) and its exploration of the heterotopic space of the hotel, the fifth season of *AHS* opens up a potential space for change in our understanding of female identity. *AHS: Hotel* queers the notions of both "space" and "identity" by choosing to focus on decidedly and proudly liminal spaces and liminal identities.

The spaces of the Murder House and the Hotel Cortez have a lot in common and this is highlighted by the show. The fourth episode of both seasons takes place during Halloween; while the ghosts of the Murder House can leave the house only at Halloween night, ghosts from outside can only visit the hotel during "Devil's night," the night before Halloween, October 30, marked with vandalism, arson, and mischief in American history. In a flashback, we watch the Countess go to the Murder House for an abortion in the 1920s but she ends up giving birth to a deformed vampiric baby. Both the Murder House and Hotel Cortez were built during the 1920s by corrupt men.[2] In the first episode, we hear a character refer to the hotel as "dead zone" because Wi-Fi does not work there. Indeed, like the Murder House, the hotel is a vortex of death, imprisoning everyone who died within its boundaries to its confines. We are told that time makes a different journey at the hotel as five years go by in a day. The power of the hotel "makes you lose your compass. Your sense of yourself" and just like the other iconic hotel in California "you don't get to leave" (E6). Added to the mix of our old formula of ghosts and human beings are vampires; these vampires are infected with an ancient blood virus that gives them a supercharged immune system. They do not get old but they can be killed; they do not have fangs but instead cut their victims to drink from them. Thus, *AHS: Hotel* takes on another type of liminal monster along with the ghosts.

On a general level, *AHS: Hotel* shows its contemporary America to be a land of addiction and crime. Most characters start with an intense need which turns into addiction (for blood, drugs, love, murder). Many of the ghostly characters in the season are made up of famous serial killers who get together every year on Devil's Night in the room of James Patrick March (Evan Peters), a prolific killer who built Hotel Cortez as his "perfectly designed torture chamber" (E2). This character is based on America's most prolific serial killer H. H. Holmes and Hotel Cortez is inspired by his murder castle.[3] Another iconic American building that inspired the hotel is the infamous Cecil Hotel in downtown LA, known for its violent history.[4] During Devil's Night celebrations, James March

---

[2] According to *AHS* lore, the Murder House was built in 1922 by the surgeon Charles Montgomery as a gift for his wife Nora. Addicted to ether, Charles performs illegal abortions on many women and then ends up insane and experiments on his own baby, creating the creature the Infantata. Similarly, Hotel Cortez was completed in 1926, built by James March (Evan Peters), a serial killer who creates the hotel to hide the bodies of his victims.

[3] Dr. H. H. Holmes is considered to be one of the first known American serial killers. He murdered many of his employees and fiancés in his hotel and collected their health insurance benefits. He is thought to have killed more than 200 man and women.

[4] The Cecil Hotel in downtown LA is seen as one of the most haunted hotels in America. The hotel saw at least sixteen murders and suicides and was, at one time, home to some serial killers like Richard Ramirez.

suggests that all the killers in the room (Dahmer, Gacy, Ramirez, Wuornos, Zodiac)[5] represent "the definition of American success." He says, "You've made your mark in history. Like the Iliad, your stories will live on forever" (E4). For Earle and Clark, this scene and the real-life inspirations for the hotel and the characters serve as "intriguing commentary" on violence and crime, exploring the darker side of American history (2019: 8).

When compared to the necrotopia that was the Murder House, the Hotel Cortez can be seen as a closer representation of Foucault's heterotopia. Foucault notes that some heterotopias are "capable of juxtaposing in a single real place several spaces, several sites that are in themselves incompatible" (1986: 25). The hotel is one of these transient spaces that combine the public sphere of the city life with the private sphere of enclosed rooms. As itself a liminal space, the hotel is fertile ground to negotiate female identity in regard to the private and the public. Moreover, Hotel Cortez serves a similar purpose to what Foucault labels "heterotopias of deviation," places like prisons, asylums, or retirement homes, where "individuals whose behavior is deviant in relation to the required mean or norm are placed" (1986: 25). Although a normal hotel would not fit this definition, since entrance to the hotel is voluntary, Hotel Cortez becomes the prison for many of the lost souls of America: outcasts, orphans, drug addicts, and criminals.

The season can be said to have the same obsession with motherhood and children, but it takes it to a campy, exaggerated place through its aesthetics and its use of vampires. This exaggerated notion of motherhood can be seen in the characters of Iris (Kathy Bates) and Alex (Chloë Sevigny). Iris is a frumpy, middle-aged woman who works at the hotel just to be close to her son Donovan (Matt Bomer), who is the Countess' lover. Donovan hates his mom intensely, but Iris continues to follow him everywhere he goes. When Donovan says he would rather "live with the addicts in the shitter's alley," Iris reminds him that she "gave [him] life" (E3). Alex, whose son is missing at the beginning of the season, finds her son turned into a vampire, and calls him as her "soulmate" (E3). Alex describes how she fell in love with her son as "a tectonic shift where everything I thought I knew about myself got rearranged" (E3). This highly

---

[5] Jeffrey Dahmer, also known as the Milwaukee Monster, murdered and dismembered seventeen men and boys between 1978 and 1991. John Wayne Gacy, the Killer Clown, raped, tortured, and murdered at least thirty-three men and boys. Richard Ramirez, the Night Stalker, terrorized California with his home invasions, murders, and sexual assaults within one year (1984–5). Aileen Wuornos shot dead and robbed seven of her clients while doing street prostitution in 1989. The never-caught Zodiac killer is thought to have killed around twenty-five people during the late 1960s although only five of his kills were confirmed.

romanticized notion of motherhood is multiplied in the figure of the hotel's master vampire, the Countess.

The Countess is not only a reproductive mother (she gives birth to a deformed vampire-baby) but she is also the nonreproductive mother who creates her progeny by letting them drink her blood. This symbolic blood suckling act signals the queer status of vampire as female monster and one that is seen to transgress gender boundaries. Creed points out that female vampire in horror is frequently represented as lesbian or bisexual, threatening to "undermine the formal and highly symbolic relations of men and women essential to the continuation of patriarchal society" (1993: 61). This is also true for the Countess, who takes on numerous lovers throughout her life, some men some women. For Creed, the female vampire "draws attention to the female blood cycle" and "reduces her captives to a state of embryonic dependency in which they must suckle blood in order to live" (1993: 83). In this formula, the vampire's lovers are also her children, and the mother vampire becomes another representation of the sadistic pre-oedipal mother who refuses to let go of her lover/child. Thus, the female vampire violates the taboo of incest and is a transgression of normative motherhood with her almost always queer identity.

The casting of Lady Gaga in the role of the Countess is also significant in the queering of female identity. Lady Gaga's "neon noir" aesthetic and her status as the "Mother Monster" outside the *AHS* universe strongly influenced her casting for this season and the styles of the hotel.[6] Foregrounding weirdness and the monstrous in her celebrity identity, Gaga can be seen as "an important contemporary figure in the expression of queer identity in terms of the perverse, the misshapen, and the abstruse" (Geczy and Karaminas 2017: 713). She is "Goth-femme, predator and parasite" (Geczy and Karaminas 2017: 714). In his book *Gaga Feminism*, Jack Halberstam suggests that Lady Gaga is a symbol for a new kind of feminism in the twenty-first century. For him, this feminism is "simultaneously a monstrous outgrowth of the unstable concept of 'woman' in feminist theory, a celebration of the joining of femininity to artifice, and a refusal of the mushy sentimentalism that has been siphoned into the category of womanhood" (2012: 6). This excessive and punk feminism is not so much about becoming women as it is about "unbecoming women"; the women here "undo the category rather than rounding it out, they dress it up and down, take it apart like a car engine and then rebuild it so that it is louder and faster" (2012: 8).

---

[6] Gaga first started to call her fans the Little Monsters during 2009 and later started calling herself the Mother Monster. She first worked with the theme of the monster on her second album to refer to different/monstrous physicality and also her fears.

It is this innovative approach to female identity, heralded by Lady Gaga, that is radically different in *AHS: Hotel* when compared to *Murder House*. *Hotel* introduces a notion of womanhood not limited by biological and essentialist categorizations and offers a critique of heteronormative society and gender distinctions. Queer strategies of drag and camp inform this season's two queer women: the Countess and Liz Taylor, a transgender woman played by Denis O'Hare. While the Countess is already queer as a bisexual female vampire, her character also openly cites Catherine Deneuve's vampire in *The Hunger*. For Geczy and Karaminas, O'Hare's Liz Taylor signals to "the instability of the category of woman" because she uses drag and performance in her identity (2017: 718). Through her long silk kaftans and Egyptian make-up, "the actor Denis O'Hare imitates a woman, Liz Taylor, who imitates Elizabeth Taylor imitating Cleopatra" (2017).

Indeed, the character of Liz Taylor, through her campy performative identity, reminds us that female identity is not limited to biological definitions. Hers is an identity of feminine excess and artifice and it is also an identity unwavering in its self-knowledge as a woman. Formerly a salesman, a husband, and a father, Liz Taylor is transformed into her true self during a business trip stay at the Cortez. The Countess helps her don her fake skin and be reborn as a woman and says, "Let me help you become who you were born to be. A goddess", in a direct reference to Gaga's song "Born This Way" (E5). Years later, when Liz Taylor finds out she has terminal cancer and decides to become one of the hotel's ghosts, it is the Countess again who helps him "transition … one last time" by cutting his throat (E12). Hence, although Liz Taylor never goes through gender reassignment surgery, she undergoes two rebirths, first as a woman, then as a ghost. Liz and her friends see her as a true woman, a fact that she reminds everyone every chance she gets. She even calls herself "the first woman in the world to have prostate cancer" (E12).

In her authentic identity and her campy humor, Liz Taylor also becomes the key to a different kind of fate for the hotel's inhabitants. After most of the characters die and the Countess is killed at the end of the penultimate episode, the last episode of the season presents us with a different kind of community in the hotel. Liz Taylor and Iris have taken over the management of the hotel, and they are trying to run a successful business, an effort constantly stultified by the murderous acts of the ghosts. Much like how the Countess has helped Liz become a woman, Liz has formerly helped Iris come to terms with losing Donovan and become a happier woman. The two now aim to help some of the hotel's ghosts find new purposes in their eternal lives since, as Liz claims, "this is California. The land of reinvention." Liz and Iris help the drug addict Sally (Sarah Paulson) become an internet sensation and the fashion designer Will Drake (Cheyenne Jackson) continue to run his fashion house from the confines of the hotel, using the ghosts as models in the fashion shows that take place in the hotel lobby.

Thus, at the end of the season the audience discover a space, a "power geometry" created as much by relations of "solidarity and co-operation" as it is by "domination and subordination" (Massey 1994: 265). In the last episode, Liz Taylor says they want the hotel to provide "a family to the friendless, a comfort to those in the cold, a beehive of acceptance." This alternative family created from all the outcasts of mainstream American society—women, children, homosexuals, bisexuals, criminals, drug addicts—brings to mind Turner's concept of "communitas," an unstructured community of equal individuals, a community where no class, caste, or rank exists (2011: 96). As liminality is a state of being "neither here nor there," it is a state out of any societal structures and hierarchies (Turner 1987: 27). As individuals are free to "play with the elements of the familiar and defamiliarize them," they create different kind of bonds with people like themselves (Turner 1987). For Turner, communitas are "homogenized," they are communities of "intense comradeship and egalitarianism" (2011: 95). He says these communities return to the "generic bond between men," and "liminality, marginality and inferiority" are the conditions of these individuals (2011: 128). In this vein, Hotel Cortez's monstrous and queer family of ghosts and vampires (everyone is dead at the end), of serial killers, drug addicts, fashion designers, and models appear as a communitas in liminality, in the purgatorial space of the hotel.

Nevertheless, Turner warns that communitas are not permanent, they only occur in "a moment in and out of time," during the liminal states in life and rituals (2011: 96). In *AHS* universe, however, as a result of liberating powers of horror, the Hotel Cortez community will live on forever, frozen in amber in the "dead zone" of the hotel. As such, the hotel, starting as a heterotopia of deviation, ends up becoming a "heterotopia of compensation," creating "a space that is other, another real space, as perfect, as meticulous, as well arranged as ours is messy, ill constructed, and jumbled" (Foucault 1986: 27). Here, liminality, marginality, and inferiority create a perfect society, a space that would be seen potentially "dangerous and anarchical by the maintainers of social structure" (Turner 2011: 109). As the space of the Hotel Cortez exists within the universe of horror and not in real life, I would like to call this a *heterotopia of potential*, presenting us with an alternative universe where womanhood is not entrapped and put in a box but is opened up and liberated to new possibilities.

Conclusion

The comparison of the house and the hotel within the *AHS* multiverse also reveals many truths about the American identity, personified in the city of LA. This is a city of "spatial apartheid," a "fragmented metropolis," "its denizens inhabiting discrete galaxies whose orbits apparently never converge" (Rosenbaum 2017: 31, 32). Together with some of the richest neighborhoods in the country like Beverly Hills and Bel Air, LA County has one of the largest prison populations and also one of the largest homeless populations in the United States. Comparing the sterile, white, upper-middle-class, suburban necrotopia of the LA Murder House to the dirty, decaying, underclass, urban heterotopia of the downtown Hotel Cortez unearths the story of privilege and exclusion written at the very heart of the American dream. Through subversive and critical lens of horror, these two worlds are turned inside out with a vengeance as *AHS* highlights the purgatorial nature of both kinds of existence.

These spaces also tell a lot about female identity in America. After all, as Elizabeth Wilson suggests, in LA, there is also Hollywood, "the world's biggest dream factory, porno factory, nightmare factory" where "the image of the perfect woman has been mass-produced since the 1920s" (1992: 145). Reading *AHS: Murder House* and *AHS: Hotel* in dialogue lets us ponder the question of where "a woman's place" might be. Massey suggests that in the West, there has always been "a joint control of spatiality and identity," evidenced in the distinction between public and private (1994: 180). *AHS* seems to suggest that if women are doomed to exist in purgatorial spaces, rather than dying in stasis as caged birds within the confines of heteronormative nuclear family, they should take their chances in the urban jungle, creating their own destinies and opening up to the possibility of a new universe where their identities are shaped by their desires, not by their anatomies.

Works Cited

Clover, C. (1987), "Her Body, Himself: Gender in the Slasher Film," *Representations*, 20: 187–228.

Creed, B. (1993), *The Monstrous-Feminine: Film, Feminism, Psychoanalysis*, New York: Routledge.

Earle, H. and J. Clark (2019), "Telling National Stories in *American Horror Story*," *European Journal of American Culture*, 38(1): 5–13.

Foucault, M. (1986), "Of Other Spaces," J. Miskowiec (trans.), *Diacritics*, 16: 22–7.

Geczy, A. and V. Karaminas (2017), "Lady Gaga: American Horror Story, Fashion, Monstrosity and the Grotesque," *Fashion Theory*, 21(6): 709–31.

Geller, T. L. and A. M. Banker (2017), "'THAT MAGIC BOX LIES': Queer Theory, Seriality, and American Horror Story," *The Velvet Light Trap*, 79: 36–49.

Hale, M. (2015), "Review: 'American Horror Story: Hotel,' as Depraved as Ever," *The New York Times*. https://www.nytimes.com/2015/10/07/arts/television/review-american-horror-story-hotel-as-depraved-as-ever.html. Accessed November 11, 2022.

Halberstam, J. J. (2012), *Gaga Feminism: Sex, Gender, and the End of Normal*, Boston: Beacon Press.

Keetley, D. (2013), "Stillborn: The Entropic Gothic of *American Horror Story*," *Gothic Studies*, 15(2): 89–107.

King, A. (2017), "A Monstrous(ly-Feminine) Whiteness: Gender, Genre, and the Abject Horror of the Past in *American Horror Story: Coven*," *Women's Studies*, 46(6): 557–73.

Komsta, M. (2014), "The Murder House, or the Archaic Mother in American Horror Story," in A. Kędra-Kardela and A. S. Kowalczyk (eds.), *Expanding the Gothic Canon: Studies in Literature, Film and New Media*, 247–68, Frankfurt: Peter Lang.

Kristeva, J. (1982), *Powers of Horror: An Essay on Abjection*, L. S. Roudiez (trans.), New York: Columbia University Press.

Lefebvre, H. (1976), "Reflections on the Politics of Space," M. Enders (trans.), *Antipode*, 8: 30–7.

Massey, D. (1994), *Space, Place, and Gender*, Minneapolis: University of Minnesota Press.

Munford, R. and M. Waters (2014), *Feminism & Popular Culture: Investigating the Postfeminist Mystique*, New Brunswick: Rutgers University Press.

Pinedo, I. (1997), *Recreational Terror: Women and the Pleasures of Horror Film Viewing*, New York: State University of New York Press.

Rosenbaum, S. (2017), *Domestic Economies: Women, Work, and the American Dream in Los Angeles*, Durham: Duke University Press.

Sevenich, R. (2015), "'Come Out, Come Out, Wherever You Are': Queering American Horror Story," *Gender Forum*, 54: N.A.

Turner, V. (1987), *From Ritual to Theatre: The Human Seriousness of Play*, New York: PAJ Publications.

Turner, V. (2011), *The Ritual Process: Structure and Anti-Structure* [1969], New Brunswick: Transaction.

van Gennep, A. (1960), *The Rites of Passage*, Chicago: University of Chicago Press.

Williams, L (2002), "When the Woman Looks," in M. Jancovich (ed.), *Horror, the Film Reader*, 61–6, London: Routledge.

Wilson, E. (1992), *The Sphinx in the City: Urban Life, the Control of Disorder, and Women*, London: Virago Press.

Wood, R. (1979), "An Introduction to the American Horror Film," in R. Wood and R. Lippe (eds.), *American Nightmare: Essays on the Horror Film*, 7–28, Toronto: Festival of Festivals.

12

"This Time I'll Get It Right": Female Coming-of-Age within Purgatorial Time Loops

Shawn Edrei

The concept of the "time loop" is a mainstay in contemporary speculative fiction, finding frequent expression in novels, comics, film and television, videogames, and more. Described by Andy Duncan as "a very personal sort of alternate history in which a part of the protagonist's life repeats itself, with variations" (James and Mendelsohn 2003: 215), the typical time loop scenario follows a highly structured formula: an individual (or a small group) becomes trapped in a spatial and temporal configuration which resets upon reaching a pre-determined terminus. Specific features of these loops tend to vary depending on genre traditions and conventions, but in most instances the protagonist retains some or all of their memories from one iteration to the next. This persistent awareness ultimately allows the trapped protagonist to use their accumulated foreknowledge and expanded understanding of the loop to either escape its confines or break the endless cycle altogether. For these protagonists, imprisonment within the loop is often explicitly depicted as a purgatorial experience; in referring to similar phenomena of "timelessness" in YA fiction, Elana Gomel refers to scenarios "in which stale traumas of yesterday are replayed with only minor variations, leading neither to a final apocalyptic collapse nor to a utopian salvation" (2018: 48). Within these spaces, the protagonist's awareness exacts a psychological toll in spite of—and sometimes because of—the impermanence of physical consequences within the loop, with escalation toward extreme violence being practically commonplace due to the supposed absence of permanent fallout. Moreover, the underlying cause of the loop tends to be unknown at first, further compounding the mental strain upon the reset-immune characters: they must conduct a long-term investigation over multiple iterations, acquiring knowledge and directly participating in the repetition in order to ultimately return to the freedom of a temporally linear existence.

In viewing these purgatorial spaces and the archetypal protagonists who tend to find themselves trapped within them, a peculiar pattern emerges among subjects who are girls or young women. For these women, the purgatorial experience is portrayed as a catalyst for a process of education and maturation, similar to the classic formula of the extinct *bildungsroman* genre, as defined by Franco Moretti:

> Mobility and interiority. Modern youth, to be sure, is many other things as well: the growing influence of education, the strengthening of bonds within generations, a new relationship with nature, youth's "spiritualization"—these features are just as important in its "real" development. Yet the *Bildungsroman* discards them as irrelevant, abstracting from "real" youth a symbolic one, epitomized, we have said, in mobility and interiority.
>
> (1987: 5)

In this configuration, the twin components of mobility and interiority are metaphorized and integrated into the process of escaping the time loop; this is not achieved by discovering a physical exit or a mechanism that breaks the cyclical repetition, but rather by the successful conclusion of a cognitive, emotional, and behavioral process, leading to some epiphany or deep understanding that the character in question did not previously possess. The end result is portrayed as a net positive despite the trials endured in the process; the protagonist's freedom doubles as an affirmation of adulthood and personal growth. This aligns with Moretti's claim that the ultimate message put forth when *bildungsroman* protagonists face contradictions is that "[t]he next step [is] not to 'solve' the contradiction, but rather to learn to live with it, and even transform it into a tool for survival" (1987: 10).

To demonstrate the particular features of the time loop narrative as *bildung* for female protagonists, this chapter will discuss three case studies which enact this particular juxtaposition of archaic coming-of-age narrative and cyclical temporal purgatory, focusing on the characters of Homura Akemi from *Puella Magi Madoka Magica*, Ophelia from *Elsinore*, and Moira McTaggart from *X-Men*. Each of these young women becomes enmeshed in cataclysmic, disastrous time loops, and suffers as a result of these repeating traumas. According to Sara Crosby, this is consistent with the inherent distinction in classical literature between male and female heroes: "One of the chief fulcrums for this oscillation is the question of the hero's 'gift.' Is it power or pain? While Joseph Campbell long ago identified part of the hero's journey as 'refusal of the call,' eventually, the male hero accepts and embraces his gift as his empowerment," whereas female heroes "often interpret their gifts as curses, and [their] journey consists of multiple, guilt-ridden, tortured refusals" (quoted in Innes 2004: 162). The experiences of women within time loops tend to differ from male characters undergoing similar cycles (as seen in films such as *Groundhog's Day*, television series like *Supernatural*, and many more examples) in two primary respects. First, these women are either aware of the conditions necessary to reset events, or are able to exact some degree of control over the loop itself; this bestows a measure of agency in a scenario that typically affords almost none, and aligns with Moretti's claim that "[t]o reach the conclusive synthesis of maturity, therefore, it is not enough to achieve 'objective' results, whatever they may be—learning a trade, establishing a reality. One must learn first and foremost ... to direct 'the plot of [his own] life's so that each moment strengthens one's *sense of belonging* to a wider community" (1987: 19). The process of ontological and chronological investigation necessary to escape the loop contains an added personal, developmental component—in enduring the crucible of repetition, these women are forced to break away from some childhood ideal or immature personality trait, emerging from the loop secure in their new roles as adults.

Debuting as a twelve-episode Japanese anime in 2011 and later branching out into manga and videogames, *Puella Magi Madoka Magica* initially presents itself as a straightforward example of the "Magical Girls" genre, popularized by series such as *Sailor Moon* (1992–1997) and *Cardcaptor Sakura* (1998–2000). As the series begins, high school student Madoka encounters an alien creature named Kyubey, who offers to grant a single wish in exchange for becoming a Magical Girl and hunting murderous, reality-warping entities known as Witches. Initially, Madoka seems enthusiastic about this possibility, delayed only by her childish inability to think of an appropriate wish. However, a mysterious new student, Homura Akemi, virulently demands that Madoka refrain from making a wish, though she herself is clearly already a Magical Girl. For most of the series, Homura is an outsider whose perspective is withheld from the viewer. She is shown to have a violent dislike of Kyubey, and an inexplicable fixation on preventing Madoka from becoming a Magical Girl at all costs. At various points Homura also seems to exhibit some awareness of future events, though her foreknowledge is clearly incomplete as key events occasionally catch her off-guard.

The truth of Homura's situation is only revealed in episode 10, titled "I Won't Rely on Anyone Anymore," which begins with a supposed repeat of Homura's introductory scene in the first episode, though key details are immediately and obviously different. In episode 1, "As If I Met Her in My Dream," Homura strides into class with her hair loose, and introduces herself to Madoka's class in a flat, disinterested tone. Moments later, she asks Madoka to accompany her to the nurse's station, though she clearly knows the way herself (despite having just transferred to the school). When Madoka questions this, Homura speaks to her in an equally detached and aloof tone: "Madoka Kaname. Do you treasure the life you currently live, and do you consider your family and your friends precious?" ("As If I Met Her in My Dream," S01, E01). When the startled Madoka answers in the affirmative, Homura continues: "Good. Because if that's the truth, then you wouldn't try changing the life you have, or the person you are. Otherwise, you'd lose everything you love. Don't change. Stay as you are, Madoka Kaname. Stay as you are, forever" ("As If I Met Her in My Dream," S01, E01).

Episode 10 reprises this introduction, but in a dramatically different configuration. Homura's posture is slouched, she wears glasses, and her hair is braided, and she shyly stammers as she attempts to introduce herself to the class. In this version, it is Madoka who first approaches Homura, offering to walk her to the nurse's station. It becomes clear to the viewer that this is not a flashback to the beginning of the series, but some alternative sequence of events: the dynamic between the two girls is completely reversed, with Madoka being confident and outspoken while Homura is awkward and hesitant. Later that day, Homura is attacked by Witches and rescued by Mami and Madoka—in full Magical Girl regalia, having already been empowered by Kyubey. Homura is awestruck by Madoka's optimism and compassionate heroism, yet in the very next scene she witnesses the deaths of both Madoka and Mami at the hands of the Witch Walpurgisnacht. Kyubey then manifests and offers Homura a similar bargain:

> **Kyubey**: Would you trade your soul to have a wish like that come true? If there's something you want badly and you're willing to accept a destiny battling Witches, then I can help you get what you want.
> **Homura**: If I make a contract with you, would you really grant me any wish?
> **Kyubey**: Absolutely. You have more than enough potential. So tell me: what is the one wish you'd have that will make your Soul Gem shine?
> **Homura**: I wish ... I wish I can meet Miss Kaname all over again, but this time instead of her protecting me, I want to be strong enough to protect her!
> ("I Won't Rely on Anyone Anymore," S01, E10)

Kyubey grants this wish by giving Homura the ability to manipulate time, which she then uses to reset events over and over. This in itself is a significant deviation from typical depictions of time loops featuring male protagonists, as Homura initiates the repeating cycle of her own volition rather than unwittingly stumble into the scenario—an expression of agency that kicks off her own process of maturation.

For the duration of the episode, the viewer witnesses Homura's attempts to prevent Madoka's death, all of which end in failure: when she joins the battle against Walpurgisnacht, Madoka becomes corrupted and transforms into a Witch herself. In the next loop, Homura attempts to reveal this to the other Magical Girls, only for Mami to become hysterically convinced that the only way to avoid this fate is to die, promptly killing their companion Kyoko and forcing Madoka to slay her in turn. Walpurgisnacht again defeats Madoka and Homura, but this time, as both girls lay dying, Madoka makes a request: "I want you to do something that I couldn't do. You can go back in time, right, Homura? You can go back and change everything so that we don't end up like this, okay? Then save me from being stupid, from getting tricked. Don't let Kyubey fool me again" ("I Won't Rely on Anyone Anymore," S01, E10). This narrows down Homura's goal during the time loop: rather than try to find a way to defeat Walpurgisnacht and save Madoka's life after the fact, Homura begins directing her efforts toward preventing Madoka's transformation in the first place. However, her next loop results in another failure, as her inability to defeat Walpurgisnacht alone results in Madoka making a wish specifically to save her, and immediately transforming into a planet-destroying Witch. Homura's subsequent reset brings the viewer back to the beginning of the series proper, now revealed to be another iteration of the loop.

Episode 10 reveals both the purgatorial nature of the time loop and its recontextualization of Homura's journey as a coming-of-age process: initially withdrawn, childlike and ineffectual, her accumulated experiences over multiple loops, involving both Madoka's death and her own, have a stark physical and mental effect on Homura. Ultimately, the resolution to this limbo-like existence requires Homura to let go of Madoka—essentially accepting the inevitable loss of a treasured relationship. However, by setting aside her single-minded objective, Homura leads Madoka to make a wish that rewrites the very fabric of reality itself, resulting in an arguably improved universe in which Magical Girls no longer suffer inevitable corruption and become Witches, instead peacefully fading away when their powers are exhausted. The final exchange between Homura and Madoka (now an ascended deity due to the immense power of her wish) reveals that the latter has gained complete knowledge of the loop and all its iterations:

Madoka: Now I can see everything that ever happened, and everything that ever will. I see all the universes that could've been, and all the universes that are waiting to be born ... I see it all, and I finally know, I know all the things you've done for me, throughout all those different timelines. All of it. All the times you cried, and all the times you got hurt, but you kept fighting for me. I'm so sorry I never knew until now. I'm so sorry.

("My Very Best Friend," S01, E12)

This admission causes Homura to break down and show emotion for the first time since her initial vow to prevent Madoka's transformation; and when the universe is recreated and the time loop finally ended, Homura remains one of only two people to remember her friend; even Kyubey's alien intelligence shows no awareness of reality having been rewritten, or of Homura's loop being broken. In accepting the loss of Madoka, rather than stubbornly insisting on imposing her will on the universe, Homura emerges as a more mature woman at the end of the narrative.

Another example of a purgatorial time loop serving as a metaphorical *bildungsroman* centers around the protagonist of Golden Glitch Studios's 2019 adventure game *Elsinore*. Based on the famous Shakespearean play *Hamlet*, *Elsinore* casts the player in the role of the doomed Ophelia and begins *in medias res*, shortly before the death of her father Polonius. At first glance, the prologue of *Elsinore* appears to be a somewhat straightforward depiction of the play's canonical sequence of events: for three days (Thursday through Saturday) Ophelia wanders the castle, converses with Hamlet and several other characters, and witnesses Hamlet's murder of her father. Only a minor divergence occurs at the end of this scenario: Ophelia is stabbed by a Norwegian spy seeking to undermine and sabotage the castle's defenses. The spy then proceeds to stage her death as a suicide by drowning (which again complies with Shakespearean canon, as Ophelia's demise is not directly dramatized in the play and there is some ambiguity as to the cause). At this point, *Elsinore* reveals its own premise and postmodern reinterpretation of *Hamlet*: Ophelia awakens in her own bed, at the start of the three-day period. Moreover, she retains a perfect memory of past events: when Hamlet enters her room again to discuss his father's murder, Ophelia is able to predict his exact words. Upon this confirmation that she is repeating past events, Ophelia begins investigating the major players at the castle, attempting to piece together both the original plot of *Hamlet* (concerning the mystery of King Hamlet's death and his haunting of Elsinore as a ghost) and the circumstances of her own imminent murder.

At first, the player's exploration of the setting and uncovering of hidden information is hampered by the spy's seeming omnipresence: no matter where the player sends Ophelia, the spy will find and kill her at the end of the third day. However, with each loop the player is able to gather more details and secrets concerning the major and minor characters at Elsinore, from King Claudius and Queen Gertrude to Irma the cook, to Hamlet's mischievous friends Rosencrantz and Guildenstern (here reimagined as Lady Rosie and Lady Guilda). Ophelia's characterization throughout this process is broadly consistent with her portrayal in *Hamlet*: she is shown to be somewhat naïve and sheltered, incapable of understanding Hamlet's anguish or the complex scenario unfolding around her. But as with Homura, Ophelia becomes determined to repeat the loop as many times as necessary in order to achieve an optimal denouement. With each iteration, she grows more accomplished and skilled at using her accumulated knowledge to manipulate circumstances and people around her, allowing her to enact various attempts at resolution: she can seduce Claudius and replace Gertrude as Queen, she can co-opt Hamlet's original plan of revealing the King's crimes through a play, she can flee Elsinore with a local barkeep revealed to be Othello, and she can even join infamous pirate queen Grace O'Malley on the high seas. Yet these solutions are consistently portrayed as imperfect and flawed: becoming Queen utterly disgusts and alienates Hamlet, Othello is destined to abandon her once he meets Desdemona, and so on. Every route concludes by resetting the loop and returning Ophelia to her bedroom at Elsinore; as with Homura and other female protagonists in this particular type of narrative, Ophelia's persistence serves as both catalyst and affirmation of her process of maturation. Her awareness expands the further she delves into other characters' lives, discovering Horatio's unrequited love for Hamlet, Bernardo's hidden passion for stage acting, Irma's absolute dedication to Gertrude, and much more.

For the player, Ophelia's emotional and psychological growth includes a mechanical evolution of the gameplay as well: namely, the ability to trigger a temporal reset at will without having to wait for the spy to assassinate Ophelia. This is of course similar to Homura's control over the shape and duration of her loop, and is key to the protagonist's assertion of agency within the repeating chain of events. Once the player has thoroughly investigated the inhabitants of Elsinore, the identity of the spy can be determined and exposed, preventing Ophelia's death; as this constitutes a significant divergence from the canonical plot of Shakespeare's play, one might assume Ophelia will therefore be freed of the purgatorial loop. Instead, the spy's arrest only extends the loop's duration for a few days, after which Ophelia is confronted with a cataclysm that cannot be prevented: the inevitable fall of Elsinore at the hands of Fortinbras and the Norwegian army (echoing the canonical end of Shakespeare's play). This complication causes Ophelia's core motivation within the loop to undergo an epistemological and ontological shift: rather than focus on avoiding her own demise, the player must now begin to interrogate the larger issue of the loop itself, the circumstances of its creation and the "rules" that govern it. With an expanded zone to explore and more people to interact with, Ophelia ultimately discovers that the loop is a kind of "curse" passed from one individual to another. The previous prisoner of this purgatorial space was Hamlet's father, who was only able to escape via his own death (thus becoming the ghost who appears to Hamlet at the start of the play); before him was his aunt Lady Simona, who initially took advantage of her temporal confinement to overthrow and supplant the reigning queen. *Elsinore* positions Simona as having completed the same process Ophelia is currently undergoing, growing and maturing to adulthood via a *bildung* process that takes place entirely within the framework of the time loop.

This discovery allows Ophelia to at last confront Quince, the supernatural entity responsible for these events. Of course, Quince's magic places him far beyond Ophelia's capacity to confront him—any attempt on her part to directly antagonize him is met with brutal humiliation and another reset (just as Madoka's inevitable corruption into a Witch empowers her beyond Homura's ability to directly confront her). The conclusion of Ophelia's purgatorial narrative makes for an interesting contrast with Homura's, even as both revolve around the acceptance of a painful emotional loss and subsequent divestment of childish attachments. Homura's release from the purgatorial loop is caused by failure: for all her efforts, she remains unable to prevent Madoka's fate, though her intervention ultimately allows for a benevolent and positive outcome which she is able to accept. Ophelia, on the other hand, quickly learns that Quince's mystical manipulations are beyond her ability to solve. While Simona was able to free herself by passing the curse of the time loop onto Hamlet's father, Ophelia instead chooses to sacrifice herself through total passivity: she ceases to take action or interact with others, denying Quince the satisfaction of seeing his victims' actions fail over and over. By removing herself as an actant in events rather than physically freeing herself, Ophelia's eternal captivity becomes an expression of strength and nobility: Quince effectively becomes *her* prisoner, and though Fortinbras's invasion remains inevitable, the conclusion of *Elsinore* nevertheless constitutes a victory for the young woman protagonist, and a successful conclusion of her purgatorial *bildungsroman*.

It is important to note that while the *bildungsroman* formula presupposes a positive conclusion based on growth and entry into adulthood, it is theoretically possible to fail this process through an inability or refusal to learn, adapt, and develop. One such example of a failed process of maturation within a purgatorial time loop is evident in the character of Moira MacTaggart, a longtime supporting cast member in the *X-Men* comics (first appearing in 1975). *X-Men*, a franchise featuring mutant superheroes fighting to save a world that hates and fears them, has had its fair share of stories featuring time travel, alternate realities, and cosmic phenomena; 2019 storyline *House of X/Powers of X* is of particular interest here, as writer Jonathan Hickman and artist Pepe Larraz reimagine Moira MacTaggart to be a mutant with the power of reincarnation. The third chapter, "The Uncanny Life of Moira X," details a series of ten lifetimes Moira experiences consecutively, being reborn with complete knowledge each time she dies: "Moira's second life began in utero. It was the *womb birth* of a **fully sentient being** who had a perfect recollection of her **prior life**" (Hickman/Larraz 2019: 94, emphasis in original). Her second life immediately proves both the value and the burden of knowledge accumulated through purgatorial loops:

> In her early years, Moira had to be careful not to let on what she really was. She had to hide what was going on in a mind that was older than the humans who made her.
>
> She knew the pride they had for their special girl would quickly turn into fear if she pulled back the curtain a little too far.
>
> But try as she might, it was impossible to completely conceal how different she was.
>
> Her teachers began to use words like "*advanced*" and "*clever*", which led to other words like "*brilliant*" and "*prodigy*", which eventually led to Moira being pushed in the direction of academia. **A life of the mind.**
>
> Moira didn't fight these efforts, as she herself wanted to understand who—and *what*—she was, and had exhausted all the possibilities the perspective of her first life offered her.
>
> (Hickman and Larraz 2019: 96, emphasis in original)

Though at this point she only possesses the information obtained from her first (largely uneventful and mundane) life, Moira is quickly able to determine the extent of her agency:

> If she simply performed her role in events as she did in her previous life—*if she was a passive participant*—then that event would proceed almost exactly as before. This proved her memories were real.
>
> But if she became an active participant, then she could change what happened.
>
> And the path of her life would **diverge**.
>
> (Hickman and Larraz 2019: 97, emphasis in original)

Moira's second life is cut short before she is able to thoroughly investigate the nature of her mutation, and so she dedicates her third life to genetics, believing the mutant gene to be a cancer and ultimately devising a cure which would strip mutants of their unique attributes. This makes her a target of the Brotherhood of Evil Mutants, a group of supervillains dedicated to mutant supremacy; more significantly, this results in a brief yet deeply significant conversation between Moira and the precognitive mutant Destiny:

> **Destiny**: You're a smart woman who is beginning to understand the potential of your power. You're starting to believe that you are in an eternal loop of some kind. That your powers give you a form of *immortality*. I want you to know **they do not**. I see ten lives, Moira. Maybe eleven if you make the right choice at the end ... **but that is all**.
> **Moira**: *How is ...* How is that possible?
> **Destiny**: You are born each time with the knowledge of your previous lives, but if you die as a child—*before your mutant powers manifest*—then you will not reincarnate. **You simply end.** Like everyone else. (Hickman and Larraz 2019: 104, emphasis in original)

This revelatory exchange adds a unique attribute to this particular time loop, especially when compared to the ones experienced by Homura and Ophelia: namely, a hard limit imposed upon the loop's overall number of iterations. Destiny's clairvoyance effectively creates a sense of urgency which runs counter to the more relaxed, long-term, and indefinite format of typical purgatorial investigation. Unlike other women in similar circumstances, who are bound only by the increasing and cumulative psychological damage they sustain within the loop, Moira is tasked with finding a way to help mutants within ten (or possibly eleven) lifetimes, after having already died twice—and then a third time, as the Brotherhood execute her for her work on the "cure."

From her fourth life onward, Moira appears to undergo a change of heart consistent with the initial stages of the *bildung* maturation process. However, that same fourth incarnation introduces a new complication "when, as Destiny had promised, the humans—*and their extinction machines*—came for them and all the children" (Hickman/Larraz 2019: 107, emphasis in original). Moira discovers that humans inevitably construct artificial intelligences known as Sentinels, which go on to decimate or utterly destroy the mutant population in each subsequent incarnation. Moira's fourth, fifth, sixth, seventh, and ninth lives all end violently, in the midst or aftermath of mutant extinction. Her foreknowledge proves inadequate to stave off this event. The prime example of this is her seventh life, where she methodically hunts down every member of the

Trask family (nominally responsible for creating the Sentinels), only to die at the machines' hands anyway: "Artificial intelligence is like fire. It's a **discovery**, not an **invention**. All she succeeded in doing was stopping a Trask from being the first human to burn their hand. *Like mutants*, the machines simply **emerge** at a certain point during societal and environmental evolution" (Hickman and Larraz 2019: 110, emphasis in original). With integration (her fourth life), isolation (her fifth), and prevention (her seventh) all having failed as viable strategies to secure the future of mutantkind, Moira spends her eighth and ninth lives aligning with canonical villains such as Magneto and Apocalypse, who use the knowledge of her multiple lifetimes to wage war against humanity. Magneto's attempt (her eighth life) fails prematurely, but Apocalypse's campaign (her ninth) against the Man-Machine Supremacy lasts for nearly a century, though mutants are never able to obtain the upper hand in the conflict and are continually pushed back until the fall of Apocalypse himself.

As her tenth life begins—the "present day" of *House of X/Powers of X* and the terminus of her personal purgatorial loop according to Destiny—Moira is forced to reevaluate all her past failures and plot a new course of action. In this, her epiphany is consistent with Homura's and Ophelia's: "After all the lives lost, after the end of all the wars, armed with the knowledge that all the old ways—*and all the old ways of thinking*—would never be enough to save her people, she decided to try something **truly revolutionary** … and in Moira's tenth life, she decided she and Charles Xavier would break all the rules" (Hickman and Larraz 2019: 115, emphasis in original). Much like Ophelia's final choice of total passivity in defiance of Quince, and Homura's ultimate acceptance that the loss of her friend is unavoidable, Moira is able to unite the fractious and divided leaders of mutantkind and their followers into a single nation—a strategy that would not have been possible had she not spent earlier loops aligning with each of said leaders in turn. This outcome appears to fit the established parameters of an optimal solution made possible at the culmination of this particular brand of *bildung*, a product of aggregated knowledge gained through suffering and maturation. Indeed, the conclusion of *House of X/Powers of X* positions Moira alongside other female protagonists at the end of their respective purgatorial journeys.

Hickman's subsequent storyline, *Inferno*, subverts this conclusion, and depicts a heretofore-unseen variation of the *bildung* time loop narrative established herein—one in which the woman at the center of the narrative regresses, essentially reverting to an earlier stage of development (and thus failing to complete the coming-of-age process). When the secret of Moira's past lives is exposed, Destiny and Mystique—at the behest of X-Men member Emma Frost—again capture and interrogate her. Moira then confesses that, despite her actions taken in defense of mutantkind, her actual goal is to recreate the cure she invented in her third life and use it on mutant children before their genetic abilities manifest at puberty—essentially condemning the mutant race to oblivion once again. To prevent this, Mystique promptly uses a unique device to strip Moira of her power, ensuring that she can be killed without resetting the timeline again. As the villainesses close in for the kill, Moira offers a rationale for her backsliding that dramatically unravels the assumption of progress and acceptance put forth at the end of *House of X/Powers of X*. Rather than evolving into a new, mature form using the totality of entire lifetimes of knowledge, the protagonist of the time loop narrative has essentially given up:

> Your hope is that with my death, you will lock in this *perfect* timeline that I have made? ... You don't know what I know. You've just seen *glimpses*. The *briefest moments* of a millennium. You don't know who **wins** and who **loses**. *I do*. It's the same thing every time. The humans win, or the machines win ... and we always lose to one, or both, of them. Losing is losing. Dying is dying. You can't say that I didn't try another way ... I did, and I failed over and over for a thousand years.
> (Hickman, Schiti and Caselli 2021–22: 22, emphasis in original)

Moira's failure here is quickly repaid with expulsion from the X-Men, entrapment in this timeline via the removal of her mutant power, and her transition to an antagonistic role in the narrative. Her actions in *Inferno* run counter to Moretti's clear definition of the end result of a successful *bildungsroman* narrative: "To reach the conclusive synthesis of maturity, therefore, it is not enough to achieve 'objective' results, whatever they may be—learning a trade, establishing a reality. One must learn first and foremost, like Wilhelm, to direct 'the plot of [his own] life' so that each moment strengths one's *sense of belonging* to a wider community" (1987: 19). Thus, unlike Homura, Ophelia, and other female protagonists who successfully complete the *bildung* process within their respective purgatorial cycles, Moira is forcibly ejected from her time loop by characters whose perspective is rarely acknowledged in narratives of this type, per Emma's classification of Moira: "At any moment, she could erase everything we've made, everything we've sacrificed, everything we've ever loved ... gone. As if it never was. And she gets to keep doing it. Over and over ... until she's satisfied, I suppose" (Hickman, Schiti and Caselli 2021–22: 16). Thus, Mystique and Destiny—products of events manipulated by Moira herself—are ultimately the characters whose agency puts an end to the atemporal purgatory and the threat of another reset, while Moira herself never achieves the cognitive and psychological clarity needed to assert control over her own personal timeline.

What makes these three case studies particularly intriguing within the larger oeuvre of time loop stories is not simply the implementation of a *bildung* process specifically for women protagonists—certainly, television series like *Russian Doll* (2019–) and episodes of *Buffy the Vampire Slayer* (1997–2003), *Charmed* (1998–2006), *Xena: Warrior Princess* (1995–2001), and more embed some type of learning process within the purgatorial repetition. Rather, as transmedia characters portrayed in film, television, graphic literature, and video games, Homura, Ophelia, and Moira exist in a unique state of multiplicity, with their respective audiences already being primed to accept different versions and variations simultaneously. For example, the *Puella Magi Madoka Magica Portable* videogame allows the player to assume the role of other girls within the loop, and alternate events may unfold in such a way that Homura herself becomes corrupted and transforms into a Witch; actor Rose Byrne's interpretation of Moira as a human CIA agent in X-Men films *First Class* (2011) and *Apocalypse* (2016) relegates her to the role of a supporting character with minimal agency and impact on the plot; and *Elsinore* is but one of many novels, films, and contemporary interpretations of *Hamlet*, most of which introduce some minor alteration to the character of Ophelia. This malleability and variation allow for a broader, deeper, and more pronounced *bildung* process, including an ontological/epistemological investigation of the loop itself, a catalyst for emotional growth, and an assertion of personal agency over the perpetual resetting of the timeline. Ultimately, their dedicated pursuit of an optimal/idealized state at the terminus of the purgatorial space/time configuration aligns with Darko Suvin's view of SF's generic imperative as a whole: "Beyond an undirected inquisitiveness, which makes for a semantic game without clear referent, this genre has always been wedded to a hope of finding in the unknown the ideal environment, tribe, state, intelligence, or other aspect of the Supreme Good" (Suvin 1979: 5).

Works Cited

Crosby, S. (2004), "The Cruelest Season: Female Heroes Snapped into Sacrificial Heroines," in S. A. Innes (ed.), *Action Chicks: New Images of Tough Women in Popular Culture*, 153–78, New York: Palgrave Macmillan.

Duncan, A. (2003), "Alternate History," in E. James and F. Mendelsohn (eds.), *The Cambridge Companion to Science Fiction*, 209–18, New York: Cambridge University Press. *Elsinore* (2019), designed by K. Chironis and C. Fallon, Golden Glitch.

Gomel, E. (2018), "A Sense of No Ending, Part 1: Never Grow Up: Narrative Formlessness and Ideological Stasis in YA Fantastic Fiction," *Dibur Literary Journal*, Issue, 6, Fall: 47–58.

Hickman, J. et al. (2019), *House of X/Powers of X*, New York: Marvel Comics.

Hickman, J. et al. (2021–22), *Inferno*, New York: Marvel Comics.

Moretti, F. (1987), *The Way of the World: The* Bildungsroman *in European Culture*, London: Verso.

Puella Magi Madoka Magica (2011), created by G. Urobuchi, Tokyo: Shaft.

Suvin, D. (1979), *Metamorphoses of Science Fiction: On the Poetics and History of a Literary Genre*, New Haven: Yale University Press.

13

The Trauma We Inherit: Sister Night, Black Female Identity, and the Parallel Racial Purgatory of *Watchmen*

Kevin J. Wetmore, Jr.

In an astonishing interview with Brazilian journalist Raphael Sassaki, graphic novel pioneer Alan Moore was asked his thoughts on contemporary superhero cinema. After denigrating the nature and purpose of such films, Moore stated:

> save for a smattering of non-white characters (and non-white creators) these books and these iconic characters are still very much white supremacist dreams of the master race ... In fact, I think that a good argument can be made for D.W. Griffith's *Birth of a Nation* as the first American superhero movie, and the point of origin for all those capes and masks.
>
> (quoted in McCarter 2019)

It is a powerful and insightful condemnation indeed to see in the "capes and masks" of American superhero/comic book characters the hood and robes of the Ku Klux Klan, particularly when the latter were framed as heroic in *Birth of a Nation*.

Moore's statement introduces several ideas useful to the purposes of this essay. First, that, like the Klan members in *Birth of a Nation*, comic book superheroes wear capes and masks to disguise themselves, to intimidate others, and to establish a "persona" as a hero for justice. Second, Moore observes a racist and anti-Black origin for the idea of masked avengers. Just as the Klan is presented as heroic for standing up to "dangerous" Black men during Reconstruction, so, too, the graphic novel hero, also often working outside the actual law, causes grievous bodily harm to villains and criminals outside of any due process and is celebrated as heroes for doing so. Third, and finally, the danger of graphic novel heroes is that they are rooted originally, therefore, in a culture of white supremacy. Unsaid by Moore is the idea that graphic novel heroes are often also rooted in ideas of gender norms and male supremacy. For every Wonder Woman there are three dozen male superheroes. Most graphic novel narratives construct the idea of hero as male protecting helpless females who rely upon such protection to keep them safe.

In recent years both the comic industry and the entertainment industry have attempted to develop properties that counter the twin elements of racism and misogyny within comic culture, both by employing more women and artists of color and by creating (or re-creating) heroes that are women, BIPOC, or both. *Black Panther* (2018), *Captain Marvel* (2019), *Eternals* (2021), *Shang Chi and the Legend of the Twelve Rings* (2021), and the ever-expanding *Avengers* circle include and center Black, Asian, multiethnic, and female characters, although straight white male characters do still continue to dominate the center of superhero cinema.

HBO's 2019 series *Watchmen* serves as a sequel to the 1986 graphic novel by Dave Gibbons and Alan Moore, created and developed by Damon Lindehoff, who refers to it not as an "adaptation" but as an "extrapolation" of the graphic novel (McDonald 2019). Eschewing the version found in the 2009 Zack Snyder film, HBO's series is set in an alternate 2019, thirty years after the events of the graphic novel, which is set in an alternate 1980s. The primary character, Angela Abar/Sister Night (Regina King), is a Tulsa, Oklahoma police officer who dresses in a black leather suit and coat, simulating a nun's habit, and uses martial arts to fight crime as a costumed police officer. She is also a Black woman, which is significant for at least two reasons.

The first is that the original graphic novel only had three characters of color: Dr. Malcolm Long, Rorschach's psychologist in prison, Dr. Long's wife, and an unnamed young African-American man who sat by the newsstand reading "Tales of the Black Freighter" in issues three, five, eight, ten, and eleven. Mary Borsellino reminds us that "all the black characters seen in *Watchmen* die horribly during the execution of Veidt's plan" (2010: 29). Indeed, after the squid attack obliterates most of New York City, the graphic novel depicts an entirely white world: Veidt, white and blonde, survives and leads the building back of the world. Dan Dreiberg and Laurie Juspeczyk disguise themselves by dying their hair blonde. Thus, all the survivors of the new world are depicted as white, blonde Aryans. This is problematic, to say the least. Placing a Black woman at the center of a new *Watchmen* narrative represents a shift in narrative dynamic and racial representation, centering both Blackness and the female perspective.

The second reason is that the series *Watchmen* centers around the investigation of the crimes perpetuated by an armed white supremacist group, the Seventh Kavalry, inspired by Rorschach's writings and masked image, that wage violent war against minorities and the police. The series explores the relationship between race and law enforcement, with a particular focus on African-American police as outside insiders who want to fight for justice within a system that is designed to be inherently racist. Whereas the graphic novel's "costumed vigilantes" operate outside of the law, and eventually are made illegal themselves by the Keene Act, Sister Night and other police officers such as Looking Glass (Tim Blake Nelson), Red Scare (Andrew Howard), and Pirate Jenny (Jessica Camacho) are all duly sworn official police with badges, serving the local municipality with uniformed beat officers who wear yellow balaclavas to hide their identities as well.

Racism, Violence, and the "Real" America

Given that much of the original graphic novel is set in and around New York—indeed, *Times Square* is ground zero for the giant, interdimensional squid that is at the heart of Adrian Veidt's plan—the setting of the HBO series is surprisingly predominantly Tulsa, Oklahoma. The reason for the shift seems rooted in two ideas. The first is the idea of the heartland as "real" America, as reflected in contemporary conservative political discourse. The coasts are too leftist and elitist—it is the center of the nation, "flyover country," that is the "real" America. Damon Lindelof, the show's creator and show runner, stated the impetus behind the "sequel" to *Watchmen* was the question, "What is it like to be an American right now?" (quoted in Braxton 2019: E6). The setting of Tulsa allows for a much more expansive exploration of American identity than the primarily New York setting of the original graphic novel.

The second is that moving the narrative to Oklahoma allows for a greater focus on race and gender in the United States. Tulsa was the site of "Black Wall Street," and the site of the Tulsa Race Massacre in 1921, one of the worst racial attacks in the early twentieth century. During the Harlem Renaissance, large numbers of Black people were migrating west and south. Close to ten thousand had settled in Tulsa, north of the railroad tracks. At this point in history, Oklahoma had a reputation for being a state friendly to Black people: "Some African-Americans participated in the land runs in the late 1800s. They included E.P. McCabe, who led a movement to make Oklahoma a majority-Black state free from white oppression" (Murphy 2021). By 1921, the Greenwood District of Tulsa, known colloquially as "Black Wall Street," was the wealthiest Black community in the United States, dominated by Black-owned businesses. On May 31, a small group of residents of Greenwood went to the sheriff's office in downtown Tulsa to stop a white mob that planned to abduct and lynch Dick Rowland, a nineteen-year-old Black man accused of assaulting a white woman in an elevator, which he denied. Rumors of a Black insurrection led to a violent attack by a white mob already resentful of Black wealth and success. An estimated ten thousand white Oklahomans descended on Greenwood and burnt it to the ground, destroying everything and killing up to three hundred Black people (see Goodwin 2021 and Murphy 2021). As Professor Karlos K. Hill observes, "The scope and scale of the violence and destruction was unprecedented" (quoted in Goodwin 2021). Although Greenwood was rebuilt, insurance claims were all denied, 1256 homes and 191 businesses were destroyed, and upwards of ten thousand Black people were left homeless. The event was never discussed nor presented in history books or outside of Oklahoma. It is the moment that the attack on Greenwood begins that *Watchmen* starts its narrative.

The first episode of the series begins with a young Black boy watching a silent movie serial of Bass Reeves (Jamal Akakpo), a Black federal marshal who arrests white criminals. "Trust in the law," he tells the audience, and the young man takes it to heart. This young man is Will Reeves (Louis Gossett, Jr./Jovan Adepo/Danny Boyd, Jr.), who will grow up to be Angela's grandfather. Angela's world is one of inherited intergenerational trauma. Her estranged grandfather, whom she never knew until she arrested him for killing Judd Crawford (Don Johnson), was both a survivor of the Tusla massacre and Hooded Justice, the first costumed superhero. Her parents were killed in a terrorist bombing in Saigon when she was a child. She works as a secret police officer in a world in which a vast conspiracy of white people from all levels of society is working to preserve white power and the permanent disenfranchisement of people of color in the United States. Angela's world is also thus one of her own trauma—witnessing the death of her parents, the violence and harm that she witnesses (and perpetuates and is on the receiving end of) as a police officer in Tulsa, and her own experiences as a woman of color in a world that devalues both aspects.

The series has as an antagonist Lady Trieu (ironically pronounced "true") (Hong Chau), Adrian Veidt's Vietnamese-American daughter by artificial insemination, who secretly plans to capture, destroy, and steal the power of Dr. Manhattan. She, too, has experienced personal and racial trauma, including her rejection by her father (when she meets Veidt, he informs her he will never call her "daughter"), a childhood marked by isolation, tough love from her mother, determined to shape her into the most intelligent person in the world, and the pressures of having to compete at a very young age.

Thus, the series has as its primary protagonist and antagonist two women of color, both of whom are the descendants of world-changing superheroes. Their identities are explored in depth across the series, slowly revealing why each woman has chosen the path she has, and how different disenfranchised ethnic groups are perceived in the United States. Gene Roddenberry, the creator of *Star Trek*, often asserted that the distancing effect of its sci-fi premise allowed him to explore social issues that would have been untouchable in a straightforward dramatic series. *Watchmen* does the same with race in America in 2019. In this essay, I propose to explore and analyze female identity for women of color in *Watchmen* with a particular focus on Sister Night, and how this is linked and explored to law enforcement and race in a parallel America.

Watchmen and Purgatorial America

Watchmen is set not just in a parallel America but in a Purgatorial America—not heaven, not hell, not paradise, not punishment, but a place in between—a place of becoming. The narrative is nonlinear, focusing on all the steps of Angela Abar's life that led to the current events. The series shifts between events in 2019 Tulsa and Tulsa in 1921, New York in 1938, 1986, and 2009, and Saigon (once Vietnam became the fifty-first state in 1985) in 1987. Each of these locations plays a particular role in the development both of the events in Tulsa in 2019 and of Angela Abar/Sister Night.

Watchmen offers three visions of America—one dominated (as it has been historically) by white supremacy—a nation by and for white people. Alternately, the series offers another vision of America in which the white supremacy of the past is challenged, and a more multicultural nation emerges, particularly as the show unmasks the past to reveal that allies, such as Judd Crawford, Chief of Police in Tulsa and Angela's mentor, are secretly members of the Seventh Kavalry. This series demonstrates the complex racial realities behind the comic book surface, such as the plot to destroy Dr. Manhattan and give his powers to the leaders of the Kavalry, and that the historic Hooded Justice, presented in the television series, was actually a Black man fighting a racist conspiracy in the New York police, rather than a simple costumed crimefighter. The third vision is that of Lady Trieu, generating a peaceful world under her benevolent rule as a god-like being that controls all of reality.

The Seventh Kalvary and its allies attempt to retain and reinforce white supremacy by literalizing it. They plan to capture and disintegrate Dr. Manhattan, sending his essence into a gathering of wealthy white politicians, business leaders, and white supremist organizations. By doing so they will literally create a "Master Race," and thus be able to assert white supremacy and white privilege all over the United States and by extension, the world. Similarly, Lady Trieu disintegrates Cyclops and the Seventh Kavalry and then plans to absorb Dr. Manhattan's powers herself. Interestingly, the show reveals that Manhattan has already placed his powers in an egg which he has left for Angela to find and consume at their home. The series ends with her eating the egg and then approaching the family pool to see if she can walk on water, thereby proving she has Manhattan's powers. The final image cuts out just as she reaches for the water. This closing image implies this continuing state of becoming—she may now have his powers, but we never quite reach a state where they manifest, thus maintaining a purgatorial reality.

Watchmen's world is purgatorial as it is neither/nor. The Seventh Kavalry envisions a white supremacist paradise; Angela and her fellow officers envision a world in which racism, system and individual, does not exist and the police exist to protect the population from the few criminals within it rather than fight an entire system, and Lady Trieu envisions a world in which she is God. Three visions of "paradise," none realized yet. The world is also purgatorial as it is not just in a state of becoming but a constant state of becoming. Just as Catholic purgatory is where the sins of those not truly deserving of damnation and not truly (yet) worthy of Heaven are slowly burned away or purged. Purgatory is a place of flames—not the fires of hell but flames designed to purge away sin. The United States and particularly Tulsa are in a constant state of becoming. The (racist) sins of the past, seen with the attack on Greenwood at the beginning and the endemic corruption of the New York police in the late thirties, are being atoned for and burnt away, even as new sins emerge in the form of the Seventh Kavalry. Paradise remains an unreachable goal; current existence offers the atonement for past sins (the series presents President Robert Redford offering reparations to Black people for slavery, Jim Crow and the violence of the past such as in Tulsa), but no actual place of rest or salvation.

In addition, Tulsa is a purgatorial place for Angela Abar. Her family is originally from there, but it was a place of great trauma. Her grandfather and grandmother fled due to the Greenwood attack. Her father and grandmother returned there when Will's obsession with being Hooded Justice broke up the family. She herself moved to Saigon as a child but was then orphaned there and subsequently adopted by her grandmother, who brought her back to Tulsa, before she returned to Saigon as a police officer. Once she met and began dating Dr. Manhattan, they decided to disguise him and hide from the world. It was to Tulsa they fled as a place both familiar to Angela but also as a place in which one might hide.

Angela's identity as Sister Night also renders *Watchmen* a Purgatorial narrative. One of the roles of the faithful is to pray for the souls in Purgatory, and there are many dead in *Watchmen*: the large-scale dead of Tulsa, Vietnam, those killed in Adrien Veidt's squid attack in New York, not to mention the police killed on "White Night" and the planned death of Dr. Manhattan. The actions of Angela (her very name suggests "Angel") and Dr. Manhattan to transform the world into a better, less systemically racist, and more inclusive society are therefore a form of prayer for the dead designed to bring peace and salvation. The episode in which the two meet and begin dating is called "A God Walks into Abar" (S01. E8), hinting both at Dr. Manhattan's divine-like existence, but also his incarnation as Calvin Abar (Yahya Abdul-Mateen II), a dead American soldier whose image and identity he takes over (thus a kind of resurrection). If Dr. Manhattan is the Christ-like figure who might save America, Angela is his avenging angel whose role is to lead the souls out of the Purgatory that is contemporary America.

She took her identity from a fake 1977 video "Sister Night" about a Black nun who fights crime. The video bears the tagline "The Nun With the Motherf**kng gun," and Angela's father forbids her to rent the film, explaining that people who wear masks are not to be trusted. But the man who planted the bomb that killed her parents wore no mask, and the police in Tulsa do. June, the grandmother who raises Angela after her parents die, also explains that Marcus, Angela's father, had a bad experience with someone who wore a mask (referring to Hooded Justice), but that sometimes one needs to wear one. Sister Night, both the video version and Angela's police identity, is a crime-fighting nun. Within the Medieval church purgatorial piety and the offering of prayers for the dead in purgatory was the special province of women in general and specifically nuns. Angela is a nun whose violence, investigations, and powers of law enforcement are brought to bear on purging America's original sin—slavery and racism—and bring a kingdom of heaven on earth in a multicultural, multiracial society.

In addition to taking place in a Purgatorial America, *Watchmen* frames its narrative as an exploration of Angela's experience as a Black woman, and especially as a Black "super woman." The series first depicts Angela in her identity as the owner of a Vietnamese bakery in Tulsa. She teaches one of her children's classes how to make a Vietnamese mooncake (S01. E01, "It's Summer and We're Running out of Ice"). From the moment of introduction, she is presented in a domestic mode—a Black woman teaching a mixed-race class of elementary school students how to make a traditional Vietnamese food.

She used to be a police officer, but allegedly resigned after the "White Night"—an attack on the police of Tulsa by militant white supremacists that resulted in the deaths of many police. As she and her husband adopted the children of two police officers who had been killed, she assumes the identity of a retired officer who runs a bakery, but instead becomes a police officer. When the baking demonstration is over, she received a mysterious call. She goes to her yet-to-open bakery to reveal it has a secret basement which contains her costume and tools to become Sister Night, employing tropes familiar from any superhero narrative, including the original *Watchmen*.

The death of a Black police officer who had pulled over a lettuce truck leads to the police discovering the conspiracy by the Seventh Kavalry. Sister Night is placed in charge of the investigation because "I got a nose for white supremacy and he smells like bleach" (S01. E01). Behind the noir-like language is the idea that Sister Night, as a Black female police officer, is more likely to perceive the presence of racism than her fellow racist cops, who may have unconscious bias. Her gender and her ethnicity are linked. Brigid Cherry observes, "One factor of identity cannot easily be analyzed without considering others: gendered identities can be strongly linked to class or racial identity ... and the one cannot be discussed without the other" (2009: 176). This is certainly true in *Watchmen*, in which Angela and Lady Trieu's gender identity is thoroughly linked to racial identity as well. Both are women of color operating in a world dominated by not just white men but white supremacists. Laurie Blake (Jean Smart), a federal agent who used to be the masked vigilante Silk Spectre II from the graphic novel, has been sent to Tulsa by the FBI to investigate the Seventh Kalvary, but also see if the conspiracy lurks within the Tulsa police itself. Her presence is proven vital, as Police Chief Crawford was indeed a leader in the Kavalry, but also seemingly killed by Will Reeves. Blake is a life-long female crimefighter who must be more confrontational than the men in order to be taken seriously. Her gender identity shapes her identity and her behavior, but her whiteness also gets her access not available to Sister Night.

Angela, Sister Night, and the Danger of the "Black Superwoman"

In her home life, Angela is the breadwinner who makes her money by secretly fighting crime while pretending to run a domestic business—a bakery. She must pretend to a more traditionally feminine occupation of baking while actually engaging in crimefighting. Cal is a house husband: he stays home and takes care of the kids, but it is as much a ruse as Angela's bakery business. He is Dr. Manhattan, the self-regenerated Jon Osterman, the most powerful being in the universe. Yet it is Angela who runs the house and fights the world.

A common, problematic trope analyzed in scholarship is the "Black Superwoman," first scrutinized in depth by Michele Wallace in *Black Macho and the Myth of the Superwoman*, in which she observed that in the wake of the Black Power Movement of the sixties there was a paradox Black women who had to be stronger, hold the family together, and be dependable to all in the community, but was confronted by a male attitude that "[s]he was too domineering, too strong, too aggressive, too outspoken, too castrating, too masculine" (1979: 91). Black women organized and ran Black familial and community life but were resented for displaying any sense of power or agency as a result. Wallace posits the misogyny in the Black Power Movement with very few notable exceptions, disenfranchised Black women from any direct role in attacking systemic racism: "[T]heir only officially designated revolutionary responsibility was to have babies" (1979: 162). She concludes that strong Black women were "terribly important to the process of keeping food on the table and clothes on the children's backs" but, "the black man slowly began to believe that if she were weaker, he might mysteriously become more powerful" (1979: 155). Or, as Kara Manke observes, "[t]he stereotype of the 'strong black woman' is more than just a cultural trope: Many black women in America report feeling pressured to act like superwomen, projecting themselves as strong, self-sacrificing, and free of emotion to cope with the stress of race- and gender-based discrimination in their daily lives" (2019).Thus, historically Black women have had to contend not only with the systemic and direct individual racism that Black men did, they had to deal with the misogyny of white and Black society as well.

Watchmen plays with this dynamic as well, demonstrating a twenty-first-century twist. Angela is the breadwinner of the family, working as both police officer and allegedly a baker, but Cal, her husband, is the caregiver, staying home and taking care of their children. The irony is that he is secretly

Dr. Manhattan, the most powerful being in the universe. He willingly gives up being that most powerful entity to partner domestically with Angela. He serves as a model for post-racial, post-patriarchal masculinity. His partner's power is no threat to his identity. The series, however, undercuts this ideal by showing that Cal/Dr. Manhattan willfully sublimates his power and when she needs help, Angela hits Cal with a hammer to release Dr. Manhattan from his disguise and evoke his full powers.

This construction, however, does not change Angela's identity as a "Black Superwoman," which, for clarity's sake, does not refer to her abilities as a superhero but rather the requirement of every Black woman to be everything everyone in her life needs. Sister Night is the best of the detectives. Looking Glass is the psych expert, Red Scare and Pirate Jenny are presented as thugs whose major attribute is violence, but Sister Night is the investigator who actually can look at the clues provided by others and solve the mysteries. When the other police are killed by the Seventh Kavalry, it is Sister Night who survives and defeats them.

Paradoxically, it is the fact that she is the best of the police that makes Angela a threat to the Kavalry. She needs to be subjugated as her very existence is a threat to their ideology and construction of reality. Dr. Kinitra D. Brooks, writing of Michonne on *The Walking Dead*, observes, "The masculinity associated with her raced blackness illustrates that her womanhood is not the only qualifier in her subjugation" (2018: 35). In other words, misogyny and racism go hand-in-hand in contemporary American society, aimed at keeping women, and especially women of color, subjugated to men. The Seventh Kavalry's racism is matched by its misogyny.

Angela/Sister Night's identity as a strong, powerful Black woman who fights and defeats misogynistic white supremacy renders her a unique character in contemporary popular culture. Black women

> exist as a marginalized, sexualized, and fetishized group. By specifically focusing on how Black women are portrayed in the media and what messages they learn, starting early in life, especially as it relates to the shade of their skin and texture of their hair, we can engage in a broader discourse that challenges these notions and assists in the development of a positive identity for Black females and even other women of color.
>
> (Robinson, Allen-Handy and Burrell-Craft 2021: 86)

In addition, Construction of Black female identity includes elements of appearance (skin tone and hair texture) which are, as Robinson, Allen-Handy, and Burrell-Craft observe, "contentious aesthetic issues related to Black females' identity" (2021: 81). Angela (and Sister Night) is not sexualized, and especially not in her role as a crimefighter. Sister Night wears a hood so that her hair is not visible. While her identity as a Black woman is not hidden (her hands are visible), her face is obscured by a black mask and further obscured by her application of a black band around her eyes so her actual skin tone is not visible (perhaps an unconscious echo of Hooded Justice?). Many female superhero narratives rely on costuming that either exposes skin or is skin-tight and revealing of curves, cleavage, and buttocks, sexualizing the female superhero. As noted above, Sister Night's costume consists of a long leather jacket resembling a nun's habit, a cowl and mask, all of which she can use to confuse an opponent during a fight, for protection, and to render herself threatening. She is not sexualized; her skin and hair are not hidden but are de-emphasized. She is obviously a Black woman, but as Sister Night her appearance as a Black woman is not what defines her.

Angela Abar/Sister Night thus literalizes the Black Superwoman trope: an adoptive mother who cares for household, family, and community, while putting food on the table and fighting against endemic and systemic racism and sexism. Donning the costume of Sister Night better equips Angela Abar to deal with the purgatorial world of 2019 America:

> [Black Women] talked about every day walking out of their houses and putting on their 'armor' in anticipation of experiencing racial discrimination," said Amani M. Allen, associate professor of community health sciences and epidemiology at the University of California, Berkeley, describing focus groups she led with African American women in the San Francisco Bay Area.
>
> (Manke 2019)

This situation results in a Super Woman identity. Cheryl L. Woods-Giscombe, a professor at the University of North Carolina at Chapel Hill's School of Nursing, argues that the superwoman schema includes five elements: feeling an obligation to present an image of strength, feeling an obligation to suppress emotions, resistance to being vulnerable, a drive to succeed despite limited resources, and feeling an obligation to help others (Manke 2019). This list doubles as guidelines for Sister Night's attributes: she projects an image of strength, hides her emotions (other than rage, but even that is kept on a tight leash), resists vulnerability, and feels obliged to help others and continue working the case long after everyone else has gone home. Anything less would merely confirm the beliefs of the racist and sexist community. She is, however, more than the problematic aspects of the Black Superwoman trope. She uses them to achieve social justice; indeed, we might argue she transcends the trope by embodying it to achieve that goal.

We might view Sister Night as the embodiment of Black feminist thought. "The goal of Black feminist theory is the realization of justice and empowerment for U.S. Black women and other groups that are similarly oppressed within society" (Robinson, Allen-Handy and Burrell-Craft 2021: 80; see also Collins 2009). Certainly, Sister Night works for justice, but her idea of justice is rooted not in the preservation of power and privilege for the monied elites but in dismantling racist structures and organizations and in empowering oppressed groups. Even the classroom demonstration of moon cake making is designed to show a younger generation that accepts as reality a Black American woman teaching a multiethnic classroom Vietnamese culture. This is also in keeping with what Robinson, Allen-Handy, and Burrell-Craft acknowledge about Black feminist theory in the twenty-first century: it focuses on "women's emerging power as agents of knowledge" (2021: 81). Sister Night is the one who learns the truth about both the Kalvary's plan and Lady Trieu's plan. She is an "agent of knowledge" due to her unique experiences in Tulsa and Vietnam and as a police officer. She also becomes an agent of knowledge through her experience of her grandfather's lived trauma.

In the episode entitled "This Extraordinary Being" (S01. E06), she relives and experiences her grandfather's experiences as Hooded Justice by ingesting his entire supply of Nostalgia—Nostalgia is an all-natural drug developed by Trieu industries that transforms one's memories into tablets that allow others to lucidly experience them. By ingesting all of her grandfather's pills at once, she must experience his most traumatic memories as if she herself is in them. The name is ironic and appropriate—the traditional meaning of "nostalgia" is a sentimental longing for the past. The actual Greek etymology means a painful homecoming. By experiencing the violence and racism that Will Reeves experienced as a young New York police officer and later as Hooded Justice, Angela better understands the man she arrested as well as her own "origin story."

His memories are experienced as black and white, like an old film, with flashes of color. She sees him discover the police in league with the racist organization the Cyclops, how his fellow officers lynch him as a warning, and how he chooses to wear the noose he was literally hung with as a symbol of the justice he seeks and was denied him. She also learns that Reeves was inspired when he saw the original *Action Comics* with Superman on the cover and felt a kinship—his parents, too, sent him away from the destruction of home (Krypton/Tulsa) to keep him safe. This inspires him, like Superman, to don a disguise and fight crime, although the crime he wants to fight is the violence toward Blacks and other historically disenfranchised people by white supremacists. He is invited by Captain Metropolis, another masked crime fighter and his eventual closeted lover, to join the Minutemen, an organization of superheroes. The Minutemen refuse to fight racial injustice. Hooded Justice must therefore pretend to be white—even his secret identity is a mask. Young Will Reeves (Jovan Adepo) puts on white makeup around his eyes, so that under the hood he appears to be Caucasian.

This entire episode seems to demonstrate a different conception of the superhero from the one Alan Moore framed in white supremacy. Hooded Justice becomes a symbol of racial justice: he fights with his fists, and a gun, and fire, burning the warehouse where the Cyclops are storing movie projectors designed to encourage violence in Blacks as part of a mind-control experiment. The *Watchmen* series offers a Black superhero narrative rooted in representation and social critique versus racial violence as spectacle for mass entertainment.

One reason for this is that the series had twelve writers: four white men and eight men and women of color. *Watchmen* thus represents a genuine attempt to represent Black female identity in the superhero genre, both through representation on screen and through the lived experiences of the creators who write and develop these characters and narratives. Much of the publicity surrounding the initial release of the show centered on Regina King and the Black women who co-wrote the scripts, focusing on Black women's voices and ideas in the development of the narrative and the character. Kinitra D. Brooks argues that because Black women "confound" boundaries of race, gender, and class, they produce "fluid fiction," which is "a racially gendered framework that revises genre fiction in that it purposefully obfuscates the boundaries of science/fiction/fantasy/horror writing" (2018: 71). In other words, the fluidity of Black women as both producer/creators (let us remember the significant number of Black women in *Watchmen*'s writer's room) and characters create a fluidity of genre. *Watchmen* is indeed a superhero narrative, but also science fiction, with elements of the Western, and the self-aware performative nature of superheroes and Black female identity as well.

Conclusion: Black Female Identity as a Way Out of Purgatory

Watchmen is part of a larger cultural project of transformative representation in the twenty-first century. The need to replace negative stereotypes (and, for that matter, absences) of Black people and especially Black women with positive representations of Black female identity is vital (Robinson, Allen-Handy and Burrell-Craft 2021: 85). *Watchmen* has at its core the idea that, as noted from the quote from Alan Moore that began this essay, law enforcement and the depiction of superheroes have both been rooted in a culture of white supremacy. The series depicts Hooded Justice, the first superhero ever, as a Black man who became a masked vigilante because the police themselves were not only racist, but actively working with white supremacist organizations to subjugate, disempower, and even kill Black people. In the America of the series, in the 1950s, Hooded Justice refuses to reveal his identity to the House Un-American Activities Committee, stating in a Black newspaper that "[f]or as long as the structures of law and order are controlled by corrupt elites whose singular, cyclopean focus is to protect and fortify the interests and flourishing of the ruling majority, I will never surrender my mission to help the invisible and the oppressed" (S01. E06). The series suggests that the purpose of masked vigilantes should be to provide racial and social justice when the institutional mechanisms of law enforcement fail to do so, rather than simply be another tool of oppression. Combined with racial justice is also the need for gender equality. The Black female superhero can fight for women, in a way that even Queer superhero Hooded Justice cannot. For just as he hides his race with makeup, he hides his sexual orientation by being closeted.

The ultimate goal of this narrative is then to reexamine our own (purgatorial) world and its history (and ongoing practice) of social injustice and systemic racism. "Like the 1619 Project, *Watchmen* pushes its audience to question the passive acceptance of white objectivity, leaving it to wonder, in the words of one Wade Tillman: Is anything true?" (McDonald 2019). I would go one step further, adding that it also asks audience to question the passive acceptance of male objectivity and even straight objectivity. Sister Night and Hooded Justice's experiences center on Blackness, female Blackness and Queer Blackness. "Neither empowerment nor social justice can be achieved without some sense of what one is trying to change," notes Collins (2009: xi), which *Watchmen* makes clear. Systemic racism is still part of the American political, social, and cultural landscapes, but positive depictions of Black female identity in this Purgatorial America go a long way toward offering models of identity, thought, and a roadmap for systemic transformation out of Purgatory.

Works Cited

Borsellino, M. (2010), "How the Ghost of You Clings: *Watchmen* and Music," in R. Bensam (ed.), *Minutes to Midnight: Twelve Essays on Watchmen*, 24–37, Edwardsville, IL: Sequart.
Braxton, G. (2019), "History of Violence," *Los Angeles Times* (October 26), E1, E6–7.

Brooks, K. D. (2018), *Searching for Sycorax: Black Women's Haunting of Contemporary Horror*, New Brunswick: Rutgers University Press.
Cherry, B. (2009), *Horror*, New York: Routledge.
Collins, P. H. (2009), *Black Feminist Thought: Knowledge, Consciousness, and the Politics of Empowerment*, 2nd ed., London: Routledge.
Goodwin, J. (2021), "100 Years Ago This Area Was Known as Black Wall Street," *CNN Business*, May 16. https://www.cnn.com/2021/05/16/success/black-wall-street-tmd/index.html.
Manke, K. (2019), "How the 'Strong Black Woman' Identity Both Helps and Hurts," *Greater Good Magazine*, December 5. https://greatergood.berkeley.edu/article/item/how_the_strong_black_woman_identity_both_helps_and_hurts.
McCarter, R. (2019), "This Seems Like a Good Time to Revisit *Watchman* Co-creator Alan Moore's Thoughts on Modern Superhero Movies," *AV Club*, November 19. http://news.avclub.com/this-seems-like-a-good-time-to-revisit-alan-moores-thou-1839942438.
McDonald, S. N. (2019), "'Watchmen' Episode Six: 'This Extraordinary Being,'" *Andscape*, November 24. https://andscape.com/features/watchmen-episode-six-this-extraordinary-being/.
Murphy, S. (2021), "100 Years after Tulsa Massacre," *Los Angeles Times*, May 27, A2.
Robinson, P. A., A. Allen-Handy and K. Burrell-Craft (2021), "Critical Media Literacy and Black Female Identity Construction: A Conceptual Framework for Empowerment, Equity, and Social Justice in Education," *Journal of Media Literacy Education*, 13(1): 79–91.
Wallace, M. (1979), *Black Macho and the Myth of the Superwoman*, New York: The Dial Press.

14

"We're Human Too, You Know": Tethered Journeys and Shadowed Struggles in Jordan Peele's *Us* (2019)

Nancy Johnson-Hunt

A Starting Point

Recurrent tropes of the "angry Black woman" have long since been employed and exploited in American popular culture. Such tropes are constructed in response to the covert socioeconomic frameworks that Black characters are relegated. These characterizations, denigrations, and perhaps even emancipation of the "angry Black woman" call attention to the complex navigation of a white world through the Black lens. In Jordan Peele's film titled *Us* (2019), main characters Red and Adelaide, both of whom are played by actor Lupita Nyong'o, are representative of the invisible and (de)humanizing position of the Black female experience in the United States. The film is an allegorical horror in every sense. While interspersed with black comedy, it represents the social, cultural, and political framework that underpins American society. The implicit attributes of America's acerbic history are reflected in a cross section of the characters who are seen to employ familiar racial tropes to convey the "absurdity in which the social realities of race and class are rooted" (Wall 2019: 458). Adelaide and Red can be interpreted as mirror images of each other: the former a willing participant in the social hierarchies of present-day America; the latter, a transgressive presence who seeks gratification through cruel and calculated means. While Adelaide personifies the docile and conforming Black woman from the outside, Red exemplifies the fraught recalcitrant Black figure who seeks vindication for her suffering. Red herself occupies the liminal spaces that exist between anger and agency and her resistance as well as persistence make her presence not just known but felt. The film illustrates how American society in particular does not always overtly recognize these emotional injuries, but how it casts Black women aside without any form of restitution or resolve (Jones and Norwood 2016). *Us* serves as a vehicle for such nuanced topics of femininity and race, while also calling attention to the racialized nature of specific emotions. Each of these Black female characters subverts social expectations, their quest for belonging marred by personal traumas, torture, and ultimately revenge.

The film *Us*, set in both 1986 and present-day Santa Cruz, chronicles the Wilson family as they experience a beach-bound summer of grim and horror-filled happenings. More specifically, this chapter will examine the characters of Adelaide Wilson and her tethered *doppelgänger*, known as Red. The use of the *doppelgänger* in this storytelling context reveals much about the construction of the underground which exists beneath the holiday location where the Wilsons are staying. According to Deborah Barnstone the *doppelgänger*, a German term that literally denotes "double-walker" is an "exact duplicate of the living person, indistinguishable from the original" (2016: 1). Barnstone further explains, the *doppelgänger* can be anything from a twin to a "mirror image, portrait, split personality, alter ego, mechanical doll, or ghostly shadow" (2016: 1). In *Us* Adelaide and Red are represented as mirror images of each other, tethered by their souls, while their bodies remain split in two. Such doubling has been traditionally predicated on the notion of evil, death, misfortune, and the dual nature of the human psyche. Since the birth of modern psychology, artists, filmmakers, and writers increasingly rely on the use of the double to signify both mental and spiritual traumas, and adjacent struggles related to identity and the ego (Barnstone 2016). As part of this exploration of Adelaide and Red, it is obvious that the conceptual nature of the *doppelgänger* has been employed to convey "unattainable goals, frustrated ambitions, and latent impulses" (Barnstone 2016: 1).

Upon Adelaide's arrival in Santa Cruz, she embodies a quiet solitude, her role as a mother and wife is reinforced as a guiding element in her determination. Adelaide later embarks on taking ownership of her destiny, an aspect of her childhood she has conveniently compartmentalized as a result of early emotional injuries. In stark contrast, Red, who is presented as a shadow-figure to Adelaide, typifies both the "angry Black woman" and "strong black woman" archetype, who seeks not only revenge but exoneration for a traumatic and troubled journey from the discarded "othered" in the underground. According to bell hooks, Blackness remains a "backdrop for otherness" (2014: 39) and historically it is Black women who must assume the mantle for strength as well as the role of object. Both Adelaide and Red represent a site of otherness through their sustained struggle, epitomized by internal and external manifestations of trauma, anger, and at times grief.

Over the course of the film Adelaide harbors disturbing memories from her childhood only to find she will eventually endure a series of macabre confrontations with Red. While Red serves as a mirror for these grim memories, she also appoints herself somewhat of a social architect, restoring what she feels is her rightful position within the social order of the above world. Although hooks argues that "theorizing black experience in the United States is a difficult task" (2014: 2), there is much to the examination of such tropes and depictions of Black female characters that remains worthy of revealing intricate critical analysis and reflection. This chapter will explore how the angry Black woman trope intersects with aspects of Black womanhood and racialized narratives. In this broader exploration, this chapter will also critically examine how the construction of Black female characters of Adelaide and Red help to amplify marginalized voices and bring light to Black female agency, empowerment, and collective resistance to structural oppression.

Tracing Anger: Exploring the Origins of the "Angry Black Woman" Trope

Negative portrayals of African-American women are not new, nor are they rare (Walley-Jean 2009). To critically examine characters Adelaide and Red, it is imperative to provide a foundation for the "angry Black woman" trope as well as the broader connections to more entrenched and prevalent stereotypes of the "Mammy," "Jezebel," and "Matriarch." The historic origins for such stereotypes in the American context begin with the image of the "Mammy," or as a residual mother-like archetype from the enslavement period, who was heralded for her loyalty as a content and obedient domestic slave (West 1995; Collins 2000; Walley-Jean 2009). The original "Mammy" character was constructed as a means to justify the "economic exploitation" while also serving as a "normative yardstick used to evaluate all Black women's behavior" (Collins 2000: 72). As Ayondela McDole (2017) observes, the "Mammy" is defined specifically by conventions that characterize her as a maternal figure, who is asexual in nature and maintains an ambiguous caretaker role to children. By the twenty-first century, these characterizations became naturalized through the white gaze as part of the popular African-American narrative. Contemporary characterizations of the "Mammy" extend beyond the realm of film and television, and may also be typified by real-life personalities, one such example is Oprah Winfrey who is seen as the "mother of America" (West 1995; Walley Jean 2009: 70). While Winfrey has no children of her own, the extensive reach of such pervasive stereotypes further illustrates that no African-American woman in any position, be that of celebrity status or social regard, remains unaffected. The "Mammy" caricature has therefore been employed to regenerate the romanticized notion by which slavery was a tolerable experience and has since been exploited both across film and in real life for decades.

The second image of the "Jezebel" was used in the branding of African-American women as sexually immoral. The "Jezebel" was conceptualized through slavery to justify sexual atrocities between white men and Black women. Atrocities such as rape and sexual assaults prolonged the reproduction of slaves and as a result rationalized the selling of mixed-race women into prostitution furthering the vicious cycle of brutality (Jewell and Staff 1993). West maintains that the "Jezebel" has become ubiquitous for its framing of "bad Black girl" imagery with sexual promiscuity (1995: 462). Descriptions of the Jezebel are more commonly associated with words that are singular in nature, from seductive and alluring to worldly and lewd (Cheers 2017). The words have since evolved into more contemporary classifications like "hood-rats," "freaks," and "hoochies," which evoke a sense of deviant behavior and subversive activities and expressions of racial identity. Additionally, it is important to note that such imagery of the "bad girl" has been applied to women from various ethnic and racialized backgrounds (West 1995). Such applications of this typification however remain more affixed to Black women than other ethnic groups; Angela Davis claims that the "image of a Black women's sexuality has never been depicted as demure or moral, vis-á-vis the historic sexual image of white women" (Davis as quoted in West 1995: 462). Indeed, as a group, white women were depicted through modes of sexual innocence, modesty, purity, and self-control while Black women were "often portrayed as innately promiscuous, even predatory" (Cheers 2017: 51). In the analysis of this chapter, neither characters Adelaide or Red are depicted through this sexualized lens, no reference is made to them as "hoochies" or "freaks" and yet the "bad Black girl" image is applied. These connections, while not overt, are still evident in their constructions as both characters are emblematic of the merging of distinct images to build a unique and still recognizable entity within Black film.

The third image of the Matriarch, also referred to as the "Sapphire," was constructed in direct opposition to the "Mammy" and is deemed a close connection to the "failed Mammy" image (Walley-Jean 2009: 71). As part of the wider cast in the situational comedy (sitcom) titled *The Amos n' Andy Show* (1928–60), the role of Sapphire Stevens during the 1940s and 1950s was created as an antithetical answer to either cheerful or subdued representations of Black femininity on-screen. Following this character's construction, the Matriarch continues to embody an overly aggressive nature, hostile, and masculinized. As Walley-Jean asserts, this image was amplified by the economic and social systems in place in the mid-twentieth century. As African-American women were forcibly designated to the workforce alongside their male counterparts, this "subsequently prevented them from fitting the standard of femininity" more associated with upper-class white women (Walley-Jean 2009: 70). Classist, racist, and sexist overtones of the white gaze in film and television have since established the frameworks of failure surrounding the lives of African-American women. The application of such images "allowed society to ignore the past and contemporary social realities" of the traumatic history of enslavement and the unreasonable demands placed on such African-American women to continue to provide for both their own and peripheral white families (Walley-Jean 2009: 71). As such, the unfeminine Matriarch with her belligerent and combative tendencies has become immortalized on screen without holding responsibility for the systemic discrimination faced by African-American women. The Matriarch or the Sapphire has increasingly dominated portrayals of Black women and has since become the genesis for what is currently deemed the "angry Black woman" caricature. For these reasons, it is evident across the scholarship that the trajectories for Black female characters in both film and television have been constructed on the basis of control, objectification, and fetishization. As Bettina Judd notes, the Matriarch or the Sapphire "produces a paradox by which Black women's knowledge and feeling is sequestered into chaotic impulse rather than controlled reason" (2019: 180). Applying this analysis of characters to Adelaide and Red it is apparent that the merging of anger and asexuality in their characters works to further dehumanize their experience and thereby their existence.

These stereotypes remain pervasive across popular culture and remain engrained into the social psyche despite there being little to no empirical evidence on how anger may be felt more strongly among Black women than any other groups. While depictions of the Black female in film embody such characterizations of anger, these may be in direct opposition to their white counterparts, with little emphasis placed on the journey they navigate as a result of this anger. As such, permeations and permutations of the "angry Black woman" trope continue to influence society's opinion of African-American women (Walley-Jean 2009). In this chapter's exploration of the film *Us*, the characters Adelaide and Red, whom both serve as constructions of the "angry Black woman" trope, can also be seen to comprise of the stereotypes such as the Mammy, Jezebel, and Matriarch. Specifically, Adelaide embodies conventions of the asexual and ambiguous caregiver role of the Mammy. While not necessarily in the jovial sense, but upon her introduction in the film, Adelaide's quiet reserve and physical presence demonstrates an inclination toward conformity and obedience. In contrast, Red's character assumes alternative forms of the Jezebel and Matriarch, making her visibly hostile, transgressive, and overly aggressive. Through this critical analysis of Us, and the characters of Adelaide and Red, their "inner lives" may help advance the narratives by which "the angry Black woman trope is meaningful" to Black women's sense of agency and selfhood (Judd 2019: 179).

In the last five years, there has been considerable scholarly attention paid to deconstruct or restore the trope of the "angry Black woman" into a figure of empowerment, strength, resilience, and ultimately liberation (Walley-Jean 2009; Allen 2015; Jones and Norwood 2016; Cheers 2017; Judd 2019; Simms 2021). It is also important to note that across both literature and film, negative stereotypes of the "angry Black woman" continue to persist (Athnasios 2021). However, there has been a significant shift in depicting the emotional complexities of the collective Black female experience through the work of Black directors and writers, such as Ava DuVernay, Jordan Peele, Shonda Rhimes, and Tyler Perry. Additionally, there is a recognition in the advancement for such scholarship to focus more closely on the trajectory between Black girlhood experiences and the "angry Black woman" trope, to ensure that such nuances are critically analyzed (Simms 2021).

The Funhouse as a Metaphorical Gateway of Black Girlhood Neglect

As demonstrated through reciprocal family dynamics, Us is inherently focused on the exchange between nature versus nurture. This importance of mutuality as Wall suggests "is underlined by the film being situated within the parameters of that most redolent and powerful of American symbols, the family" (2019: 459). The Wilson family plays an important foundation for closeness and mutuality, a dynamic that is critical in their survival and escape from their underground *doppelgängers*. However, as the film proceeds, we see this dynamic evolve as Adelaide's true identity reveals itself.

In the beginning of the film, we are introduced to a young Adelaide at the Santa Cruz boardwalk as she walks through the amusement park. There is a tangible rift between her parents, who are referred to only in flashbacks as nameless characters. While they argue, the camera is intent on focusing on Adelaide's presumably blank stare and there is no overt or discernible reaction at her parents quarreling in front of her. This lack of emotion can be seen as Adelaide's disassociation from her parent's troubled relationship. Her childhood innocence is challenged through having to manage such a volatile relationship, a view that is corroborated by Michael Dumas and Christina Sharpe who observe that "Black girls are never granted innocence or the state of being a child" (Sharpe as cited in Halliday 2019: 22). Her father becomes increasingly aggravated by her mother's assertion to look out for Adelaide as she leaves to find a bathroom. Her father's inattention coupled with her mother's insistence highlight the subtleties of neglect that are commonly used through Black girlhood narratives. As Ruth Nicole Brown (2009) further notes, the struggle faced by Black girls is inherently tied to their race, class, sexuality, and gender, and as such does not prevent them from facing such negative and harmful experiences as part of this journey. In this instance, Adelaide, like many young Black girls have to navigate a childhood that is rife with fear, misunderstanding, and loneliness while simultaneously yearning to belong (hooks 1997).

According to Simms the pervasive nature of the "angry Black woman" trope "is rarely placed in a context that considers Black girlhood" (Simms 2021: 1); however, the film captures both the origins of such girlhood trauma and its trajectory into adulthood (Simms 2021). Adelaide's character navigates these complexities, even though she is risking her life in the process. As Adelaide abandons her father in pursuit of entertainment, she happens upon the "Funhouse," a mirror maze that leads her to an untimely encounter with what is implied to be her *doppelgänger*. She later resurfaces, unwilling to speak. At this point of transition, her mother discovers that this new Adelaide no longer speaks; her voice disappears leaving both parents distressed as to what may have occurred during her disappearance. Adelaide's mother visits a child psychologist in the hope that her daughter's speech may return. She believes that the trauma of the subsequent events that transpired in the funhouse has left her speechless. As we learn through the film, this Adelaide does not speak because she does not want to but because this version of Adelaide has never been taught. It is later revealed that the original Adelaide never escapes the funhouse and is replaced by her clone/double who assumes her position in the "above ground"; this is who we later discover is Red. This is the foundation for which Red enacts her revenge in pursuit of vindication. While Red later demonstrates how crucial the inequalities of being raised in the underground may be, it is evident upon this replacement of Black bodies, one child is nurtured back into a worthy life while the "other" suffers in a purgatorial space underground.

In addressing the inequalities of Black girlhood specifically, Audrey Lorde (1984) argues, "[I]t is the right of children to be able to play at living ... but for a Black child every act can have deadly serious consequences and for a Black girl child, even more so" (as cited in Halliday 2019: 23). The traumatic events that transpire in the underground become the foundation for the "angry Black women" trope to materialize, but, as Judd (2019) maintains, can also be the focus for more meaningful practice of self-hood.

Within the beginning of the film, Adelaide experiences sudden vivid memories of her childhood in Santa Cruz. It is not discernible in these flashback sequences that a switch occurred between herself and Red in the past. However, it is inferred on multiple occasions that these memories are key to a disturbing event which transpired and, in many ways, is the cause for residual trauma in the adult version of Adelaide. Prior to Adelaide's admission to her husband Gabe (Winston Duke) that something untoward happened during her childhood at the Santa Cruz pier, she is inflicted with deeply troubled memories. However, for the sake of her family and to ensure that their beach vacation remains unaffected, Adelaide, like many Black female characters, illustrates a sense of quiet resolve in the face of adversity. Simms explains that in these instances and in ironic fashion, "Black girls are often stripped of their girlhood and innocence while simultaneously burdened with family and community labels of strength and responsibility" (2021: 8).

Generally speaking, there are clear cultural expectations that suggest that most children are worthy of innocent childhood experiences that absolve them from adult responsibilities. However, "the presumption of innocence for Black girls, on the other hand, is tenuous at best" (2021). While the adult Adelaide demonstrates a certain stoicism during these flashback scenes, for most Black girls into womanhood, silence is used as a coping mechanism in light of the traumas they have to face (Simms 2021). Upon having these flashbacks, Adelaide's silence speaks to these residual traumas. As Simm's maintains when Black girls and women "choose to speak out, they are often ridiculed, accused of lying, or ignored altogether" (2021: 9), which is the exact reaction that Gabe exhibits when Adelaide reveals this encounter with her childhood *doppelgänger*. For these reasons, Adelaide learns to not only silence herself in the process but is also unable to take ownership of being rightfully angry at the systemic injustices that exist in her world. This anger is then transferred to Red, as Red uses her voice to speak out on the atrocities of the underground. As such, over the course of the film we witness Adelaide and Red not only mirror each other in their childhood experiences, but how rage replaces silence in a bid to win back some semblance of agency.

Mirroring Rage: A (De)Construction of Dualities

The subterranean underworld in *Us* denotes a thinly veiled allegory for white supremacy, that in order to succeed as a Black woman, you must conform quietly and without tension or resistance. Peele's presentation of Black female marginalization in *Us* explicitly weaves together critical components of race, class, and gender as "equally determinant and (mutually supporting) social formations" (Wall 2019: 459). This is exemplified through the tethered shadow people relegated to America's mutual migrant basement which is arguably a metaphor for the lower or even "other" class. Adelaide and Red are emblematic of the journey for those deemed as second-class citizens and the eventual triumph over the systemic obstacles built for the purpose of sustained marginalization. As hallmarks of these racial tragedies, we witness the brutality of conformity and the challenges faced by Black women when rage is the only outcome for such traumatic events. These emotions have become racialized on-screen and have become exploited for decades. As Sherrie Allen suggests, "the 'angry Black woman' is a myth that continues to be rehashed using stereotypes to perpetuate the oppression of Black womanhood" (2015: iv). The story of *Us* explores how Adelaide and Red play the role of the "angry Black women" but also how they choose to navigate their pain in idiosyncratic ways. Such idiosyncrasies are not commonly represented on Black film or through Black female characters as these roles are commonly depicted for their recognizable archetypal constructions. What makes *Us* unique is how rage is constructed, at times more nuanced and subtle but also blatant and hostile. Adelaide while seemingly portrayed as aloof, secretive, and reticent by nature is countered through Red who functions as a darker and more extreme mirror image of the two. Thus, the "anger and rage black women carry possibly offers new solutions to modern problems that plague them" and can be used as a vehicle for how agency is an antidote to rage (Allen 2015: 10).

In many ways, the film addresses the racialized experiences and gendered struggles of navigating Black girlhood into womanhood, while simultaneously having to own anger in the process. When we are first introduced to Adelaide, she is joined by her family driving down to their holiday home in Santa Cruz, California. Adelaide is seated quietly in the front of the car, while not seeming to share her husband's enthusiasm for a summer vacation. Her attention, while preoccupied, circles between her husband and her children. As the visual framing suggests, Adelaide is constructed as a Black woman with a seemingly ordinary life. She belongs to a small nuclear family with a holiday home and motorboat which are used as peripheral signifiers of reasonable wealth and leisure. Over the course of the film, Adelaide's calm demeanor slowly unravels on screen as the imminent threat of her past resurfaces in ruinous ways. The threat of losing all she has worked hard for is simply minutes from entering her home.

As part of this introductory scene, we then meet Red along with the Wilson family *doppelgängers* in their Santa Cruz beach house a third of the way into the film. Emerging as a hostile group, Red's whispered restraint in her pursuit of revenge is terrifyingly calculated in inflicting pain. Red is a Black woman whose rage is measured in approximations; her actions with her signature razor-sharp gold scissors are contemplative but nonetheless a terrifying figure to behold. Adelaide and Red's mutual and mirrored rage is the result of a collective reckoning as opposed to a united front. As Wall suggests, the film is not a (re)presentation of "we're all in this together" but rather "if attention is not paid and inequalities addressed, the exploited underclass will visit upon those above ground" (2019: 458).

As Red situates herself in Adelaide's home, her menacing nature is evident upon her distorted oration. Her voice is broken and ominous as she narrates, while stroking her deformed male child across his head, the fire crackling in the background. She begins:

> Once upon a time, there was a girl and the girl had a shadow, the two were connected, tethered together, and when the girl ate, the food was given to her warm and tasty, but when the shadow was hungry, she had to eat rabbit raw and bloody.
>
> (Peele 2019)

As part of this dystopian fairy-tale, we see a comparison emerge between Red and Adelaide, with one life prioritized while the other forgotten, diminished in parts to suffering and pain. As Red continues her monologue, she highlights how the "shadow" had no bodily autonomy, from her subjugation to faux matrimony, to the tortures of childbirth and subsequent birth traumas. She continues, "[S]o you see, the shadow hated the girl, so much for so long until one day the shadow realized she was being tested by God" (Peele 2019). Throughout Red's recital, Adelaide remains still, cold, and emotionless. While a single tear is shown to drop from her eyes, Adelaide's husband, Gabe, offers his wallet as compensation for Red's suffering. His unawareness of the gravity of Red's story only further amplifies the extent of ignorance of the existence of "others" and especially those who are relegated to the underground. As Samuel Kimbles suggests, "we tend to be unconscious of our complexes until suffering makes us aware of their existence and organizing power in our daily lives" (Kimbles cited in Allen 2015: 159). In what is constructed like an amusing scenario, Gabe's delicate mockery speaks volumes and is symptomatic of the general criticism Black women are faced with when bringing attention to their pain.

According to Lupita Nyong'o, the quality of Red's voice was employed as a storytelling device for her raw rage (Ugwu 2019). Developed as part of the condition known as spasmodic dysphonia, Peele (2019) describes the broken voice as one that has not been used in years, calling further attention to the forgotten bodies and voices situated in the underground (Ugwu 2019). As a symbolic and physical manifestation of this broken system, Jones and Norwood propose that "even if a Black woman is saying the very things that others are saying, her voice on certain topics (particularly those involving discrimination and inequality) is viewed with skepticism, as if her Blackness and womanness disqualify her from speaking" (2016: 2037). This marginalization is amplified through Red's broken voice box, which struggles to verbalize the story in a clear and distinct manner. While the words may be deemed in earnest, the speech is neutralized by the lowered volume. The muted and hushed tenor is symbolic of how difficult the trajectory of trauma may be. As implied by her entrance Red's journey is ultimately undone by her broken voice. For these reasons, it can be understood that such encounters contribute to the continued criticism against other "Black women who push against exclusionary hierarchies instead of the root causes of the problem (i.e., the exclusionary hierarchies)" (Jones and Norwood 2016: 2037). As a result, the gendered and raced voices of Black women become problematic, as opposed to the underlying issues to which they are trying to bring attention to. Therefore, Red not only embodies the "angry Black woman" trope through her physical performance but by which her very words signify the Black female struggle is yet to be understood and therefore believed.

According to Judd the "angry Black woman" trope is most recognizable during the moment in which Black women are expected to verbalize their emotions, and further elaborates that the trope "delegitimizes Black women's speech and emotions whether we are angry or not" (2019: 187). Additionally, Judd maintains that anger is marked as symptomatic of a Black woman's pathology, ingrained in the natural state of being as opposed to the shared experiences of marginalization. These characterizations also connect to broader issues surrounding female emotion entirely. According to Teresa Bernardez (1988) women within Western cultures have shown an inability to present anger, without it challenging predisposed notions of control and emotional regulation (cited in Allen 2015: 11). As Bernardez reiterates, "women's expression of anger is usually thwarted, inhibited, or diverted in our culture. This phenomenon acquires the character of a cultural prohibition ... the view that women's anger is a destructive emotion" (Allen 2015). As such, this typification of anger as inherent in the Black woman's experience is further enhanced by Red's contained performance. Her premeditated approach to anger, as demonstrated through her monologue and subsequent attacks, is seen as crazed and delusional in the face of Adelaide's entire family, as they remain dismissive of the underlying reasoning for Red's arrival. Through this hostile interaction, there is not a single Wilson family member who questions what Red must have gone through, but rather see her as villainous in her attempt to vindicate herself.

It is important to note that the reliance on the "angry Black woman" trope can be detrimental both in erasing the complexities of Black women's emotions and evading the deeper impacts of white supremacy and systemic racism. The exploitation of such tropes through the white gaze further results in severe socioeconomic disparities within the Black population. However, from this analysis, it is evident that both Red and Adelaide, through their construction in a Black directed film, their anger, and other nuanced emotions such as fear and grief, are capable of challenging as well as dismantling the hegemonic structures of oppression. Celeste Walley-Jean (2009) describes this anger as a source of empowerment, as a means of self-preservation and protection from unfair treatment and subsequent micro-aggressions. Like numerous depictions Black female characters in literature and popular incarnations, the "angry Black woman" trope may also create space for which strength and resilience underpin the outward manifestation of anger. While Simms argues the trope "simultaneously delegitimizes real and justified experiences of anger" (2021: 2), Allen (2015) suggests that it can be employed to reframe rage and redirect anger in a bid to find and amplify the Black female voice. As such, Adelaide and Red's anger and resistance to patriarchal conventions help them reclaim their bodily autonomy and agency in the process.

Reconstructing the "Angry Black Woman" Trope: Does Agency Legitimize Anger?

As part of Adelaide's first adult interaction with Red, she begins by asking what Red wants and Red responds, "We want to take our time, we have been waiting for this day for so long," and concedes, "I call it the untethering" (Peele 2019). From this scene onwards and over the course of the rest of the film, Red and Adelaide enact a cat and mouse-style chase. Red and her signature razor-edged gold scissors, an instrument gifted in the underground, is used to untether herself from both the bodies of the aboveground but also the symbolic systems of oppression that have led to the abandonment of the tethered. Prior to the final conflict scene, Adelaide follows Red into the underground. As suggested through her familiarity with her surroundings, it is evident that Adelaide has been in the underground before. Indeed, as Jeffries also confirms, Adelaide's motion is that of "military precision," which further reinforces that Adelaide may be just as calculated in her desire for autonomy (2020: 294). Ultimately, after a prolonged cat and mouse sequence ensues, they eventually find themselves in America's purgatorial basement. Rabbits from the cages are seen roaming the corridors of the basement, after they have been seemingly set free. The rabbits, as Red mentions in her verbal prelude to the Wilson family aboveground, were not only presented as a meal, but their docile nature in what are cages in a laboratory style basement speaks to the insidious nature of the underground. The rabbits symbolize what experiments may have presumably taken place. Eventually, we see Adelaide and Red in what looks like a classroom. Here, Red remains cutting paper into an undisclosed shape facing a big blackboard with her back to Adelaide, Adelaide carefully stalking toward Red, only stopping when she speaks. Red, in her signature broken drawl, says, "How it must have been to grow up with the sky. To feel the sun, the wind, the trees. But your people took it for granted. We're human too, you know. Eyes, teeth, hands, blood. Exactly like you" (Peele 2019). As Adelaide stalks Red from behind, Red continues:

> And yet, it was humans that built this place. I believe they figured out how to make a copy of the body, but not the soul. The soul remains one, shared by two. They created the Tethered so they could use them to control the ones above. Like puppets. But they failed and they abandoned the Tethered. For generations, the Tethered continued without direction. They all went mad down here.
>
> (Peele 2019)

Harry Olafsen argues that the "Tethered girl uses her time under what is essentially colonial rule to upend the aboveground girl and swap places with her" (2020: 23). This claim that time is bound by colonial rule suggests that oppression is a paradigm that requires incisive change, which Red takes it upon herself to facilitate. However, as indicated through the film, colonially engrained and systemic structures are difficult to dismantle, even if Red exercises her agency to do so. As Olafsen elaborates, "while Red may be the savior for the Tethered, she also plays a role in their subjugation, while she, herself, is continuously oppressed by Adelaide and the rest of the aboveground people" (2020: 26). hooks (2014) claims that this internalized subjugation is not uncommon within the Black collective experience, and that these traumas are especially deeply engrained in Black women. As hooks further observes, "among black women, such deeply internalized pain and self-rejection informs the aggression inflicted on the mirror image—other black women" (2014: 42). As Red and Adelaide engage in the final fight scene, Red enacts a dance sequence of sorts, with Adelaide while circling her in the underground classroom. During this fight sequence, there are also flashbacks of Red and Adelaide dancing as children, highlighting the mimicry of the tethered underground. They continue this scene through the corridors eventually ending up in the basement bedroom, bunkers lining the room. Here as Red stalks behind, Adelaide strikes puncturing Red through the abdomen, the fight ends with Red hugging Adelaide while whistling the same tune she was found doing as she entered the funhouse. In the end, Red is strangled by Adelaide using handcuffs. As she dies, Adelaide lets out a grimace and then a sustained breathless laugh; she has saved herself from the very place she was initially tethered (Peele 2019). In many ways, this scene indicates that Black characters do not have be constructed as loudmouthed archetypes as perpetuated in the media (Abdurraqib 2017). In Red and Adelaide's case, they can be decisive, incisive even, and that ultimately a reconstruction of Black female anger is imperative as part of the peripheral emotions that their characters embody. In this case, Adelaide has always been the winner right from the initial swapping of places.

In the film, internalized pain and suffering resurfaces through rage but is reconstructed with the idea of inner strength. This inner strength is then employed in a means to form a sense of individual agency, the kind of agency that drives Red and Adelaide to overcome obstacles in a bid to create a different world for themselves. While they are both seemingly oppressed through the wider lens of racial oppression, there is something to be said about how they both envision a different future for themselves. For Adelaide it was literally to swap positions with the original inhabitant of the above world, while Red premeditates a plan for herself over the course of her underground oppression. In the entirety of the film, this journey of self-actualization was never about whether Red or Adelaide would succeed in the aboveground, it was about whether they would overcome their oppression. As Samaa Abdurraqib (2017) describes, this strength was (and continues to be) crucial, "serving to bind black families and communities and to heal black people from outside racist attacks" (cited in Chappell and Young 2017: 231). In many ways, while strength and anger can be seen as an impediment in Black female narratives, it can also be seen as equally liberating as it is evident that both characters can survive without male support. For instance, more recent Black horror films have been led by either a Black male protagonist or antagonist. Jordan Peele's 2017 *Get Out* and Nia Da Costa's 2021 directorial reimagining of *Candyman* are both Black horror films which have been constructed through the Black male lens, although one could argue that Black traumas are a shared spectrum of experience, be it through micro-aggressions or through the infliction of racial violence. As Bellot, Cox, and McKinney (2021) elaborate, these recent horror films redress racial violence "by capturing, in various ways, what it feels like to experience horror as a Black American, when your mere *presence* can itself be a source of terror to others" (par 3).

In *Us* however, Red and Adelaide's Black identities, and womanhood foster a shared experience of agency and influence. For Red, this is shown through her leadership of the underground, while Adelaide's influence is felt by her family as the matriarch. As part of this Black female agency, their characters are constructed in a way that reshapes race and gender dynamics, in particular the paradigm of Black horror that has been typically cast through the Black male lens.

Concluding Remarks

Us is an allegorical representation of how the deeply ingrained systems of oppression can only be dismantled on account of Red's rage and her knowing appropriation of the trope of the "angry Black woman." Her liminal existence, in being from above, but raised below, is symbolic of the purgatorial structure of the underground, where all those within it are labeled as the "Tethered" and therefore lacking the soul to be considered as human. This dehumanization of the tethered as the allegorical and mirrored "other" serves as justification for the atrocities of slavery during early American colonization and subsequent growth as a nation. As noted above, the "angry Black woman" trope serves to continue the subjugation of Black female bodies, while also being a symptom of the physical, sexual, and mental abuse they have continually suffered at the hands of American white supremacy and privilege. *Us* then reveals that this anger is justified, but also that the trope itself is one that can be mimicked and reappropriated by Black women to find agency and freedom from the purgatory they continue to find themselves in; Red's bitterness is used to temper the inequality she has faced and is eventually brought, quite literally, to the surface freeing her from the underground. However, due to Red's uncontainable desire for revenge, she and Adelaide are unable to both exist in the aboveground. And so it is ultimately Adelaide's controlled anger that wins out and allows her to maintain her agency and freedom, even if only for herself. In contrast, however Red's escape from the underground has served as an example to the rest of the Tethered who have followed her and her anger into the sunlight.

Works Cited

Abdurraqib, H. (2017), *They Can't Kill Us Until They Kill Us*, Columbus: Two Dollar Radio.

Allen, S. S. (2015), "Transforming Rage: Revisioning the Myth of the Angry Black Woman," *ProQuest Dissertations and Theses*. Ph.D., California: Pacifica Graduate Institute. https://www.proquest.com/docview/1778844116/abstract/6C818C2BBD424525PQ/1.

Athnasios, A. (2021), "Mammy and Aunt Jemima: Keeping the Old South Alive in Popular Visual Culture," *Honors College Theses*, August 3, 2021. https://digitalcommons.wayne.edu/honorstheses/76.

Barnstone, D. A. (2016), *The Doppelgaenger*, Bern: Peter Lang GmbH, Internationaler Verlag der Wissenschaften.

Bellot, Gabrielle, Renee Cox and Danielle McKinney (2021), "How Black Horror Became America's Most Powerful Cinematic Genre," *The New York Times*, November 10, sec. *T Magazine*. https://www.nytimes.com/2021/11/10/t-magazine/black-horror-films-get-out.html.

Bernardez, T. (1988), *Women and Anger: Cultural Prohibitions and the Feminine Ideal*, Stone Center for Developmental Services and Studies, Wellesley College. http://wcwonline.org/vmfiles/31sc.pdf.

Chappell, J. and M. Young (2017), *Bad Girls and Transgressive Women in Popular Television, Fiction, and Film*, New York: Springer International Publishing.

Cheers, I. M. (2017), *The Evolution of Black Women in Television: Mammies, Matriarchs and Mistresses*, London: Taylor & Francis Group.

Collins, P. H. (2000), *Black Feminist Thought: Knowledge, Consciousness, and the Politics of Empowerment*, London: Psychology Press.

Halliday, A. S. (2019), *The Black Girlhood Studies Collection*, Toronto: Canadian Scholars' Press.

hooks, b. (1997), "From Bone Black: Memories of Girlhood," *Critical Quarterly*, 39(3): 80–3. doi:10.1111/1467-8705.00110.

hooks, b. (2014), *Black Looks: Race and Representation*, London: Taylor & Francis Group.

Jeffries, J. L. (2020), "Jordan Peele (Dir.), Us (Motion Picture), Universal Pictures," *Journal of African American Studies*, 24(2): 288–96.

Jewell, K. S. (1993), *From Mammy to Miss America and Beyond: Cultural Images and the Shaping of US Social Policy*, London: Psychology Press.

Jones, T. and K. J. Norwood (2016), "Aggressive Encounters & White Fragility: Deconstructing the Trope of the Angry Black Woman," *Iowa Law Review*, 102(5): 2017–70.

Judd, B. (2019), "Sapphire as Praxis: Toward a Methodology of Anger," *Feminist Studies*, 45(1): 178–208.

McDole, A. (2017), "Mammy Representations in the 21st Century" Theses - ALL, 194. https://surface.syr.edu/thesis/194.

Olafsen, H. (2020), "'It's Us:' Mimicry in Jordan Peele's Us," *Iowa Journal of Cultural Studies*, 20(1): 20–32.

Peele, J. (Dir.). (2019), *Us*, Universal City: Universal Pictures.

Simms, S. (2021), "The Trope of the Angry Black Woman: From Girlhood to Womanhood," M.A., Maryland: University of Maryland, Baltimore County. https://www.proquest.com/docview/2622807931/abstract/E018BA80582C4030PQ/1.

Ugwu, R. (2019), "Why Lupita Nyong'o's 'Us' Voice Sounds So Creepy," *The New York Times*, March 24. https://www.nytimes.com/2019/03/24/movies/why-lupita-nyongos-us-voice-sounds-so-creepy.html.

Wall, D. C. (2019), "Us," *Black Camera*, 11(1): 457–61.

Walley-Jean, J. C. (2009), "Debunking the Myth of the 'Angry Black Woman': An Exploration of Anger in Young African American Women," *Black Women, Gender + Families*, 3(2): 68–86.

West, C. M. (1995), "Mammy, Sapphire, and Jezebel: Historical Images of Black Women and Their Implications for Psychotherapy," *Psychotherapy: Theory, Research, Practice, Training*, 32(3): 458–66.

Index

#MeToo 1–3, 5, 7–9

abject 71, 89, 132, 163, 178–9
absence 32, 60, 62, 96, 126, 160, 191, 217
abuse 1–3, 6–7, 14, 36, 63, 65, 72, 74, 76,
    83, 95, 106, 118, 120–1, 123, 152,
    159, 161, 163, 236
addicted 182–4, 187
African American 16–17, 116, 206–7, 215,
    223–5
angel 73, 81, 153, 168, 211
anger 86, 93–4, 221, 223, 225, 229–30,
    232, 235–6
apocalypse 14, 23, 27, 34, 35, 75, 117, 124,
    191, 201, 203
    post 30, 33, 159
asexual 223, 225–6
ash 11, 23–4, 29–31, 38, 75, 85, 104–5
assault 47, 78, 82, 208
    sexual 8, 72, 80, 184, 224

bisexual 185–7
Black American 4, 216, 223
    anti 215
Black Lives Matter 1
black (space) 23, 32, 35–6, 38, 46, 62
Black Women 206, 211–18, 221–36
blackness 1, 35, 206–10, 214, 217–18
blank 169, 227
blood 23, 48, 76, 81, 109, 111, 135, 144,
    181, 183, 185, 230, 233
body 25, 35–6, 41, 56, 65, 76, 78, 87, 132,
    139, 146, 151, 166, 233
    brown 66
    female 7, 57, 60, 63, 76, 81, 133, 138,
    178–80
    politic 46
bondage 126
border 4, 8, 14, 17, 55–6, 61–3, 85, 109,
    135, 166, 178, 181
borderland 55, 56, 58–60, 64–6
bound 78, 80, 126, 130, 134, 138, 150, 200,
    224, 232

boundary 29–30, 32, 48, 57, 97, 104, 108,
    121, 137, 139, 175, 177, 183, 185,
    217

cannibalism 42, 47, 51, 53, 107, 109
captive 185, 198
Chicana 14, 55, 57
childhood 14, 48, 193, 222–3, 227
children 6, 9, 14, 28, 36, 55, 57, 59–61,
    64–6, 72–4, 66–7, 80, 82–3, 85,
    88–91, 105–7, 109, 110, 119–20, 131,
    145, 147, 151, 160, 163, 167, 175,
    179–81, 184–5, 195, 198, 200, 202,
    208, 211–13, 223–4, 227–30, 234
colonial 55–61, 63, 65–6, 234
    post 55
    pre 57, 59
community 74, 103, 107, 126, 163, 186
confinement 36, 55, 66, 130–1, 133–4,
    138, 168–9, 177, 179, 182–3, 187–8,
    191, 198
conservative 3–4, 6, 8, 13–17, 154, 207
contagion 24, 27
corridor 92–3, 144, 233–4
Creed, Barbara 88, 96, 132–4, 138–40, 152,
    175–6, 178–81, 185
cruel 24, 36, 49, 77, 79, 92, 102, 159,
    165–7, 178, 221
cult 41, 49–51, 73–8, 81–2, 120, 176
culture 1, 4, 5, 8, 10, 35, 41, 43–4, 55, 61,
    66, 143–5, 150, 153–4, 175–6, 178,
    204, 214, 216, 218, 221, 232
    counter 161

danger 9, 25, 75, 80, 105, 109, 137–8, 165
dangerous 12–13, 89, 102, 107, 118, 121,
    151, 159, 161, 164, 166–7, 187, 205,
    213
darkness 4, 23, 31, 35–6, 41, 43, 45, 49, 53,
    73, 82, 107, 169–70, 180
daughter 9, 12, 13, 14, 16, 30, 57–8, 61,
    63–5, 71, 76, 80, 82–3, 85–6, 89, 97,
    103, 122, 160–1, 177, 179, 208, 226

Index

death 11, 24, 27, 37, 41, 42, 55–6, 59–62, 65, 74, 75, 78, 82, 85, 86–7, 88, 91–2, 94–6, 106, 108, 110–11, 123, 131, 136, 138, 148, 150–1, 153, 159, 163–4, 176–83, 195–8, 208, 211–12, 222
decay 23, 27, 29, 31, 34–6, 38, 73–4, 78, 133, 138–9, 145, 179, 181, 188
degeneration 44, 125
dehumanize 36, 56, 61, 63, 225, 235
demon 15, 30, 42, 51, 60, 80–1, 152–3
demonic 9, 48–9, 143, 145–7, 151, 154
depression 27, 52, 94
desire 41, 46, 82, 87–90, 96, 119–20, 125, 135, 150, 168, 178, 181, 188, 233, 236
despair 24, 92, 125, 151–2, 154
desperation 86, 136
devil 73, 146, 183
dirt 66, 168, 188
discrimination 1, 4, 8, 56, 213, 215, 227, 231
disease 12–13, 23–8, 79, 179
disenfranchised 2, 4, 6–7, 35, 64, 208–9, 213, 216
dismember 62–3, 180, 184
divine 80, 108, 110, 150
divine Comedy, The 42–3, 47, 72, 74, 117, 157, 164
dystopia 4, 16, 45, 159, 167–8, 230

embody 14, 49, 51, 55, 57, 59–63, 131, 134, 136, 138–9, 148, 164–6, 182, 215, 222, 225–6, 231, 234
  dis 61
empty 1, 30, 32–4, 58, 62, 74, 92–3, 104, 121–2, 125, 131
environmental 23–4, 28–30, 36, 38, 119, 201
escape 9–11, 13, 45, 73, 85–7, 111, 121–2, 158–60, 162, 165, 167, 191–3, 198, 226, 236
  no 7, 14, 16, 26, 91, 130, 157, 160, 227
eternal 16, 49, 52, 56, 135, 186, 198, 200
evangelical 3, 6, 7, 8, 9, 60
evil 12, 24, 37–8, 43, 46–8, 55, 88, 95, 104–5, 110–11, 132, 134, 136, 138–9, 146, 154, 167–80, 200, 222
excess 5, 8, 13–14, 166, 185–6
existence 25, 29, 34, 45, 48, 56, 65, 74, 110, 131, 136, 139, 148, 164, 181, 188, 191, 195, 210–11, 214, 231, 235
  non 58

existential 3, 12, 105
extremism 9, 14–16, 112, 152

fairytale 48, 123, 134, 230
fanatic 36
fantasy 8, 10, 29–30, 41, 48, 85, 105, 111, 119, 121, 126, 143–5, 147–50, 168
father 11, 16, 45–7, 86–7, 89–90, 96–7, 106–8, 111, 126, 152, 178, 186, 196, 198, 208, 210–11, 216, 227
fear 27, 41–6, 63, 75, 88, 90–1, 93, 108, 119, 133, 136–9, 152, 166, 168, 179, 185, 199, 137, 232
feminine 13, 45–6, 89, 104, 179, 186, 213
  monstrous 129–34, 136–7, 176, 178
femininity 41–4, 47, 49–50, 53, 185, 222, 225
fetus 139
flashback 37, 38, 80, 176, 178, 183, 194, 227, 228, 234
fundamentalism 14, 101, 103, 106–8, 110–12, 158, 162, 166
future 8, 14–5, 34, 44–6, 49, 51, 109, 111, 137, 139, 157, 162, 164, 166, 168–70, 177–8, 193, 201, 234

gender 41–3, 45, 47, 49–53, 56, 58, 60, 63–4, 66, 101, 104, 110, 112, 120, 132, 134, 144, 152, 165, 175, 185–6, 206–7, 212–13, 217–18, 227, 229, 231, 235
ghost 15, 30, 55–61, 66, 73, 75, 86, 91, 95–6, 105, 137, 143, 151, 164, 177–80, 183, 186–7, 196, 198, 222
ghoul 48, 101
girl 9, 11, 13, 17, 31, 36, 55–6, 58, 60–2, 64, 66, 85–6, 108–9, 111, 143, 148, 152, 160–1, 163, 178, 192, 203, 224, 230, 234
  final 152–3
  hood 226–9
  magical 193–5
God 11, 49, 72, 76, 78, 90, 92, 106–11, 117, 121, 146, 150, 210, 211, 221
  like 52, 209
  ling 49
goddess 41, 50–3, 55, 57, 63, 186
gods 92, 126

gothic 24, 29–30, 42, 44–6, 48, 52, 91, 95, 133–4, 144, 154, 168, 170
grave 48, 62, 154

harassment 7
haunt 30, 44, 55–6, 59, 61, 65–6, 91, 96, 105, 111, 133, 137, 147–8, 150–1, 164, 177, 179, 183, 196
heaven 41, 72–4, 107, 209–11
hell 11, 13–14, 30, 41–5, 48–50, 53, 72–80, 83, 104–5, 117, 119, 122, 126, 157, 164, 209–10
homosexual 187
hope 3–4, 5, 15–17, 49, 137–8, 146
horror 8–9, 12, 13, 23–4, 28–30, 36, 38, 42–5, 47–8, 50, 52–3, 61, 71, 75–6, 79, 88–92, 96, 101, 104, 108, 111, 125, 131, 143–50, 152–5, 175–81, 185, 187–8, 221–2, 235
hostile 13, 24, 31, 130, 225–6, 229–30, 232
hybrid 51, 111

identity 9–11, 13, 15–16, 50–1, 56, 58, 65, 73, 82, 85, 90, 96, 118–19, 125, 129–33, 139, 165, 175–8, 180, 182, 184–6, 188, 207, 209, 211–12, 214–15, 217–18, 222, 224, 226, 235
ideology 12, 14, 48–9, 51, 63, 66, 88, 143, 154, 163, 175, 178, 180, 182, 214
imperialism 37, 42, 44–6, 48, 50, 52
imprison 36, 66, 98, 134, 152, 165, 179, 181, 183, 191
indigenous 1, 2, 57, 60
infect 6, 26–8, 78, 183
inhospitable 30, 34, 36

jailer 134
judgement 2–4

kidnap 33, 35, 120, 152
killer 26, 42, 52, 73, 86, 89, 93, 95, 125, 132, 151, 183–4, 186–7, 197, 202, 208, 211–12, 214

lesbian 185
liminal 10, 31, 32, 35, 42, 45, 47, 50, 85, 89, 91, 96–7, 129, 134–9, 176–8, 182–4, 187, 221, 235

masculine 13, 50, 61, 72, 97, 104, 213, 225
masculinity 42–3, 45, 47, 49, 214

massacre 90, 207–8
maternal 14, 46, 58, 85, 96–7, 120, 178, 180, 223
matriarch 50–2, 86, 89, 95, 97, 223–6, 235
melancholy 89, 95
memory 47, 49, 58, 65, 93, 125–6, 151–2, 160–1, 164–5, 169, 196
milieu 24, 30–1, 34
misogyny 6, 44–5, 57, 60, 154, 159, 163, 166, 206, 213–14
monstrosity 9, 14–16, 29, 41, 45, 48, 50, 55, 132–4, 136–7, 139
monstrous 9, 15, 31, 34–5, 44, 46, 51, 52–3, 78, 81, 88–9, 129–30, 132–6, 139, 152–3, 176, 178–80, 185, 187
morality 27, 29, 37, 48, 81–2, 101, 108–9, 123–5, 131–4, 139, 144–6, 168, 224
mother 4, 6–7, 9, 12–3, 16, 36, 43, 47, 57–9, 63–5, 76, 80–2, 85–91, 95–8, 107, 110, 120, 130, 149, 151–3, 165, 188, 208, 217, 224–7
  hood 14, 55, 61, 88, 181–2, 184–5
  monstrous 50–3, 89, 96, 132, 181
mourning 56, 58–9, 64, 66, 89, 107
murder 48, 51, 55–6, 91, 109–10, 124, 144, 151–2, 178–9, 183, 186, 193, 196
murdered 56, 58–66, 86, 183–4
mutilate 56, 62, 65
myth 8, 41, 43, 46, 48–50, 57, 63, 134, 138, 143, 148–51, 154, 168, 229

neoliberalism 5, 9, 29, 38, 49, 64
nostalgia 53, 103, 108, 216

oppress 36, 46, 60, 96, 101, 144, 154, 157, 160, 166–7, 175, 179, 207, 216, 218, 223, 229, 232–5
outcast 86, 184, 187
outsider 86, 101, 104, 139, 193

pain 10, 38, 57–9, 66, 75, 82, 86, 91, 94–5, 107, 121, 125, 151, 162–3, 180, 192, 198, 216, 229–31, 234
particulate 13, 23, 28, 30, 32–6, 38
passage 137
patriarchal 2, 8, 9, 11, 14, 59–61, 63, 66, 89, 96–7, 110, 122–4, 127, 139, 145, 154, 158–9, 162, 175, 178–80, 185, 214, 232

politics 1, 4–5, 8, 10, 12–13, 16, 26, 28, 38, 41–2, 46–8, 53, 56, 59–60, 64–6, 102, 122, 133, 143, 146–7, 154, 159–60, 182, 207, 210, 218
possession 15, 94, 132–3, 136, 139, 146, 151–2
pregnant 6, 49, 72, 177–8
prison 35–6, 66, 87, 98, 130–1, 152, 165, 179–81, 183–4, 188, 191, 202
prisoner 134, 146, 198
psychic 13, 31–2, 36, 41, 120, 143, 151–3
psychology 8, 43–4, 72, 75, 88, 91, 98, 120, 125–6, 140, 160, 179, 191, 197, 200, 203, 206, 222, 227
punish 57, 60, 63, 78–9, 85, 87, 91–2, 94, 98, 106, 117, 119, 157, 160–1, 164, 169, 209
purgatory 5–6, 8–17, 55–6, 58, 64–6, 72–4, 80, 82–3, 85, 91–2, 94, 97, 103–8, 110, 117–19, 121–3, 126, 130–1, 134, 136–9, 148, 150, 159–161, 163–66, 169–71, 175, 177–8, 180–2, 187–8, 191–2, 195–6, 198–203, 209–11, 215, 218, 228, 233, 235–6

queen 51–2, 134–5, 197–8
queer 176, 182, 185–7, 218

racism 16, 35, 38, 44, 48, 55, 57, 60, 66, 163, 205–7, 209–16, 218, 225, 232, 235
rebirth 13, 41–2, 186
redemption 91–2, 96, 124, 158
religion 12, 14, 27, 51, 65, 76, 81, 102, 104, 108, 133, 145–6
 anti 162
religious 11, 14, 43, 48, 76, 101, 103, 105–7, 109–11, 120, 149–51, 159, 162, 164, 166, 169
repress 33, 41, 44, 59, 72, 80, 158, 162, 166, 175
revenge 73, 77, 81–2, 87, 90, 98, 111, 121, 161, 166, 169, 222, 228, 236
ritual 51, 63, 74, 86–7, 107, 109, 111, 125, 131, 137, 177, 187

sacrifice 12, 14, 16–17, 50, 60, 72, 85, 87–8, 96–7, 110–11, 121, 124–5, 181, 198, 202, 213

Satan 48–50
sexism 55, 57, 215
sexual 2–3, 6–8, 49, 56, 63–5, 72, 78, 80, 83, 118, 122, 132, 139, 163, 178, 184, 214–15, 224, 236
sexuality 60, 133, 175, 185–7, 218, 223, 225–7
Silent Hill 8–9, 12–14, 23, 30–3, 35–6, 38, 71–82, 85–7, 89–92, 95–8, 101, 103–11
sins 57, 60, 76, 78, 85, 106, 117, 123, 168, 177, 210
slavery 35–6, 160, 163, 210–11, 224, 236
soul 72–3, 75, 82, 103, 117, 119, 130–3, 135–8, 150, 152, 184, 194, 211, 222, 233, 235
 less 45
specter 55, 61, 212
spirit 37–8, 148–53, 166–7, 169–70
spirituality 125, 146, 150, 192, 222
storytelling 14, 15, 90, 222, 231
subterranean 11, 41–5, 47–50, 52, 74, 229
suffering 10, 43, 57, 61, 79, 81, 88, 91–2, 97, 103, 110, 117, 123, 145, 151, 192, 201, 221, 228, 230–1, 234, 236
suicide 163, 178, 183, 196
symbolic 11, 35, 38, 41–2, 45–6, 50, 52, 63, 75, 88–9, 93–4, 96–7, 102, 105, 132, 175–80, 182, 185, 192, 216–17, 226, 231, 233, 235

torment 77, 151–2, 157–8, 165
torture 36, 42, 46–7, 63, 65, 91, 98, 103, 105–6, 121, 126, 146–7, 150, 157, 180, 183–4, 193, 222, 230
toxic 16, 29–32, 34–6, 45, 74, 118
transform 65, 80, 87, 117, 134, 178, 186, 192, 195–6, 203, 211, 216
transformative 43, 87, 163, 195, 217–18
transgress 9, 15, 43, 60–2, 64, 75, 85, 91, 97, 120–1, 175, 185, 221, 226
trapped 9–11, 13–15, 55, 65, 75, 78, 81, 85, 90–1, 94, 97, 122–3, 131, 136–7, 139, 150–2, 182, 187, 191–2
trauma 13–14, 16, 38, 47, 72, 74, 77–8, 80–1, 83, 86, 91, 93–4, 120, 147, 154, 159, 161–6, 168, 191–2, 208, 210, 216, 222, 225, 227–31, 234–5

trial 2–3, 81, 192
tunnel 33, 48

underground 13, 41–6, 50, 53, 74, 118, 123, 160, 222, 226, 228–9, 231, 233–6
urban 25–6, 42, 64, 144, 188
utopia 87, 131, 191

vampire 10, 15, 48, 129–39, 145, 149, 152, 182–7, 203
villain 81, 131–2, 136, 138–9, 145, 147, 160, 200–2, 205, 232

violence 2, 7–8, 12–13, 38, 42, 45–6, 48–51, 56, 59, 62–4, 66, 81, 86, 89–91, 95–6, 105–6, 110, 120, 146, 152, 154, 160, 163, 167, 178, 182–4, 191, 193, 200, 207–8, 210–1, 214, 216–17, 235

wild 28, 52
witness 37, 97, 157, 159, 161–4, 168–70, 194–6, 208, 229
womb 41, 132, 152, 179–81, 199

www.ingramcontent.com/pod-product-compliance
Lightning Source LLC
Chambersburg PA
CBHW071824300426
44116CB00009B/1427